★★★★ THE ★★★★
US ARMY
★★★★★ IN ★★★★★
VIETNAM

★★★★ THE ★★★★
US ARMY
★★★★★ IN ★★★★★
VIETNAM

Leroy Thompson

A David & Charles Military Book

CREDIT
All photographs in this book
are US Army Official, unless
otherwise credited.

British Library Cataloguing in Publication Data
Thompson, Leroy
  US Army in Vietnam.
  1. Vietnamese wars. Army operations by United States.
  Army 1961–1975
  I. Title

  ISBN 0–7153–9219–0

Phototypeset by ABM Typographics Ltd, Hull
and printed in Great Britain
by Butler & Tanner Ltd, Frome
for David & Charles Publishers plc
Brunel House   Newton Abbot   Devon

Distributed in the United States by
Sterling Publishing Co. Inc,
2, Park Avenue, New York, NY 10016

CONTENTS

INTRODUCTION: AMERICA'S LONGEST AND MOST UNPOPULAR WAR

Various starting points might be identified for America's involvement in Indochina, but perhaps April 1945, when an agent of the OSS made contact with Ho Chi Minh, is most noteworthy from the point of view of the massive place Indochina would later assume in the military and the political history of the United States. From the beginning, the American OSS men found Ho Chi Minh remarkably friendly towards the USA, a feeling that was reciprocated by the agents. Virtually all the agents recommended US backing for Ho, who was generally viewed as a nationalist first and a Communist second. This view has resulted in a debate which has now lasted for over 40 years as to whether handled correctly Ho Chi Minh would have become a Vietnamese Tito rather than a confirmed enemy of the United States.

In any case, members of the OSS had been secretly ordered not to aid the French in re-colonizing Indochina, which resulted in strained relations between representatives of the two powers in the area. However, as anti-Communism became the watchword during the later 1940s and early 1950s, material and financial support was given to the French in the war against the Viet Minh, Ho Chi Minh's Communist guerrillas. On 8 February 1950, the United States recognized Vietnam, Laos, and Cambodia, created from former French colonies. Throughout the fighting taking place in Indochina, the United States had military observers with the French. However, during the early stages of the conflict in Indochina, the United States was far more concerned with the fighting in Korea. Only after the end of the Korean conflict did the United States begin to consider military action in Indochina, consideration that at one point even included discussion of using nuclear weapons in support of the French. On 17 February 1954, the US did make an offer to help train the Vietnamese, to a major extent as part of the preliminaries to filling the power vacuum likely to be left upon the departure of the French. Then, in April 1954, the possibility of US combat troops being committed seemed real, though with the announcement of the fall of Dien Bien Phu on 8 May 1954, the United States instead

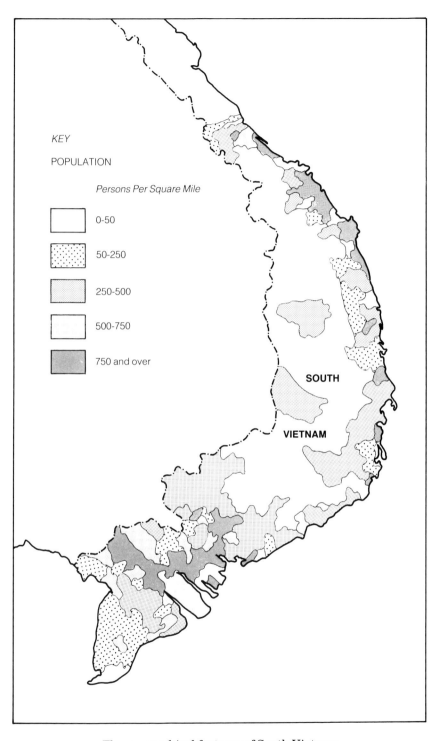

SOUTH

VIETNAM

The geographical features of South Vietnam.

helped work out the ceasefire over the next two months, resulting in the armistice of 21 July, which divided the country at the 17th Parallel, thus creating North and South Vietnam. US Navy ships were then used to evacuate many non-Communists from the North to the South.

Just as NATO had been formed to block Communist expansion in Europe, SEATO (Southeast Asia Treaty Organization) was formed on 8 September 1954 as a bastion against Communist ambitions in Southeast Asia. The original eight members of the alliance were the United States, Britain, France, Pakistan, Thailand, New Zealand, Australia and the Philippines.

In February 1955, a US training mission began operating in South Vietnam under Lt Gen John O'Daniel, who had a staff of about three hundred Americans operating under the overall command of French Gen. Paul Ely. O'Daniel, himself, had a mixed American/French training command. Symptomatic of the power struggles which would continue to plague South Vietnam and contribute to its fall, in April 1955, there was an attempt by Bao Dai to take power from Premier Diem; it was unsuccessful.

Under the dynamic new American President, John F. Kennedy, countering Communist insurgencies achieved a new priority. This resulted in the visit by Vice President Johnson to South Vietnam in May 1961 where he spoke to the National Assembly and assured them of US support against the Communists to the North and waging a guerrilla war within South Vietnam. A few months later, in November, 1961, the United States began making good on its promises as aid was increased to South Vietnam, including helicopters and fighters, and instructors in their use. President Kennedy's favorite soldiers, the Special Forces, were now fully involved in training in Vietnam and elsewhere in Southeast Asia.

By early in 1962, it was becoming apparent that President Diem was losing control of the country. In February, his palace was bombed by planes of the South Vietnamese Air Force, while in the countryside, Communist successes were mounting. The Buddhist protests against the government, which were growing more and more strident by late summer of 1963, increased doubts among US experts on Southeast Asia that Diem could maintain control. As a result, in November 1963, President Diem and his brother were ousted and killed with tacit US approval. The junta which replaced him lasted only three months and the government of South Vietnam remained unstable for the next two years as regime after regime took office until Marshal Nguyen Cao Ky and General Nguyen Van Thieu brought some semblance of stability to the country's government. The Communists, ever quick to seize an advantage, had stepped up their operations within South Vietnam during the period of government instability. Among the more obvious results of the perceived Communist threat was an increase in the number of US advisors by 5,000 to a total of 21,000.

With the Gulf of Tonkin Incident at the beginning of August 1964, in which North Vietnamese gunboats purportedly fired on a US destroyer, followed by retaliatory US air attacks, the United States took a giant step towards the full commitment of American troops to combat in Vietnam. On the diplomatic front, in the United Nations the United States accused North Vietnam of aggression. In a graphic illustration of the mood of the American Congress at that point, on 7 August 1964, the House of Representatives voted 411 to 0 and the Senate 88 to 2 in favor a resolution backing President Johnson on his retaliatory moves against North Vietnam. The Communists were capable of moves of retaliation themselves, however, as a few days later they blew up a US barracks inflicting US casualties. The United States again upped the ante sending 160 US and South Vietnamese planes against the North a few days later.

On 30 March 1965, a bomb exploded at the US Embassy, no doubt playing at least some part in President Johnson's offer on 7 April 1965 to talk directly with the North Vietnamese about the security of South Vietnam. However, this offer also proved a preliminary to increasing the United States direct military support to South Vietnam as on 17 June 1965, B-52s began flying missions against the VC within South Vietnam. Then on 28 July 1965, the President ordered 50,000 more men to Vietnam and doubled the draft, thus beginning the commitment of ground combat troops which would eventually see 2.8 million troops serve in Vietnam and 57,000 die there.

During the next three years, the enthusiasm of the American public for the war in Vietnam began to wane, culminating with the shock of the Tet Offensive and invasion of the American Embassy compound. Seeing the war up close each night on the evening news certainly helped erode any broad-based militancy as well. As a result of his declining popularity, primarily because of his association with the escalation of the war, on 31 March 1968, Lyndon Johnson announced that he would not run for re-election. A few days later, perhaps feeling that as a lame duck Johnson would be more conciliatory, Hanoi proposed direct talks with the USA. As a result, on 14 May 1968, the Paris Peace Talks opened.

In late August 1968, the battlefield once more dominated American television screens, but this time the battlefield was Chicago, Illinois, as anti-war protesters disrupted the Democratic Convention. Rioting in American cities would become somewhat endemic during the later 1960s and early 1970s, partially attributable to a militancy in the Civil Rights Movement and partially to anti-war sentiment. The feeling that Blacks were fighting a disproportionate part of the war often contributed to the riots. One of the largest riots – in Detroit – in fact evolved from a welcome home party for Black veterans.

Although the US troop level in Vietnam peaked at 549,500 in January 1969, reductions were near as the new President – Richard Nixon – took office. On 13 May 1969, Nixon announced that in an attempt to make the draft more equitable a lottery would be instituted which would call nineteen year olds first rather than taking the oldest eligible men first. Less than a month later, on 8 June 1969, Nixon ordered the first US troop reductions in Vietnam as 25,000 men were scheduled for rotation home. At home in the USA, the anti-war movement was growing as on October 1969, a Vietnam moratorium was observed nationwide, including major rallies. This was followed on 15 November by the descent of 250,000 anti-war protesters on Washington. Although the anti-war movement never represented a majority of Americans, it was a very vocal minority.

Throughout 1970, the protests continued as did the American troop pullout. One of the most lasting scars of the war would be inflicted on 4 May 1970 during protests over the expansion of the US ground war into Cambodia when Ohio National Guard troops fired on protesters at Kent State University, killing four and wounding eleven, most of them innocent bystanders not even involved in the protests. The rather lame claims that protesters had fired on the Guardsmen proved unfounded, but, in what was in actuality as great an injustice as Mai Lai, no one was punished. The battle lines between those who supported the war and those who did not were more clearly drawn, however, and the event drew heavy criticism from Vietnam War veterans opposed to the war since they appreciated more than most the incompetence shown by the National Guardsmen. Moving towards a complete US withdrawal, the process of turning the fighting of the war over to the Vietnamese – 'Vietnamization' – had been continuing, and on 7 October 1970 President Nixon proposed a supervised truce in Vietnam, Cambodia and Laos and a more comprehensive peace conference.

Public confidence in the government's handling of the war suffered another blow in July 1971, when the Pentagon Papers scandal occupied the front pages of American newspapers. However, while Nixon continued to remove troops, he stepped up the bombing of the North during April and May 1972. The trustworthiness of the North

Vietnamese had been graphically illustrated when their Easter Offensive pushed south on 30 March 1972. It was clear to the North Vietnamese that the US wanted out of Vietnam and was not likely to begin sending troops back into the conflict. As a result, although US air power assisted the South during the offensive, US ground troops continued to leave. On 30 December 1972, bombing was halted north of the 20th Parallel, with peace talks resuming in January 1973. These talks culminated on 23 January 1973, with President Nixon's announcement of 'Peace with Honor' a phrase which would be quoted with irony over the next decade by both supporters and opponents of the war. As a key part of the agreement, on 29 March 1973 the 'last' POWs held in the North were freed and the last US Troops were pulled out of Vietnam. To this day there are still serious doubts that the North Vietnamese really released all prisoners they were holding, another one of the unhealed wounds of the Vietnam War.

There were attempts, however, to heal another wound as on 17 September 1974, President Ford offered amnesty to draft evaders and deserters willing to do two years public service as part of his 'earned re-entry program.' This offer, including a 'penance' as it did, received little criticism from veterans' groups, in contrast to Jimmy Carter's 1977 pardon of draft evaders which was vilified by those who had fought and seen comrades die. Opening new wounds was the December 1974 revelation, as part of the Watergate fallout, that the CIA had kept files on dissidents during the Vietnam War. As the CIA came under the microscope, other accusations, including their active support of drug dealing in Southeast Asia, would arise as well.

On 11 March 1975, the North Vietnamese launched their final thrust into South Vietnam, resulting in the hasty evacuation of Americans on 29 April and the fall of Saigon on 30 April. After three decades, the Vietnamese Communists, though Ho was no longer alive to see the success, had unified the country. The United States commitment of millions of troops and billions of dollars had bought the South Vietnamese at least another decade (as well as South Vietnamese profiteers and black marketeers numerous villas and Swiss bank accounts) and broken the Viet Cong, resulting in the defeat being an invasion rather than an insurgency. Those who had fought in Vietnam and those who had not, however, asked the same question: Was it worth it? The question is still being asked, and the effects of the War are still being felt. It was that same generation that fought and died in Vietnam and demonstrated in Chicago that overwhelmingly elected Ronald Reagan to the White House with the tacit mission of refurbishing both American pride and the American armed forces.

1
THE US MILITARY MACHINE
OF THE 1960s

Normally, when one discusses the organisation of an army historically, one does it from the top down. However, since Vietnam, more than most wars, was fought by the guys at the bottom it might be best to look at the structure of the US Army from the point of view of the line doggie – the grunt – the PFC. As early as basic training, the American soldier had to learn the chain of command and be able to recite it or drop for 100 pushups. He was expected to know each command level in the chain and the person occupying that slot. In practicality, above company commander, it didn't really matter to the grunt, but he had to know anyway. The grunt's chain of command, then, was:

Fire Team Leader, Squad Leader, Platoon Leader, Company Commander, Battalion Commander, Brigade Commander, Division Commander, Corps Commander, Army Commander, Army Group Commander, Theater Commander, Army Chief of Staff, Secretary of the Army, Secretary of Defense, and President of the United States.

During the Vietnam War period, the US Army consisted of the Regular US Army, the Army Reserve and the National Guard. Prior to the massive commitment of troops to Vietnam it was assumed that the Regular Army would blunt initial Communist thrusts in Korea or Western Europe while the reserves and National Guard would be mobilised and fed in to 'roundout' units or replace losses. Draftees would then receive their initial training and form new units or act as replacements for those units already committed to combat. The Army Reserve and National Guard contained a particularly substantial percentage of service and support troops since the Regular Army was oriented heavily towards combat arms – Armor/Cavalry, Artillery and Infantry. The Combat Support Arms – Engineers, Military Intelligence, Military Police and Signals – were especially dependent upon the Reserves to reach wartime strength, while the Service Arms – Finance, Quartermaster, Medical, Ordnance, Chemical, and Transportation – would also draw on reservists to reach full capability to supply an Army in the field. However, with few exceptions, neither the Army Reserve nor the National Guard were mobilised, forcing the Regular Army to feed draftees into units in Vietnam more quickly than anticipated. This was the result of a combination of factors. The President did not want to send the Soviets the signal that US defense capabilities were stretched thin, which mobilising the reserves might have done. There was the need to retain a reserve to deal with possible problems elsewhere in the world, as well as the political pressure at home, since the National Guard and Reserves did offer somewhat of a haven for the sons of the more affluent elements of society. Thus the President did not mobilise the Reserves or Guard in large numbers.

Although total US Army strength would increase by about 50 per cent between 1965 and 1970, from 966,000 to 1,432,000, this rise certainly represented nowhere near a maximum mobilisation of manpower. With a far smaller population to draw upon, the US Army in 1945, for example, numbered 8,131,000. The Marine Corps which bore a disproportionate amount of combat for its numbers increased somewhat more, numbering 190,000 in 1965 and 295,000 in 1970. Still, there is no doubt that the Vietnam War stretched the US armed forces thin, especially in aviation support and in elite, mobile assault troops such as the airborne, airmobile, and amphibious brigades and divisions.

The Department of the Army and Its Major Commands

The Secretary of the Army was the politically appointed head of the US Army. Operating under his supervision were three staffs – Chief of Staff, General Staff and Special Staff. Controlling all Army personnel with the exception of those assigned to the three staffs or a few on special assignment were thirteen commands as follows:

US Continental Army Command This command included the Military District of Washington and the five Armies – 1st, 3rd, 4th, 5th and 6th, covering the contiguous United States.

US Army Combat Developments Command This command developed doctrine, concepts, and requirements for the Army and, as a result, ran the Army service schools.

US Army Material Command This command was charged with development, testing, evaluation, procurement, distribution and maintenance of Army equipment.

US Army Security Agency This command handled the Army's Signal's intelligence and worked closely with NSA.

US Army Strategic Communications Command This command handled the Army's share of the Defense Communications System.

US Army Intelligence Command   This command was in charge of intelligence and counterintelligence for the Army.

Military Traffic Management and Terminal Service   This command handled transportation for the Army.

US Army Air Defense Command   This command supplied the Army contingent to the Continental Air Defense Command.

US Army Forces Strike Command   This command provided the Army's strategic reserve forces as part of the multi-service Strike Command for deployment wherever needed in a crisis.

US Army, Alaska   This command provided the Army portion of the US Alaskan Command.

US Army Forces, Southern Command   This command provided the Army portion of the US Southern Command, based in the Panama Canal Zone and targeted towards Latin America and the Caribbean.

US Army, Europe   Part of the US European Command, this command was the primary deterrent force in Western Europe and included the 7th Army, V Corps and VII Corps in Germany as well as other units in Europe.

US Army Pacific   This command was part of the US Army Pacific Command. During the Vietnam War, it was of special importance since it controlled all of the Army forces in Vietnam as well as the 8th Army and I Corps in Korea and other Army elements on Okinawa, in Japan and in Thailand.

US Army Vietnam

US Army Vietnam, despite its size, was considered a subsidiary command under MACV (Military Assistance Command Vietnam). Though USMACV had operational control of the Army forces in Vietnam, US Army, Pacific also maintained control based on its responsibility for all Army forces in the theater.

The CARS System

In an attempt to develop a more permanent regimental system and the resulting pride in past unit achievements, the US Army in 1957 adopted Combat Arms Regimental System (CARS) which allowed traditional regiments to exist without neglecting the need for flexible organisations within the division. As a result, for the armor/cavalry, infantry and artillery, the regiments with the longest traditions within the US Army were broken down with each troop, company or battery forming the basis for a battalion or squadron of the resulting CARS regiment. This system resulted in the presence of ten cavalry regiments, nineteen armored regiments, sixty-one infantry regiments, seventy-five artillery regiments and one Special Forces regiment. Battalions of any of the regiments might serve within different divisions, while retaining the regimental traditions and honors.

(For purposes of designation within this book when referring to battalions or squadrons, their number will be given first and the regimental number second. For example, the 1st Battalion of the 503rd Airborne Infantry Regiment, which served with the 173rd Airborne Brigade, would be referred to as the 1/503. Throughout this work this system will be used to identify battalions or troops assigned to Vietnam.)

The ROAD Concept

As of April 1961, US Army divisions were reorganized along the Reorganization Objective Army Division (ROAD) system from the former Pentomic system, which had been designed for use in a nuclear war situation, and which was based on five battle groups. Under the ROAD system, divisions had a fixed divisional base augmented by a mix of infantry, armor and cavalry maneuver battalions to fit the division's mission. Normally, these maneuver elements were organised into three brigades each composed of three battalions, though separate brigades would frequently have a fourth battalion assigned. The divisional base for the infantry, mechanised infantry and armored division were basically identical, though there were slight differences in manpower. For example, the division base for the infantry division comprised 8,024 troops, the mechanised infantry division 8,264 troops, and the armored division 8,372 troops. Comprising the division base for each of the three types of division were: HQ and HQ Company, MP Company, Engineer Battalion, Signals Battalion, Armored Cavalry Squadron, Divisional Artillery, Support Command, and three Brigade HQ and HQ Companies. Additionally, the infantry division base included an Aviation Battalion.

US Army Deployment Outside of Vietnam

Deployment of major units to Vietnam is discussed later in this book, but in understanding how the US Army maintained its commitments elsewhere in the world during the War, a look at where major divisional and brigade formations not sent to Vietnam were stationed might be useful.

CONUS (Continental United States)   1st Armored Division was based at Fort Hood during most of the War but in 1971 replaced the 4th Armored Division in Germany; 2nd Armored Division was also at Fort Hood; 5th Infantry Division (Mechanized) was stationed at Fort Carson, though one brigade served in Vietnam; 6th Infantry Division was at Fort Campbell with one brigade in Hawaii; 24th Infantry Division (Mechanized) was based at Fort Riley with elements in Germany; 82nd Airborne Division remained at Fort Bragg – although one brigade was deployed to Vietnam in response to the Tet Offensive, a fourth brigade was formed to keep the 82nd at full strength as the key element of the strategic reserve; 6th Armored Cavalry Regiment was at Fort Meade; 194th Armored Brigade was at Fort Knox; 197th Infantry Brigade was stationed at Fort Benning.

Additionally, the bulk of the 3rd, 6th, and 7th Special Forces Groups were based in the USA at Fort Bragg.

Not included in those units in CONUS are Reserve and National Guard units.

Germany   3rd Armored Division; 4th Armored Division (until replaced by the 1st Armored Division in 1971); 3rd Infantry Division (Mechanized); 8th Infantry Division (Mechanized); 2nd Armored Cavalry Regiment; 14th Armored Cavalry Regiment; BERLIN Brigade.

Korea   2nd Infantry Division; 7th Infantry Division;

Elsewhere – Alaska   171st Infantry Brigade (Mechanized); 172nd Infantry Brigade (Mechanized);

Panama Canal Zone   193rd Infantry Brigade.

Although it should be obvious from this enumeration that theoretically strong US Forces still remained in Germany and Korea it should be understood that in many cases these divisions or brigades had been heavily denuded of personnel, especially experienced NCOs, for service in Vietnam. Their aviation assets had also been severely drained as available pilots were sent to Vietnam. As of mid-1968, for example, of Aviation General Support Companies in the US Army one was in the USA, seven in Vietnam and two throughout the rest of the world; of Medium Helicopter Companies three were in the US, thirteen in Vietnam and three throughout the rest of the world. In many cases, those aviation units still assigned in Germany or Korea were severely understrength. Should a serious threat have arisen in Europe or Korea, too, US reserves were stretched very thin, particularly as the threat of rioting in US cities tied down portions of units such as the 82nd Airborne Division on internal security duties.

The '2½ War' Concept

Under the Kennedy Administration and later the Johnson Administration there had been an expansion of US Army strength on the basis of contingency planning for a '2½ War' possibility. Under this concept the possibility had to be planned for that the USA would become involved in a war in Europe, another war in Asia, and possibly a counterinsurgency in Latin America, all simultaneously. By 1965, the plan called for a force of twenty eight and one third divisions comprised of three USMC divisions, sixteen and one third active Army divisions and nine reserve divisions to deal with these potential threats.

As of 1965, the strategic concept called for the five divisions already deployed to Europe to hold while the four divisions in CONUS reinforced and then the eight reserve divisions earmarked for Europe were mobilised. This concept also was predicated on a war lasting only three months. The use of US nuclear weapons always played an important part in contingency planning in Europe, too. This was 'War #1.' Simultaneously, should the Chinese have attacked in Asia ('War #2'), the four divisions already deployed would hold while the three in CONUS earmarked for reinforcement arrived. In both 'Wars #1 and #2', it was assumed that the forces in place would fight a holding action in conjunction with allies while the forces in CONUS were deployed. Planning for 'War #2' in Asia did not consider the possibility either of a simultaneous attack by the North Koreans/Chinese/North Vietnamese. 'War #3' was the one-half war, generally hypothesised to be a counterinsurgency war in the Western Hemisphere. Allocated to deal with this contingency were three and a third divisions of the Strategic Reserve and one reserve division.

Initially, when US ground troops were commited to Vietnam it was viewed in US contingency planning as a '½ War' which would only absorb a limited amount of manpower and equipment. By 1967, however, since the reserves were not being mobilised and the troop commitment to Vietnam was growing, substantial portions of troops designated as CONUS reinforcements for Europe and as the Strategic Reserve were being committed to Vietnam. This resulted in draining most of the strategic reserve and making Vietnam certainly a full 'war' and perhaps a '1¼ War.' Just prior to the Tet Offensive in early 1968, the Strategic Reserve consisted of only the 82nd Airborne Division, one brigade of which was then committed in reaction to the Tet Offensive.

The resulting '2½ War' Strategic Concept as of 1968 then was drastically altered from 1965, assuming that 'War #1' in Europe would be fought by the five divisions already deployed, the six in CONUS and eight reserve divisions. 'War #2' in Asia was being fought by the twelve divisions already deployed (including Army forces in Korea and Marine forces on Okinawa). To deal with 'War #3,' the '½ war'/counterinsurgency, all that remained was two thirds of the 82nd Airborne Division (though a fourth brigade was raised to bring the division to full strength in CONUS while the 3rd Brigade fought in Vietnam) and one reserve division.

At this stage the Joint Chiefs were pressuring the President for the mobilization of the Reserves; however, though a few reserve units were mobilized, for the most part President Johnson resisted these pressures. Nevertheless, this was the military situation which would cause President Johnson not to seek re-election and President Nixon to begin the process of Vietnamization so that US forces could begin pulling out.

The combination of Congressional disenchantment with the military in the later stages of the Vietnam War and the need to cut military costs as troops were being pulled out led to the adoption in 1969 of a scaled down '1½ War' Strategic Concept, though other options considered included: the maintenance of only a small token force in Asia with US emphasis being almost entirely on a European War in support of NATO; maintenance of the '2½ War' Strategy; expanding to deal with a '3½ War' Strategy, which would assume a major war in Europe, Northern Asia, and Southern Asia; or emphasis on strong conventional capability in both Asia and Europe to move away from the emphasis on nuclear weapons.

By 1973, when the United States was out of Vietnam, force allocation for '1½ War' still considered the option of having to fight in Europe, Asia and a brushfire war but only sixteen regular Army and Marine divisions and nine reserve divisions would be committed as follows: To Europe four and one third were already deployed to be reinforced by four and two thirds in CONUS and eight reserve divisions; to Asia one and two thirds divisions already deployed to be reinforced by two and one third divisions in CONUS; to any other contingency, now including the Middle East, Africa, and Latin America, the three divisions of the Strategic Reserve and one reserve division.

Although hawks during the Vietnam War often pushed for a more vigorous prosecution of the land war – the invasion of the North, for example – the realisation of how thinly stretched the thin olive drab line was, especially during the period 1967-1969, and the possibility of having to deal with the commitment of Chinese troops should

North Vietnam be invaded certainly offers a better understanding of the caution with which operations north of the DMZ were pursued. With US troops so heavily committed to Vietnam, the US conventional shield in Germany and Korea was even less of a deterrent than usual, a fact which would have forced the US to resort to the nuclear option much more quickly in response to an invasion at either point. No doubt, Soviet analysts were aware of this fact as well, but it was still a sobering thought for the President and the Joint Chiefs of Staff.

2
THE MEN WHO FOUGHT THE WAR

Although the Vietnam War was fought by a heterogeneous group, the group was far less heterogeneous than that which had fought America's previous wars. Except for the officer corps, the middle class was not present in percentages approaching their proportion of the population, while, with the exception of a few members of the professional officer corps coming from traditional military families, the upper classes managed to avoid the war almost entirely. The US Selective Service System, which supplied conscripts to fill the ranks during the war, theoretically operated impartially, but the various types of deferments available tacitly allowed many to slip through the net of conscription, especially since local draft boards were locally administered, thus allowing for far different criteria in different areas.

Just as an example of the potential for avoiding service, the Selective Service System at the beginning of the Vietnam conflict offered the following draft classifications:

> **I-A:** available for military service (during the Vietnam War this classification would almost certainly result in being called);
> **I-A-O:** conscientious objector available only for non-combat military service;
> **I-C:** a serving member of the armed forces;
> **I-D:** member of the reserves or a student taking military training;
> **1-0:** conscientious objector available for civilian work in hospitals or other service work;
> **1-S:** student deferred (one of the most widely used methods of avoiding service during the Vietnam War, especially with draft boards that would allow more than four years of deferment for graduate degrees, law degrees, etc);
> **I-W:** conscientious objector performing civilian health work or other service work;
> **II-A:** deferred because of civilian occupation (among professions which allowed many to avoid the draft were engineering, especially in defence work; teaching; law enforcement; etc);
> **II-C:** deferred because of an agricultural occupation (the offspring of at least some 'gentlemen farmers' were so deferred);
> **II-S:** deferred because of special studies, including research, etc;
> **III-A:** deferred because of having children or because of hardship on dependents (the actor George Hamilton, for example, received such a deferment as the sole support of his mother!);
> **IV-A:** a registrant who had completed military service or was the sole surviving son;
> **IV-B:** an official deferred by law;

IV-C: an alien (actually a substantial number of resident aliens were drafted and served in Vietnam);

IV-D: a minister of religion or divinity student (in cases of some affluent families sons had attacks of devoutness and felt the calling of the cloth until the end of conscription);

IV-F: physically, mentally or morally unfit to serve (although many deferments were for valid medical reasons, the large number of professional athletes who escaped the draft under this deferment is indicative of how loosely it was sometimes applied, additionally, there was a large underground market in punctured eardrums or other deferrable maladies);

V-A: over the age of liability for military service.

Especially in the later stages of the Vietnam War, a disproportionate number of draftees were from the lower classes, particularly Blacks and Hispanics. The draft system also helped create the youngest Army the US had ever sent to war, as the average age for most enlisted personnel in Vietnam was around nineteen. Gone were the privates and corporals of twenty-five to thirty who in World War Two would have been nicknamed 'Pop' or, if they had some education, 'Professor' and who would have exerted a calming influence on the younger troops. The few men in their mid-twenties who were drafted were normally those whose student deferment had

Members of the 503rd Infantry (Airborne) of the 173rd Airborne Brigade take cover under enemy fire.

run out, and they rarely were sent to Vietnam or, if they were, they ended up in rear echelon service units as clerks. The very inequality of the system of manning the US Army in Vietnam would have a telling effect in the later years of the war. It should be pointed out that well over fifty per cent of the men who served in Vietnam were not conscripts but volunteers. However, this figure which runs to almost seventy five per cent is misleading since the Air Force and Navy were entirely composed of volunteers, and the Marine Corps was predominantly volunteer as well. A large number of Army combat troops remained conscripts, despite a leavening of volunteers in the airborne and Special Forces and among career soldiers.

As the bulk of combat troops were pulled from the poorer less well-educated portions of society, racism, insubordination, drug abuse and atrocities would become more endemic, though even during 1972 and 1973 effective leadership still could counter these tendencies in the better units.

The Officer Corps

Leadership, especially by junior officers, was of critical importance in Vietnam since the war was normally fought at the platoon and company level. Good lieutenants and captains would lead their men into combat and be followed, while bad ones were likely to order their men into combat and be disobeyed. The rapid expansion of the US Army put a strain on the ability of the Army to supply junior officers, particularly since the normal source of 2nd lieutenants in an emergency was the college campuses of America, the very places where the war was least popular.

There were normally three sources of officers for the Army. First was the US Military Academy at West Point, which turned out the core of the corps, as it were. From the ranks of West Point graduates came many of the professional Regular Army (RA) soldiers. During Vietnam, West Point could not come near meeting the great demand for officers. Ironically, too, by the very fact that they were the most professionally trained officers, they were often the most distrusted by the conscripts whom they were likely to be commanding. Often viewed as 'ticket-punching-lifers' out to write a name for themselves in the blood of their men, many grunts automatically distrusted the West Point ring and what it stood for.

The second primary source for officers was the Reserve Officers Training Corps (ROTC) Program present on many university campuses. As the war grew more and more unpopular, however, enrollment dropped in ROTC programs, and many campuses asked the ROTC program to leave. Ironically, too, many of the best ROTC graduates subtly tried to avoid combat service in Vietnam as well by volunteering for non-combat arms.* In addition to attending military classes and drilling during the school term, ROTC trainees attended two six-week summer sessions during their university career prior to being commissioned upon receiving their university degree. Normally, these new 2nd Lieutenants would then proceed for their specialised branch training. Those top graduates – (Distinguished Military Graduates (DMGs)) – were eligible to apply for Regular Army commissions as opposed to reserve commissions. The advantage of a Regular Army commission was that it was much more desirable should the officer aspire to a career in the Army since it would protect him more readily from cuts in manpower and grant other career advantages. Other ROTC graduates received reserve commissions which allowed them to serve on active duty, perhaps for more than twenty years but without quite the status or career potential of those with RA commissions.

The third route to a commission was through Officers Candidate School (OCS), an intensive twelve-week course leading to a commission as a 2nd lieutenant. OCS was designed to allow college graduates who had attended a college not offering ROTC or who had chosen not to enroll in ROTC to be trained for a commission. As the Vietnam War became a voracious devourer of lieutenants and captains, standards for OCS were lowered somewhat, allowing those with only two years of college or perhaps even less to qualify for a commission. OCS was also the route by which many top-notch Army NCOs who had attended college while serving were enabled to be commissioned. As an ironic result, though the Army's career officer corps viewed OCS graduates with a certain amount of disdain, many of the enlisted men in Vietnam preferred to be commanded by OCS graduates, whom they viewed as more akin to themselves, particularly if they were combat experienced NCOs prior to commissioning.

A fourth route to a commission was in place in Vietnam, though it was rarely used. The 'Battlefield Commission' which occurred fairly frequently in World War Two amidst the attrition of 'service for the duration' was rarely used in Vietnam since the one-year tour

---

*A friend of the author's who graduated in the top ten ROTC graduates from a prestigious university was the only volunteer for the infantry. Only one other of the top ten volunteered for a combat arm, and it was armor, one not particularly likely to see service in Vietnam. Ironically in this case, the top graduate volunteered for the Finance Corps, seemingly an extremely safe branch, yet found himself in Vietnam flying dangerous missions to isolated Special Forces camps to pay the irregulars.

A young captain and members of the 173rd Airborne Brigade search a hooch during a search and clear operation in South Vietnam. This officer carries an M16, the same as his men. Reliance upon great weight of fire was a characteristic of US forces in Vietnam.

allowed new junior officers to be rotated in more easily. Still, very occasionally, direct battlefield commissions were granted in Vietnam. Other direct commissions were occasionally given in non-combat arms as well to individuals with special qualifications. Doctors, for example, did not have to go through a full OCS program to receive their commissions, instead having an 'orientation' program.

At the beginning of the US Army buildup in 1965, the officer corps and, in fact, the entire US Army was of quite high caliber. Most field grade officers had seen combat in World War Two or Korea, while junior officers were in the Army because they had so chosen. The combination of the Cold War, the Cuban Missile Crisis and the Dominican Republic operation had given training an immediacy which helped keep both officers and men sharp. Although when first committed to Vietnam some junior officers reacted slowly in ambush situations and had to learn the techniques of 'area warfare,' by the later stages of the war most officers holding the rank of captain, major or lieutenant colonel had already done at least one tour in Vietnam and had learned many of the combat lessons to be taught by that conflict. However, just as the one-year tour of duty diluted the pool of experience among enlisted personnel a special quirk of the officer's tour diluted his experience even more. Most infantry lieutenants and captains serving in Vietnam actually only served their first six months on the line; then spent their second six months on staff. This policy was justified because of the heavy casualties taken by infantry lieutenants and captains, schooled in leading from the front – 496 2nd lieutenants, 1,468 1st lieutenants, and 1,009 captains killed in Vietnam of all branches, but predominantly infantry and aviation. Once again it meant that new lieutenants and captains were rotating into most line infantry units every six months, thus turning the 'old man' into the 'butter bar cherry.'

In the early days, particularly, officers took casualties as the VC/NVA zeroed in on radio antennas, thus hitting at command groups. New officers were soon briefed on the value of dispersing to limit such casualties. Company commanders, too, had to learn that maps frequently did not show what was located beneath the jungle canopy where their men would be moving. Personal reconnaissance or the use of LRRPs by the battalion or higher authority helped overcome this disadvantage.

The young officer, often only twenty one or twenty two years old himself, in Vietnam found himself facing often conflicting decisions. He was under pressure to carry out his missions, often to bring in a 'respectable body count,' yet to limit casualties. As a result, whenever possible, he used firepower from artillery or aircraft rather than expend his men. Ironically, however, this tactic often led to increased casualties from misdirected ordnance or other accidents. The young officer, too, who was generally from a middle class background, often southern, might find himself commanding a platoon with heavy concentrations of lower class whites and blacks. The latter, especially, would be suspicious of him, particularly if he had a 'cracker' accent. A new lieutenant had to win the confidence of his men while retaining the aloofness necessary to command, never an easy task but especially difficult in Vietnam.

Of course, if junior officers, who were at least in the boonies with the men, had trouble winning the confidence of the men, senior officers who often lived in incredibly cushy conditions in rear areas had even greater difficulty relating to the men. A common practice by ranking officers in some units was to buy the men's respect with medals, a practice, which along with the practice among many clerks of writing themselves, their friends and visiting officers up for medals, particularly cheapened the bronze star and air medal in Vietnam. Nevertheless, there were good field grade officers who as battalion commanders went into combat with their men or were lost while directing battles from their helicopters. The toll of 228 Army majors and 111 lieutenant colonels killed in Vietnam indicates that not all stayed away from the action, though once again helicopter losses either as pilots or passengers counted for a substantial percentage of these deaths.

Warrant Officers

Warrant officers occupied a position between commissioned officers and non-commissioned officers, commanding through a warrant rather than a commission. There were four warrant officer ranks – Warrant Officer 1, the lowest, through Warrant Officer 4, the highest. Normally, all warrant officers were reserve rather than regular officers and normally had less stringent educational requirements than commissioned officers. Traditionally, warrant officers had occupied specialised technical positions filling such slots in the TOE as Unit Supply Technician, Criminal Investigator, Aviation Technician, etc. However, the demand for helicopter pilots during the Vietnam War – 2,931 Army helicopter crewmen were killed in Vietnam – led to a greatly expanded warrant officer program to provide helicopter pilots. As a result, the sight of twenty-year-old warrant officers piloting helicopters loaded with nineteen-year-old infantrymen became all too common by 1968. For many young men who had not attended a university or who had attended only for a year or two, the warrant officer program was their only chance to become aviators and they volunteered in large quantities. In other cases the most promising graduates of various Army enlisted training centers were approached about becoming warrant officer/aviators. Sent to Fort Rucker for flight training, these young aviators made excellent chopper pilots for Vietnam service, their very youth letting them fly with the recklessness and daring needed to survive many of their missions. Nevertheless, many of these young pilots gave their lives – a total of 901 W-1, 277 W-2 and 29 W-3 died in Vietnam; the bulk of these warrant officer deaths were among aircrewmen.

Enlisted Personnel

To a large extent the American enlisted soldier in Vietnam has taken a bum rap. The stereotype has remained of a burned out, drug dependent misfit when in actuality most American enlisted personnel in Vietnam served dutifully and with no more nor less courage than young soldiers in other wars. Those in most of the line combat units especially had to be disciplined to survive. As a result, racism, drug usage and disobedience of orders was rarely a problem with line combat units, particularly during the period prior to 1969 or 1970 when most enlisted personnel felt they were fighting for something, even if they were not always sure what.

The real backbone of any Army is its NCOs, and the career NCOs the US Army entered the war with were good. Many were, in fact, combat veterans of World War Two or Korea. As the war progressed, however, this solid foundation of sergeants began to collapse as some of the best were sent to OCS, others were killed, or, most often, the

Showing the youth and mixture of front line troops in Vietnam in a war with no front line, members of the 9th Infantry Division engaging the enemy near Saigon in May 1968.

rapid expansion of the Army outpaced their numbers. By the late 1960s frequently the only real career NCOs in an infantry company were usually the first sergeant and the operations sergeant. The remainder were either junior NCOs serving in slots beyond their rank due to the shortage of NCOs – for example, SP4s or corporals as squad leaders or sergeants or staff sergeants as platoon sergeants – or 'shake and bakes.' ('Shake and bake,' a term based on an instant food available in the USA, referred to graduates of the Non Commissioned Officers School at Fort Benning who were promoted to E-5 upon graduation, E-6 if an honor graduate.)

In addition to the drain on NCOs which Vietnam itself created, the need to train troops for Vietnam put an even greater strain on the NCO corps as sergeants were assigned to training cadres in increasing numbers. As a result, NCOs were pulled from units in Europe, Korea and the Continental United States, leaving the US Army outside of Vietnam even shorter of experienced NCOs. Even units in training for Vietnam were not immune from having their NCO complement denuded. The 196th Infantry Brigade, for example, while in training had 120 critical NCOs and junior officers who were supervising the training taken away for Vietnam service. This was the same 196th Infantry Brigade which would later have numerous problems while assigned to the Americal Division. How much better the unit would have performed had it not been denuded of command personnel is, of course, speculative.

By the later years of the war, most senior NCOs were on their second or third tour and were able to pass on the expertise they had gained to some of their younger subordinates. Some of these second tour NCOs or even first tour ones even found themselves temporarily filling officer's slots as they commanded platoons. Losses among NCOs were high, too, particularly among E-5s (sergeants), 5,123 of whom lost their lives in Vietnam. An additional 2,335 E-6s (staff sergeants) also died in Vietnam. US lieutenants and sergeants were trained to lead from the front, and their casualty figures show they performed according to their training.

Below the sergeants were the privates and corporals who fought and died in the greatest numbers. Normally, every trooper serving in Vietnam had been promoted to Private First Class (PFC), though some had been busted back to private. The PFC (E-3) died in the greatest numbers of any rank in Vietnam, 12,803 paying the price. Corporals (E-4) were close behind in the number of dead with 11,494.

Many preferred being privates, with the minimal amount of responsibility and thinking to do. The exigencies of war, however, eroded the training and competency level of even the lowly private

If a soldier were wounded in Vietnam, he had a better chance of surviving the wound than in either World War Two or Korea, and a better chance of receiving medical attention without a frighteningly long delay and uncomfortable journey largely due to the innovation of helicopter medevac. The UH-19 Chicksaw – the US Army variant of the Sikorsky S-55 used by the French in Indochina in the 1950s – saw limited use by the US Army in Vietnam, before being superseded by more modern more capable helicopters, part of the process of replacing human beings with technology.

as training was carried out at an accelerated pace with the training cycle shortened by many weeks. In an attempt to fill the need for ground pounders to carry out all of those sweeps in Vietnam, infantry training centers were operating at full capacity at Fort Benning, Georgia; Fort Bragg, North Carolina; Fort Campbell, Kentucky; Fort Dix, New Jersey; Fort Gordon, Georgia; Fort Jackson, South Carolina; Fort Lewis, WA; Fort McClellelan, Alabama; Fort Ord, California; and Fort Polk, Louisiana. Gen Westmoreland's limitation of the combat tour to 365 days definitely helped morale as each trooper knew as soon as he arrived in Vietnam when he would be leaving, but it also meant that each 365 days a replacement would be needed as well.

In fact, when one considers the abbreviated training some troops received, their performance was nothing short of remarkable. The 1st Cavalry Division (Airmobile), for example, was still training on the ships deploying the division to Vietnam, yet the 1st Cav would soon build a reputation among the most glorious in American military history; while the 9th Infantry Division, which would perform exceptionally well in the Delta as amphibious infantry, had twelve weeks cut off their training schedule to get the division to Vietnam sooner. In good divisions, with good leadership, the US trooper was tough and motivated, even if his political masters in Washington were not. Fortunately, too, the Continental Army Command, which was in charge of training, had developed a tough, realistic training regimen in response to the Cold War of the early 1960s and thus was relatively well-prepared to expand to deal with the huge demands of the war.

Despite their youth, the grunts who fought the war in Vietnam had to learn the life-and-death lessons of combat and become hardened to death and destruction quickly in order to survive. They had to learn that the VC snipers would purposely wound a soldier then kill those trying to go to his aid; learn that every step could bring death or dismemberment from booby traps; yet, at nineteen or twenty years old, they would be expected to respect the niceties in dealing with prisoners. Likewise, they had to learn lessons about the Army they were serving in – such as that while his line unit might be at only sixty or seventy per cent of authorised strength, rear echelon units were almost always overstrength with an abundance of REMFs (Rear Echelon Mother Fuckers).

As the numbers of black troopers in line units grew there was some tension due to the riots in the ghettos at home, but generally combat troops helped each other stay alive and worried about such items as race only in rear areas. The frustrations of the war began to tell on the poorly educated troopers as the frustrations of booby trap losses often eroded any minimal desire to treat Vietnamese suspected of Communist sympathies with understanding.

Among the more 'elite' units such as the 173rd Airborne Brigade, 1st Air Cavalry Division, or 101st Airborne Division, the mystique of being paratroopers or air cavalrymen and pride of unit helped keep the troops sharp, but the very fact these units saw the most combat made it difficult to replace their losses with equally well-trained troops. The shortage of parachute troops made it difficult to keep even the 173rd Airborne Brigade on full parachute status, while the airborne brigades of the 1st Cav and the 101st Airborne Divisions were soon getting replacements who were non-para-troopers. Arriving in Vietnam as 'Airborne, Unassigned' normally guaranteed that graduates of jump school would soon be where the action was since they would normally be sent to the airborne unit seeing the heaviest action and, hence, needing the largest infusion from the repo depo. Even some of the esprit de corps of the most 'elite' units began to erode when the troopers saw their comrades' lives wasted. In the wake of the Battle for Ap Bia Mountain (Hill 937) – best known as 'Hamburger Hill' – in May 1969, even some members of the 101st Airborne Division refused to advance.

The greatest disintegration in morale among the enlisted troops in Vietnam, however, occurred during the period from 1971 on when the American combat commitment was obviously drawing to a close and troops were being used much less aggressively in the field. There was a far higher percentage of fraggings, shootings and accidents during this period than during the earlier heavy combat days of the 1967 and 1968. The inaction of these final years also contributed to the much more prevalent drug abuse, crime, racial problems and disobedience as the troops fell prey to their frustration and resentment. Personnel turnover and the shortage of officers and NCOs contributed to problems as well, once again especially during the final two years.

Other units outside of Vietnam were affected by the malaise of the early 1970s, too, as they frequently became either holding units for those veterans of Vietnam awaiting discharge or as manpower pools from which levies for Vietnam could be pulled.

Despite the frustrations and inequalities of the war, however, the average enlisted man fought well in a war with no front lines in the traditional sense. Though the War in Vietnam produced the disillusioned members of Vietnam Veterans Against the War, it also produced the toughened combat vets who would form the basis for the post-Vietnam highly professional Army. Though the emphasis on 'body count' beyond a doubt caused much senseless killing, there is also little doubt that US troops inflicted horrendous casualties on the VC and NVA, despite the fact they were normally fighting at the place and time of the Communists' choosing.

Perhaps the best way to end a discussion of the men who fought the war in Vietnam is to point out that most do not view themselves as losers. They know that when they met the enemy they usually prevailed; they learned the lesson which combat soldiers have learned throughout history – one can continue fighting despite numbing fear and can win. But they also learned that courage and dedication on the battlefield are not enough if not backed by political will. The men who fought the war are now the generation which views politicians as the least trustworthy group in American society; they learned the hard way that the men who fight the war are not the men who control the war, and the men who controlled the war in Vietnam certainly aren't the men whose blood flowed there.

Ironically, there was much distrust between the veterans of World War Two and Korean and Vietnam veterans during the Vietnam era and the years right after the US pullout. Few Vietnam veterans joined organizations such as the VFW or the American Legion and many members of these organisations viewed the Vietnam veteran as not quite the soldier they had been. As time has passed, however, Vietnam veterans have gained acceptance and like the veterans of earlier wars have found that for the guy burying his face in the mud as bullets whizz overhead the name of the war does not matter that much. The guys that died with the 1st Infantry Division in World War One are just as dead as the ones who died in World War Two with the same division or as the far greater numbers that died in Vietnam with the Big Red One.

The radio code in Vietnam for the command 'continue mission' was 'Charlie Mike' and US troops Charlie Miked from 1965 until 1972. It was not until they were gone that the South fell; the NVA and VC had learned the hard way that they could not stand against the US Army, but the US Army had learned the hard way that it could not stand against the American electorate and their representatives in Washington.

Separate Infantry Brigade

Mission
To destroy military forces and to control land area including population and resources.

Assignment
As determined by Department of the Army and Theater Commanders.

Capability
a. Command, control and administration of up to five maneuver battalions in independent offensive and defensive combat operations in nuclear and nonnuclear war;
b. Sustained combat operations against similarly, or less well equipped land forces in areas where a military force of less than a division size is required, or as a part of a larger force;
c. Operations in difficult weather or terrain:
d. Army airborne operations;
e. Operate as a part of a joint amphibious force;
f. Operate as a part of a joint airborne force;
g. Control of enemy populations;
h. Restorations of order;
i. Operations with limited logistical support;

j. May be attached to an operated as part of a division;

k. Individuals of this organization, except medical and chaplain personnel, can engage in effective, coordinated defense of the unit's area or installation.

Limitations

This unit has the following organic limitations:

a. No air defense artillery;

b. Limited airlift capability;

c. Limited mobility;

d. Limited protection against armor;

e. Limited protection against artillery and nuclear effects;

f. This unit requires appropriate signal augmentation for an external signal communications capability.

Infantry Battalion (Mechanized)

Mission

To close with the enemy by means of fire and maneuver in order to destroy or capture him or to repel his assault by fire, close combat and counterattack.

Assignment

Organic to Infantry Division (Mechanized), TOE 37G, Separate Infantry Brigade, TOE 7-100, Separate Infantry Brigade (Mechanized), TIE 37-100G, Armored Division, TOE 17G, or Separate Armored Brigade, TOE 17-100G.

Capabilities

a. A base of fire and maneuver elements;

b. The means to seize and hold terrain;

c. The capability to conduct independent operations on a limited scale;

d. Limited antitank defense;

e. Indirect fire support for organic and atttached units;

f. Long range patrolling when properly equipped;

g. A high degree of cross-country mobility to successfully exploit the effects of nuclear and nonnuclear weapons;

h. A force that complements and enhances the inherent capabilities of tank elements, when employed in tank/infantry teams;

i. A force that can participate in airmobile operations when provided with air transport;

j. When this battalion is transferred or detached from the division, or separate brigade, a personnel section from the Personnel Services Division, AG Section, Administration Company, TOE 12-37G or TOE 12-177G, will be transferred with or attached to this battalion. This personnel section will be composed of those individuals who regularly maintain this battalion's records in the Personnel Service Division;

k. Chaplain support is required from brigade headquarters;

l. Unit is dependent upon the U.S. Air Force to provide a forward air controller (FAC) for directing tactical air support;

m. Individuals of this organization, except medical personnel can engage in effective, coordinated defense of the unit's area or installations;

n. One hundred percent mobile in organic transportation.

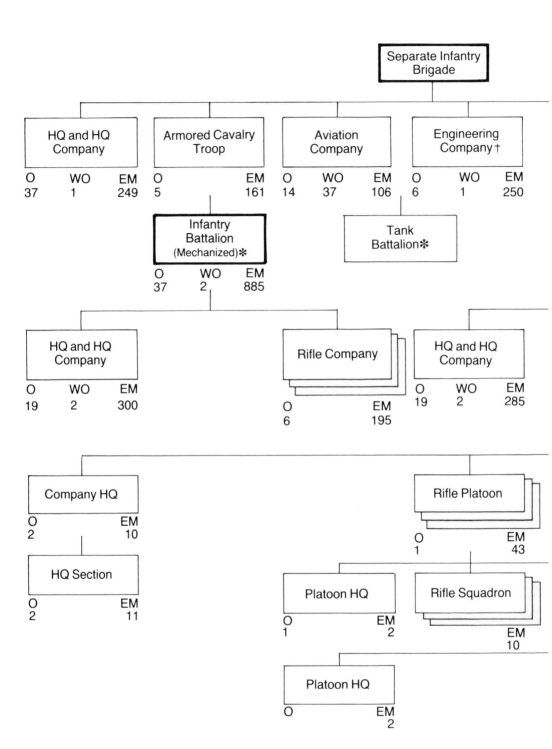

Separate Infantry Brigade

HQ and HQ Company
O 37
WO 1
EM 249

Armored Cavalry Troop
O 5
EM 161

Aviation Company
O 14
WO 37
EM 106

Engineering Company †
O 6
WO 1
EM 250

Infantry Battalion (Mechanized)✻
O 37
WO 2
EM 885

Tank Battalion✻

HQ and HQ Company
O 19
WO 2
EM 300

Rifle Company
O 6
EM 195

HQ and HQ Company
O 19
WO 2
EM 285

Company HQ
O 2
EM 10

HQ Section
O 2
EM 11

Rifle Platoon
O 1
EM 43

Platoon HQ
O 1
EM 2

Rifle Squadron
EM 10

Platoon HQ
O
EM 2

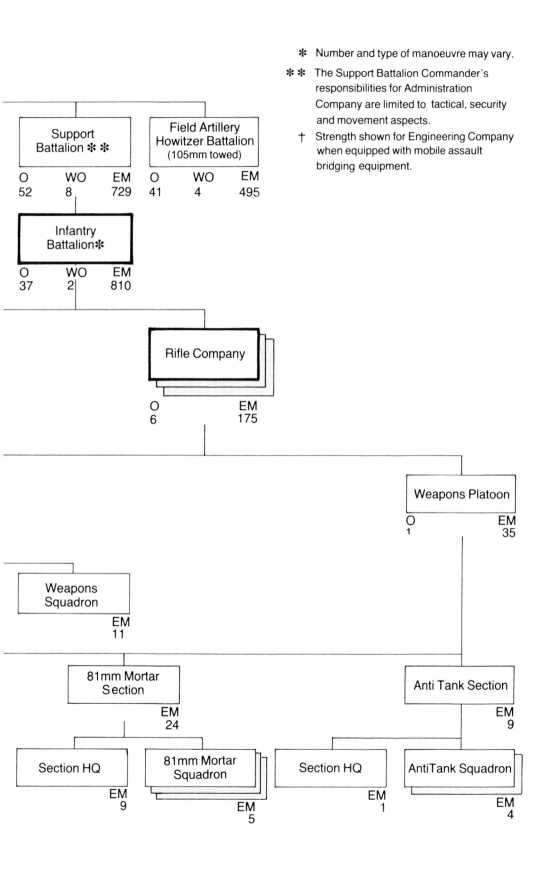

* Number and type of manoeuvre may vary.

** The Support Battalion Commander's responsibilities for Administration Company are limited to tactical, security and movement aspects.

† Strength shown for Engineering Company when equipped with mobile assault bridging equipment.

Support Battalion **

O	WO	EM
52	8	729

Field Artillery Howitzer Battalion (105mm towed)

O	WO	EM
41	4	495

Infantry Battalion*

O	WO	EM
37	2	810

Rifle Company

O	EM
6	175

Weapons Platoon

O	EM
1	35

Weapons Squadron

EM
11

81mm Mortar Section

EM
24

Anti Tank Section

EM
9

Section HQ

EM
9

81mm Mortar Squadron

EM
5

Section HQ

EM
1

AntiTank Squadron

EM
4

Infantry Battalion

Mission
To close with the enemy by means of fire and maneuver in order to destroy or capture him or to repel his assault by fire, close combat or counterattack.

Assignment
Organic to Infantry Division, TOE 7G, and Separate Infantry Brigade, TOE 7-100G.

Capabilities
a. A base of fire and maneuver elements;
b. The means to seize and hold terrain;
c. The capability to conduct independent operations on a limited scale;
d. Limited antitank protection;
e. Indirect fire support for organic and attached units;
f. Long range patrolling when properly equipped;
g. A force that can participate in motorized, mechanized, and joint airborne operations when provided with sufficient transportation;
h. A force that can participate in airmobile operations when provided with sufficient air transport;
i. The capability to maneuver in all suitable types of terrain under all climatic conditions;
j. Dependent upon the Headquarters and Headquarters Company, Infantry Division Brigade, TOE 7-42G, for chaplain support;
k. Individuals of his organization can engage in effective, coordinated defense of the unit's area or installation;
l. For mobility of the components of this battalion see applicable TOE.

Rifle Company

Mission
To close with the enemy by means of fire and maneuver to destroy or capture him or to repel his assualt by fire, close combat and counterattack.

Assignment
Organic to Infantry Battalion, Infantry Division or Infantry Battalion, Separate Infantry Brigade, TOE 7-15G.

Capabilities
a. Providing a base of fire and maneuver;
b. Seizing and holding terrain;
c. Maneuvring in all types of terrain and under all climatic conditions;
d. Capitalizing on all forms of mobility;
e. This unit is dependent upon the Headquarters and Headquarters Company, Infantry Battalion, TOE 7-16, for provision of mess facilities when centralized at battalion level;
f. Fifteen percent mobile.

3
COMMAND AND CONTROL WITHIN VIETNAM

The initial US command within Vietnam was the Military Assistance Advisory Group-Indochina (MAAG-Indochina), which served from 17 September 1950 to 31 October 1955. Present during the final stages of French rule and the first stages of Vietnamese independence, MAAG-Indochina was replaced by MAAG-Vietnam on 1 November 1955. MAAG-Vietnam would serve until 15 May 1960 providing training to Vietnamese combat troops and furnishing field advisors to Vietnamese units. Although Military Assistance Command Vietnam (MACV) came into existence on 8 February 1962, MAAG-Vietnam continued to function for an additional two years, primarily since its advisory effort was already in place. MACV would, however, become the major command within Vietnam, controlling the massive troop commitment which would come beginning in 1965. During the approximately eleven years of MACV's existence before its departure from Vietnam on 29 March 1973, MACV had four commanders. The first was Paul D. Harkins, but the second and third commanders, Gen William Westmoreland and Gen Creighton Abrams who commanded respectively from June 1964 to July 1968, and July 1968 to June 1973, were the best known since they commanded during the time of major US effort. The last commander of MACV was Gen Frederick Weyand. Westmoreland, the tough ex-paratrooper, was associated most closely with the early optimistic commitment of US troops to hold the line and give the Vietnamese armed forces time to mature, while the less colorful Abrams was the military architect of 'Vietnamization.'

It should be understood that although MACV was commanded by an Army general it was a joint services command for all military forces in Vietnam to include the Seventh Air Force, III Marine Amphibious Force, the various Army and Navy units, and various special activities. Also falling under MACV was the Field Advisory Element, which by 1968 was providing almost 9,500 advisors to training schools, district officials, Regional and Popular Forces (known to US troops as 'Ruff Puffs'), to regiments and battalions of the Vietnamese Army and Marine Corps and to squadrons and

Gen Creighton Abrams along with Viet and American Special forces officers.

Flotillas of the Vietnamese Air Force and Navy. In many cases the advisor's lot was not an enviable one as he was frequently located away from other American troops, often with units whose reliability was questionable: yet the Field Advisory Element did a remarkable job in keeping ARVN units in the field and fighting.

Also falling under the MACV commander was US Army Vietnam (USARV), the command created in July 1965 to control support and logistical units for the Army combat units in Vietnam. Among the USARV components, but by no means all, were: Department of the Army Combat Development Command Liaison Field Office; Department of the Army Special Security Groups; US Army Material Command Communications System, Saigon; US Army Material Command Electronics Command Field Service Activity; US Army Material Command Logistics Assistance Office, Long Binh; US Army Material Command Office of Procurement and Material, Army Area; US Army Material Command Weapons Command, Vietnam; US Army China Beach Rest and Recuperation Center, Da Nang; US Army Engineer Command, Vietnam; US

Army Engineer Construction Agency; US Army Medical Command, Vietnam; US Army Postal Group, Vietnam; US Army Procurement Agency; and numerous others. As the US military effort in Vietnam wound down, USARV was replaced by USARV/MACV Support Command which operated from 15 May 1972 until 28 March 1973.

The Field Forces and Other Corps Level Commands

As the US Army moved from the advisory to the combat role, it became necessary to have a command between MACV and the divisional level. The first such unit – Field Force, Vietnam – became operational on 15 November 1965. This unit evolved from the original provisional field force HQ, Task Force ALPHA (Provisional), which had been formed in August 1965. Both units were responsible for Army units operating in the II Corps Tactical Zone. Although the normal US Army procedure would have been to use a corps HQ to control divisions and separate brigades, the more flexible Field Force was adopted in Vietnam to avoid confusion with the Vietnamese corps structure, to supervise logistical and support functions as well as combat, and to allow the adding of various subordinate headquarters, including corps HQs.

On 15 March 1966, Field Force, Vietnam became I Field Force, Vietnam with responsibility for operational control of US and allied units in II Corps Tactical Zone as well as giving combat assistance to the Vietnamese within II Corps TZ. Among the US units which would fall under I Field Force command at one time or another were: 1st Cavalry Division (Airmobile); 3rd Brigade, 25th Infantry Division; 1st Brigade, 101st Airborne Division; 4th Infantry Division; and 173rd Airborne Brigade. Additionally, Task Force SOUTH, composed of units drawn from the 4th Infantry Division, 173rd Airborne Brigade and 101st Airborne Division, fell under I Field Force during its existence as well.

Formed simultaneously with I Field Force was II Field Force, Vietnam to control allied and US units in III Corps Tactical Zone. Since this Tactical Zone contained Saigon and other critical areas, II Field Force would become the largest US Army combat command in Vietnam. Units which fell under II Field Force control at some point included: 1st Infantry Division; 3rd Brigade, 4th Infantry Division; 3rd Brigade, 82nd Airborne Division; 11th Armored Cavalry Regiment; 196th Infantry Brigade (Light); 199th Infantry Brigade (Light); 1st Cavalry Division (Airmobile); 9th Infantry Division; 25th Infantry Division; 101st Airborne Division; and 173rd Airborne Brigade.

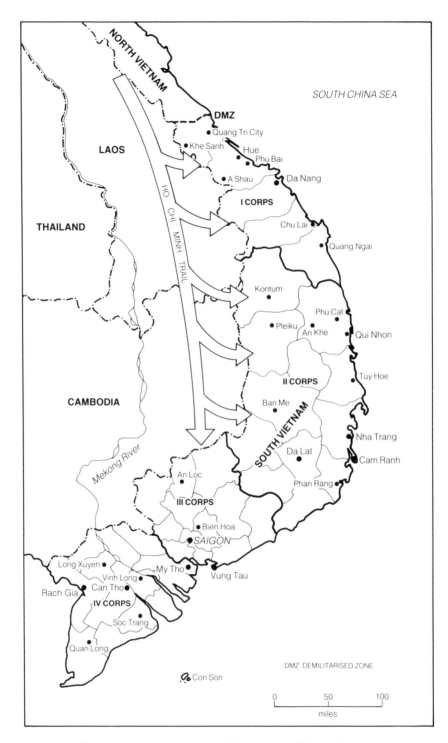

NORTH VIETNAM

LAOS

THAILAND

CAMBODIA

DMZ

Quang Tri City
Khe Sanh
Hue
Phu Bai
A Shau
Da Nang

I CORPS

Chu Lai
Quang Ngai

Kontum

Phu Cat
Pleiku
An Khe
Qui Nhon

II CORPS
Tuy Hoe

Ban Me

SOUTH VIETNAM

Da Lat
Nha Trang
Cam Ranh

Mekong River

An Loc
Phan Rang

III CORPS

Bien Hoa
SAIGON

Long Xuyen
My Tho
Vung Tau
Vinh Long
Rach Gia
Can Tho

IV CORPS

Soc Trang

Quan Long

Con Son

SOUTH CHINA SEA

HO CHI MINH TRAIL

DMZ: DEMILITARISED ZONE

0   50   100
miles

The Corps Tactical Areas and Provinces of South Vietnam.

One US Army corps did serve in Vietnam – XXIV Corps. Activated in Vietnam on 15 August 1968, XXIV Corps was consolidated with Provisional Corps, Vietnam, which had been established in March 1968, from MACV Forward, the command established on 9 February 1968 to counter the NVA/VC Tet Offensive. Under the operational control of III Marine Amphibious Force, XXIV Corps controlled Army units in the I Corps Tactical Zone, at various times including: 23rd Infantry (American) Division; 1st Brigade, 5th Infantry Division (Mechanized); 3rd Brigade, 82nd Airborne Division; 1st Cavalry Division (Airmobile); 101st Airborne Division (Airmobile); and 196th Infantry Brigade (separate). Although I Field Force, Vietnam and II Field Force, Vietnam departed in late April/early May, 1971, XXIV Corps, controlling the residual US combat presence, remained operational until 30 June 1972.

It is interesting to note that the 1st Cavalry Division (Airmobile) served under each of the three corps level commands at some time during its sojourn in Vietnam, an indication of its use wherever its airmobility would be most valuable at a given point in the war.

4
INFANTRY

Although he may have been frequently delivered to battle via helicopter, Vietnam was still an infantryman's war. Due to the terrain in Vietnam and the counterinsurgency nature of the war, it was not just an infantry war but an infantry war at a very basic level. The squad, platoon, and company were the units offering the most effective control in search and destroy missions and patrolling. The infantryman faced myriad problems in fighting the war in Vietnam, not the least of which was that his traditional mission of taking ground and holding it did not apply. Frequently, he might have to take the same ground a dozen times, then retreat from it back to his base camp.

The infantryman did the best job of taking the war to the enemy of any of the conventional US forces fighting in Vietnam, but most of the engagements still only took place if the enemy chose to fight. As a result, the infantry war in Vietnam was a very frustrating one. Facing boobytraps, snipers, and an enemy indistinguishable from the local villagers, it is easy to understand why the infantryman was often the most cynical soldier in Vietnam. While it seemed to the Grunt that the bulk of the US military establishment in Vietnam consisted of 'REMFs' basking in safe rear areas making money on the black market and living with attractive Vietnamese girls, the infantryman, often poor and uneducated, faced danger with radios that worked only intermittently, many senior officers who were only 'ticket punchers,' and a population both at home and in Vietnam that did not support him. By 1970, if the average infantryman had been asked to list his enemies in order the lists would have probably run something like: the South Vietnamese, the Pentagon, REMFs, the American public, Jane Fonda, leeches, and finally the NVA/VC. Nevertheless, though younger, less well-educated, and with a far more nebulous mission than his predecessors in World War Two or Korea, the American infantryman in Vietnam fought well.

Infantry Unit Organization

Conventional Infantry
According to TOE 7G, the infantry division circa 1967 had a strength of approximately 18,500 men. Each division could be subdivided into

three brigades, each with three infantry battalions, each with three companies, each with three platoons, each with three squads. TOE 7-15G set the strength for an infantry battalion at thirty-seven officers, two warrant officers and 810 enlisted men. The battalion was divided into an HQ and HQ Company with nineteen officers, two warrant officers and 285 enlisted men and three rifle companies, each with six officers and 175 enlisted men. Among the specialist functions within the HQ and HQ Company were the Battalion Ground Surveillance Section, the Battalion Communications Platoon, the Battalion Recon Platoon, the Battalion Heavy Mortar Platoon, the Battalion Anti-Tank Platoon, the Battalion Support Platoon, the Battalion Maintenance Platoon, the Battalion Medical Platoon, the Battalion Air Control Team, *et al.* Each rifle company was divided into a company HQ with two officers and ten enlisted men, a company weapons platoon with three 81mm mortar squads and two anti-tank squads with 106mm recoilless rifles and three rifle platoons. Each rifle platoon with one officer and forty-three enlisted men was broken into a platoon HQ, three ten- man rifle squads, and an eleven-man weapons squad.

Additionally, divisional units included the HQ and HQ Company, the MP Company, the Aviation Battalion, the Engineer Battalion, the Signal Battalion, the Armored Cavalry Squadron, the Divisional Artillery and the Support Command. Along with the three brigade HQ and HQ Companies, these units formed the division base which accounted for slightly over fifty per cent of the division's strength.

In actuality, divisions serving in Vietnam usually had strengths twenty-five per cent or more higher than the standard TO&E due to certain augmentations. The infantry battalion as normally organised in Vietnam offers a good example. Since the heavier weapons were normally not needed on most missions in Vietnam, helicopter gunships, 'fast movers' (USAF ground support aircraft) or artillery instead supplying support, a fourth rifle company was normally organised within each battalion. The resulting battalion had a HQ and HQ Company with fifteen officers, two warrant officers and 147 enlisted men; four rifle companies with six officers and 158 enlisted men; and a combat support company with four officers and ninety six enlisted men. This organisation resulted in allowing more 'Grunts' to function as light infantryman for airmobile and/or patrolling operations, thus making it a TOE better suited for the war in Vietnam. Carrying this organisation to its logical conclusion, brigades in Vietnam frequently added a fourth battalion as well.

Also serving in Vietnam were four light infantry brigades, the strength of which varied depending upon the number of infantry

Members of the 173rd Airborne Brigade take cover from enemy fire during the Battle for Hill 875 in November 1967.

battalions (light) assigned. Since normally four infantry battalions were assigned to such brigades, strength will be given based on this assumption. Authorised strength of a typical light infantry brigade would then be 280 officers, forty one warrant officers and 4,293 enlisted men. Each infantry battalion would have an authorised strength of thirty seven officers, one warrant officer and 731 enlisted men, and would be broken into three rifle companies, an HQ and HQ Company and a Combat Support Company. In Vietnam the battalion might be organised with a fourth rifle company.

Airborne Infantry

The airborne division circa 1967 was substantially smaller and more lightly equipped than a regular infantry division. The airborne division TOE called for 844 officers, 174 warrant officers and 12,431 enlisted men. Each of the nine airborne infantry battalions consisted of thirty-six officers, two warrant officers and 771 enlisted men.

Divisional troops included the HQ and HQ Company, the MP Company, Aviation Battalion, Engineer Battalion, Signal Battalion, Armored Cavalry Squadron, Divisional Artillery, Support Command Brigade HQ and HQ Company. The HQ and HQ Company of the Airborne Battalion contained eighteen officers, two warrant officers and 243 enlisted men, while each of the three Airborne Rifle Companies contained six officers and 176 enlisted men. The rifle company was broken into three 45-man rifle platoons, a 32-man weapons platoon, and a 15-man HQ section. The only airborne division which served in Vietnam in its entirety was the 101st Airborne which was converted in 1968 into an airmobile division. While serving in Vietnam its TO&E was adjusted, though not as much as the conventional Infantry division's since the airborne TO&E was already designed around light, highly mobile troops.

Two separate airborne brigades – the 173rd Airborne Brigade and the 3rd Brigade, 82nd Airborne Division served in Vietnam so a discussion of the TOE of separate airborne brigades should also be of interest. According to TOE 57-100G the separate airborne brigade had a strength of 244 officers, thirty-seven warrant officers and 3,860 enlisted men. In actuality, the 173rd Airborne Brigade, for example, in Vietnam often ran five hundred to one thousand over this number. According to the TOE, each of the three airborne infantry battalions of the brigade had the same strength as battalions in an airborne division. Specialist brigade troops included the HQ and HQ Company, the Armored Cavalry Troop, the Engineer Company, the Support Battalion and the Field Artillery Battalion. For Vietnam service, an aviation company would normally have been assigned.

Airmobile Infantry
Because the airmobile divisions were termed air cavalry in Vietnam, it is easy to forget that once delivered to battle by their helicopters they were still infantrymen. In fact, the best way to think of the air cavalryman is probably as an air dragoon, who once dismounted became a rifleman. The airmobile division's aviation complement will receive substantial discussion in the chapter on aviation; this section will concentrate on the infantry elements of the division.

Total manpower of the airmobile division according to TOE 67-T was 1,167 officers, 670 warrant officers and 13,944 enlisted personnel. The greater number of officers and warrant officers proportionally can be explained by the larger complement of

aviators within the airmobile division. Divisional troops included
the HQ and HQ Company, MP Company, Aviation Group, Signal
Battalion, Engineer Battalion, Air Cavalry Squadron, Divisional
Artillery, Support Command, and two Airmobile Brigade HQ and
HQ Companies and one Airborne Brigade HQ and HQ Company.
Note that one brigade was authorised as an airborne brigade. Rather
than nine infantry battalions as one would expect, the airmobile
division was authorised eight, three of them airborne battalions. In
the 1st Cavalry, at least, these battalions were known as squadrons.
In Vietnam service, the ninth battalion was normally added to allow
each brigade three maneuver battalions.

Each airmobile or airborne infantry battalion within the
airmobile division was, according to TOE 7-55T, authorised 37
officers, 1 warrant officer and 729 enlisted men. These were divided
into an HQ and HQ Company with 14 officers, 1 warrant officer and
119 enlisted men; three rifle companies each with 6 officers and 164
enlisted men, and a combat support company with 5 officers and 118
enlisted men. This combat support company included the Recon
Platoon, Mortar Platoon and Anti-Tank Platoon. Each rifle company
consisted of the company HQ, three rifle platoons, and a mortar
platoon. The 45-man rifle platoon could be broken into three rifle
squads, each of 10 men, and a weapons squad of 11 men.

Airborne and airmobile divisions, because of the caliber of their
troops and because of their ability for rapid response generally, saw
a great deal of combat. As a result, they were frequently below
authorised strength, particularly after a major action. Infantrymen
who were airborne qualified and who arrived in country 'airborne
unassigned' soon learned that they were likely to join whichever of
the airborne/airmobile divisions was most heavily engaged at the
time since that was the unit which would have suffered the most
casualties and, hence, would need the most replacements.

The Infantryman's Tools: Weapons and Equipment

As the war progressed, the infantryman's gear progressed along
with it. In some cases, weapons or equipment which had been
designed primarily with a land war in Europe in mind proved
inappropriate for the fighting in Vietnam. In other cases, weapons or
equipment proved themselves in combat and have continued in
service until today. Since operations were frequently carried out at
the company level, this discussion will limit itself to the weapons
likely to be encountered in a typical rifle company in Vietnam.

81mm mortarmen firing from a mortar pit at Dalat, Republic of Vietnam.

The infantryman's basic weapon has traditionally been the rifle. Vietnam was no exception, and it was the new infantry rifle in Vietnam which proved most controversial. At the start of the US infantry commitment to the Vietnam War, the M14 was the standard US Infantry weapon. Heavy and bulky for jungle fighting, the M14 fired the 7.62mm NATO round. Although the M14 was a selective-fire weapon allowing either semi- or full-automatic fire, the selector switch was normally locked on most weapons: however, on the M14E2, which was designed as a squad automatic weapon to replace the old Browning Automatic Rifle, the switch was operable.

When the 173rd Airborne arrived in Vietnam, the M16 was already being issued to airborne units. About ten per cent shorter than the M14, at 99cm; and just over half the weight with a fully loaded 30-round magazine, at 3.82kg, the M16 was much better suited for the war in Vietnam. The lighter 5.56mm cartridge could be carried in greater quantity, too, an advantage when supply was frequently via limited helicopter lift. An unstated advantage from the point of view of the US attrition strategy against the the VC/

NVA was that the 5.56 round tended to cause nasty wounds creating a drain on the limited Communist medical resources. There were some initial problems with the M16 caused by a switch to a powder which fouled the bore more heavily, combined with the wet climate in Vietnam and the poor maintenance of the weapons by some users. As a result, the chambers became pitted causing cases to stick rendering the weapon inoperable or causing the bolt to fail to go all the way forward due to fouling. In addition to educating the troops in the necessity of better maintaining the weapons, the M16A1 was introduced which incorporated a bolt assist to allow the bolt to be pushed into battery if necessary. Chambers were also chromed to make them more durable. The M16 was 'select fire' and was much more controllable in full automatic than the M14 had been. Still, US infantrymen had too much of a tendency to fire their weapons on 'Rock and Roll' rather than aiming and hitting their target. With each squad member having full auto capability, the two automatic riflemen were replaced with M60 machinegunners in some squads.

The **XM177E2**, which was also known as the CAR-I5, was a shorter version of the M16 with only an 11.5 inch (29.2cm) barrel and telescoping stock, very popular with special operations troops but normally seeing only limited use with line infantry units. The XM21 sniper's rifle, which was an accurised version of the M14 did see highly successful service with Army snipers throughout the war. A Redfield three to nine-power variable telescopic sight was standard with this version.

Although pistols are normally derided by staff officers and other non-combatants, the infantryman has always realised that the pistol makes a good insurance policy, one which can be with him even when it is inconvenient to have his rifle present. As a result, many infantrymen in Vietnam had pistols, either authorized or unauthorized, though later in the war the use of unauthorized pistols was cracked down upon. The standard issue pistol for those infantrymen allowed them by the TOE was the 1911A1 .45 automatic. With a magazine capacity of seven rounds of .45 caliber ammunition, the Government Model auto was a deadly close-quarters weapon best remembered for its stopping power and reliability, though in the hands of troops not really trained to shoot it, accuracy was sometimes difficult. Just as the 'Grunts' who were not authorized a pistol frequently managed to 'promote' one from somewhere, company or platoon officers who were authorized a

Opposite: This photograph helps portray the jungle conditions the US infantryman faced in Vietnam. (*Larry Dring*)

pistol normally supplemented it with a rifle, realising a pistol made a poor primary weapon in combat.

Two other weapons which saw more use with special operations units than with line infantry units were the submachinegun and the fighting shotgun. The standard US Army issue SMG in Vietnam was the **M3A1** 'Grease Gun.' Chambered for the same .45 acp round as the Government Model pistol, the Grease Gun could deliver its 30-round magazine with surprising accuracy in the hands of a skilled user. Trench/Riot shotguns such as the **Ithaca Model** 37 were sometimes carried by the point man on patrol who would rely on the scattergun's devastating close range fire to sweep the trail clear if coming upon the enemy unexpectedly. Once again, however, this weapon saw far more use with special operations units.

The **M60 GPMG** saw very wide use in Vietnam on armored vehicles and helicopters and as an infantry weapon. M60 gunners were usually selected for their size and strength since humping the 10.48kg weapon on patrol took stamina. In firefights, however, its 550 rounds per minute were greatly appreciated. Normally, for squad/platoon use, the M60 was used with the bipod and was frequently carried slung around the gunner's neck. Though it could be fired from the hip, it was far more effective when fired prone using the bipod and sights. Since the M60 used the 7.62mm NATO round from a link belt, ammunition supply was somewhat of a problem in units armed with M16s; hence, the ubiquitous photographs of troops in Vietnam carrying extra belts for the M60.

The **M79** Grenade Launcher, affectionately known as 'Thumper' among infantrymen in Vietnam, was one of the most useful squad weapons in the war since it gave each squad two integral indirect fire weapons. Capable of firing HE (High Explosive) or smoke rounds accurately out to 400m in the hands of a skilled user, the M79 was a single-shot break open 40mm weapon. Skilled 'Thumper' men were highly regarded among Grunts in Vietnam.

Also firing the 40mm grenade was the **M203** launcher, which was mounted directly below the handguard on an M16 rifle. The advantage of the M203 was that it allowed the grenadier to function as a rifleman as well. The only real disadvantage of the M203 was that its range was 50-100m less than that of the M79.

Opposite above: Paratroopers of the 173rd Airborne Brigade along with a dog and handler of the 39th Scout Dog Platoon during the fighting for Hill 875.

Opposite below: During operation OREGON, members of the 1st Air Cav prepare to air assault into an LZ. The air cavalrymen are on the chopper's skids ready to disembark rapidly.

An M60 machinegunner with his 'hog' during a sweep in Vietnam.

The **M72** LAW (Light Anti-Tank Weapon) was almost never used in the anti-tank role in Vietnam, but it did prove extremely useful against entrenched enemy or as a bunker-buster. The LAW's 1kg rocket had a maximum effective range of 300m.

Although a company's mortars were frequently left behind on patrolling operations, the **M29** 81mm mortar saw wide enough use that it should be mentioned. Weighing 48.5kg in firing position, the M29 could be broken down into the barrel (12.7kg), bipod (14kg) and baseplate (21.7kg) for transport. Using HE rounds, the M29 had a maximum range of 3,500m and a maximum rate of fire of 30 rounds per minute. In addition to HE, smoke and illuminating rounds were also available.

Of the various hand grenades in service with the US Army in Vietnam, three types are of special interest. For the average infantryman, the most important may have been the **M18** colored smoke grenade. Available in red, green, yellow, or violet, this grenade which emitted smoke for 60-90 seconds, was used to mark helicopter LZs for extraction, to mark positions for air support, and in other cases where it was necessary to identify the unit's location to friendly forces. The choice of colors helped prevent the enemy from using captured smoke grenades to decoy in helicopters. For offensive use the **M26** grenade was a fragmentation grenade with four to five second fuse. It was intended that the M26 be carried on or in ammunition pouches, each pouch holding three grenades within the pouch and one on each side. Because of the tangle of vines and branches in many operational areas in Vietnam, troops avoided clipping grenades to webbed gear, packs, etc where a branch might conceivably pull the pin and detonate the grenade. For clearing bunkers or tunnels, the M-34 incendiary grenade (also known as the 'Willie Pete' because of its white phosphorous content) was especially useful as it also had a fragmentation effect, which

An M60 machinegunner, his ammo belt draped across his shoulder, fords a stream.

combined with the burning phosphorous particles flying over a 35-meter area, to wreak havoc with the enemy in any confined area.

The **M18A1** Anti-Personnel Mine was so widely used in Vietnam that it must be mentioned in any discussion of infantry weapons. Using seven hundred steel balls imbedded in a plastic matrix and backed by an explosive charge, the M18A1 was a formidable area defensive weapon. Emplaced around fire bases, on patrols at night around positions, or flanking the killing zone on ambushes; the Claymore could be devastating out to as far as 50m when initiated by its trip wire or hand-held initiator. With his typical ingenuity, the infantryman also discovered that the plastic explosive from inside the Claymore could be used in small quantities to heat his C-rations.

The Infantry Arrives

Infantry advisors had been serving with the Vietnamese Forces since the French withdrawal and had been serving down to regimental level as early as 1959 but it was not until after President Johnson designated Vietnam a Combat Zone in late April 1965 that the stage was set for US Army and Marine infantrymen to begin carrying out their own operations in Vietnam. The first Army Infantry unit to arrive was the 173rd Airborne Brigade, which was deployed to Bien Hoa from Okinawa on 7 May 1965. The 173rd, which had been the primary rapid reinforcement unit in the Far East, was an excellent choice since the unit was highly motivated and highly trained, particularly in jungle warfare.

About a month after the arrival of the 'Sky Soldiers,' Gen Westmoreland requested forty-four US and allied infantry battalions to help stabilise the deteriorating situation in Vietnam. This request was followed on 26 June by Westmoreland receiving much broader authority to use US troops in combat. As a result, the 173rd Airborne Brigade was committed along with ARVN para-troopers and members of the Royal Australian Regiment against the VC on 28 June in War Zone D, a traditional VC stronghold. Although this initial action was not particularly auspicious for the paratroopers, the 173rd would soon establish itself as a very tough competent unit, a unit which became a 'fire brigade' to be used anywhere it was needed.

The next US infantry unit to arrive was the 2nd Brigade of the famous 1st Infantry Division – the 'Big Red One' – the Brigade HQ of which became operational in country on 11 July. Initially, one battalion of this brigade was assigned to provide security at Cam Ranh Bay, while the other two infantry battalions helped secure the

M79 grenadiers of the 4th Infantry Division give suppressive fire during Operation OREGON.

giant airbase at Bien Hoa. This acclimatisation period during which units dug in and provided security before starting active patrolling would become standard as new units rotated into Vietnam. Back in the States, the remainder of the 1st Infantry Division was ordered to be combat ready by 1 September 1965 in preparation for following its point brigade to Vietnam, a deployment which was completed by late October.

In realisation that the US buildup would make it tough if not impossible to win the war, the VC/NVA stepped up their attacks in response to the first US ground operations, thus starting the cycle which would continue to bring even more US Infantry rapidly into Vietnam. The 1st Brigade of the 101st Airborne arrived in country very late in July to put three US infantry brigades in the field against the Communists. On the same day that the 1st Brigade of the 101st's HQ went operational – 29 July 1965 – President Johnson doubled the draft call to 35,000 men per month. He thus indicated the US intent to send even more men.

The next deployment did not take place until September 1965, but it was an especially important deployment as the 1st Cavalry Division (Airmobile) became the first entire division sent as well as the first of a new type combat division – the airmobile infantry division. Sent both to offer the airmobility needed to fix the enemy in Vietnam and to test the airmobility concept the air cavalrymen would be watched by the US military establishment as well as friend and foe alike overseas, all interested to see if they were marking the dawn of a new age of mounted combat.

Sent to the Central Highlands to help counter the Communist threat to this highly critical area of Vietnam, the 1st Cav operated out of An Khe. The Cav's move into An Khe was covered by the now battle-toughened men of the 173rd Airborne, who managed to kill over two hundred VC during the Cav's relocation. It would fall to the 1st Cav, however, to take part in the first really major US infantry action of the Vietnam conflict.

In response to the presence of three NVA regiments around Pleiku, one infantry battalion and an artillery battery of the 1st Cav were initially moved to Pleiku but were soon followed by the remainder of the 1st Brigade. Meanwhile, the Plei Me Special Forces camp had come under heavy attack; necessitating a relief operation supported by the 1st Cav. To follow up on the relief of Plei Me, the 1st Cav began to search actively for the NVA to the south of Pleiku. By late October, contact with the enemy indicated that the NVA were assembling in the Ia Drang Valley. As the 3rd Brigade of the 1st Cav replaced the 1st in the area on 9 November the stage was almost set for the first major test of the airmobile warriors. On 14 November, the 1st Battalion/7th Cavalry made heavy contact in the valley, coming under heavy attack before being reinforced. In fact, had it not been for the Air Cav's ability to heli-lift reinforcements quickly to the site of contact, the situation would have been very grave indeed. Instead, the NVA found themselves in a meatgrinder that inflicted 634 KIA upon the Communist troops. Throughout the remainder of November, the 3rd Brigade, then the 2nd Brigade, of the 1st Cav was engaged in the area, eventually driving the NVA across the border into Cambodia after killing almost one thousand eight hundred of them. Among the infantry lessons to emerge from this first major US ground battle were the necessity to properly maintain the M16 to avoid malfunctions in combat, the sensitivity of

US radios to moisture which rendered them inoperable at critical times, and the inadequacies of the US-issued poncho, which proved to be too loud and too heavy for use in Vietnam.

Infantry on the Offensive

The Ia Drang Valley operation had shown that US troops could take the initiative against the VC/NVA. As a result, it was planned substantially to step up US ground combat operations in 1966. The availability of more and more infantry battalions also allowed somewhat more flexibility as well. The 25th Infantry Division had begun arriving in Vietnam at the end of December 1965 and would continue until April 1966. The first major unit in country had been the 3rd Brigade, 25th Infantry Division, which was already committed to combat in January 1966, when it carried out sweeps along with the 173rd Airborne Brigade near the Cambodian border. Although only occasional contact was made with the enemy, these sweeps did result in the capture of substantial numbers of enemy weapons and supply caches. The 173rd Airborne also gained the distinction of being the first US infantry unit to move into the Mekong Delta. In addition to contacts against the enemy while on sweeps, the 25th Infantry Division discovered it had problems to face within its own base camp, which it turned out contained the extensive Cu Chi tunnel complex. As a result, the troops of the Tropic Lightning Division quickly began learning the skills of the tunnel rat, though it still took them to the end of the year before the complex was completely cleared.

Despite its excellent reputation, the 1st Infantry Division had not been performing up to expectations in Vietnam. As a result, command was given to Maj Gen William DePuy (though he was still a brigadier general when he took command). DePuy immediately began instilling a more aggressive attitude in the division, replacing brigade and battalion commanders when necessary. Among the officers he brought in was future US Secretary of State LTC Alexander Haig, who commanded the 1st Battalion, 26th Infantry. By April, DePuy's influence was being felt as the division was involved far more aggressively against the enemy.

Generally, the NVA/VC had already learned that they could not stand against US firepower and avoided major confrontations. However, one major operation in early 1966 (January-March) – MASHER/WHITE WING – once again showed that the mobility of the 1st Cavalry Division (Airmobile) gave it the best chance to bleed the enemy. Carried out in conjunction with the (ROK) Republic of

A machinegunner of the 9th Infantry Division looks out over his .50 MG which has a Starlight scope mounted for night use.

Korea and the ARVN troops, this operation accounted for almost two thousand four hundred enemy casualties.

The next major operation for US infantry units was PAUL REVERE which ran between May and July 1966. Involving the 3rd Brigade of the 25th Infantry Division as well as ARVN and ROK troops, this operation inflicted almost five hundred and fifty enemy casualties. Beginning during the midst of PAUL REVERE, the 1st Brigade, 101st Airborne Division's Operation HAWTHORNE accounted for another 531 enemy casualties.

The 173rd Airborne was already a formidable combat force. In June, it gained even more striking power with the arrival of the 4th Battalion, 503 Airborne Infantry Regiment.

Throughout the war, the defense of Saigon would tie down a substantial portion of US infantrymen. For example, between early June and mid July, the 1st Infantry Division was kept busy in Bing Lang Province against the VC 9th Division in EL PASO. This operation showed the results of DePuy's leadership as the Big Red One, making skillful use of ambush and airmobility, fought four battles during which they inflicted 855 enemy casualties.

August 1966, proved to be a big month for arrival of new infantry units as the 196th Infantry Brigade (Light) arrived – it was the first of the brigades raised specifically for service in Vietnam. The 2nd Brigade of the 4th Infantry Division also arrived in August, followed by the rest of the division in September and October. In a departure from normal procedure, the 4th which had been vastly understrength when tabbed for Vietnam service, trained eight thousand draftees slated to join the division under divisional supervision at Fort Lewis, thus instilling much more sense of unit pride than was frequently the case with conscripts.

Following almost immediately upon its arrival in country, the 196th Infantry Brigade began Operation ATTLEBORO – the first major search and destroy operation – against the remnants of the VC 9th Division in September. The operation did not really began to roll, however, until 19 October when a major enemy base area was discovered. By early November, elements of the 25th Infantry Division, 4th Infantry Division, 1st Infantry Division, 173rd Airborne Brigade, and ARVNs had all become embroiled in what was turning out to be the largest operation of the war up to that point. By the time ATTLEBORO ended on 24 November, over three thousand of the enemy had become casualties.

As US infantry units were becoming heavily involved in Operation ATTLEBORO during October, the 1st Cavalry was launching Operation IRVING to clear coastal areas in Binh Ding Province of the VC. While the ROKs and ARVNs set up blocking positions around the area of operations, the air cavalrymen sent two of their brigades into the area to hunt down the enemy. On 13 October, the air cavalrymen located the VC Province HQ in an underground complex, which gave the cavalrymen a chance to turn their own tunnel rats loose. Throughout 1966, as more and more tunnel complexes were being located, Standard Operating Procedures (SOP) were being developed for tunnel rats so that those sent into the dark underground chambers would have a better chance of survival and of finding important documents. In addition to effectively clearing the area of VC, IRVING inflicted 681 enemy casualties and proved invaluable in further developing air mobile tactics.

Irving also illustrated the importance of psy ops, population control, and civic action when working in heavily populated areas. Commanders of other infantry divisions, noting the successes of Operation IRVING began to appreciate that air mobility would increase their speed and flexibility of operations, extend their area of influence and allow rapid buildup of forces. By IRVING, too, procedures for planning air mobile operations were becoming sophisticated, normally involving in inverse order: 1. the ground tactical plan, 2. the landing plan, 3. the air movement plan, and 4. the loading plan.

The last really major operation by US Army infantrymen in 1966 was PAUL REVERE IV involving the 4th Infantry Division in their first major operation, the 25th Infantry Division and the 1st Air Cav. This operation along the Cambodian border west of Pleiku ran from 18 October-30 December and resulted in around one thousand enemy casualties, a figure which would have been substantially greater had the enemy not been able to flee into Cambodia.

As 1966 came to a close, the 3rd Brigade of the 9th Infantry Division – the division slated for operations in the Mekong Delta – began arriving, as did the 199th Infantry Brigade (Light). The 199th Infantry Brigade had been slated for Vietnam service from the start and accordingly had been trained rapidly at the Infantry School at Fort Benning, Georgia, prior to being deployed to Vietnam where it arrived on 10 December 1966. So rapid had been the 199th's training, in fact, that when 4th Battalion, 12th Infantry carried out a combat helicopter assault on 17 December *that* was their first airmobile operation.

Although US infantry had attempted to become more aggressive at searching out and engaging the enemy during 1966, it is important to note that during the year eighty-eight per cent of all firefights were initiated by the enemy, in a majority of cases from entrenched positions. Obviously, the initiative was still with the enemy. Nevertheless, US infantrymen were gaining important experience and learning important lessons. In addition to developing procedures for tunnel rats and perfecting airmobile tactics, the officers and troops were acquiring field tactical experience under fire, experience that no training could duplicate. They were learning that since the VC/NVA normally instituted the contact, the enemy would have an initial advantage for a few minutes, but then US artillery support or air support could be brought to bear quickly turning the tide. Infantrymen learned, too, that when engaged they normally had to press the attack against the Communists to keep them from using delaying tactics while other ambushes or booby traps were set. Finally, the infantryman began to learn to fight and survive in the jungle.

1967 and Divisional Sized Operations

Beginning on 12 January 1967, 199th Light Infantry Brigade began FAIRFAX/RANG DANG in conjunction with ARVN Rangers in a test of what would come to be known as Vietnamization. For most of the rest of the year, the 199th would find itself patrolling the villages around Saigon on security duties.

Perhaps the most noteworthy operation of the year, however, was CEDAR FALLS followed by JUNCTION CITY. These operations, which began on 8 January, were an attempt to use larger US formations to 'conventionalize' the war. The objective was to clear the 'Iron Triangle', a notorious VC haven. The operation opened with a surprise air assault by the 1st Battalion, 26th Infantry, commanded by LTC Alexander Haig, against the village of Ben Suc, a VC logistics center which would be razed to the ground as part of the operation.

Other units involved in CEDAR FALLS included elements of the 25th Infantry Division, 196th Infantry Brigade, 1st Infantry Division, 173rd Airborne Brigade and 11th Armored Cavalry Regiment. As these major units took up blocking positions around the 'Iron Triangle' to block escape, maneuver units began advancing inward to constrict the triangle. During the three weeks this tightening of the cordon took, about seven hundred enemy casualties were inflicted, not many really considering the size of the US effort. Aggressive patrolling by the 173rd Airborne Brigade had proven an especially important aspect of the operation. As a result, the enemy had been cleared from the area, the sympathetic population had been relocated and one thousand one hundred enemy bunkers and five hundred enemy tunnels had been discovered, cleared and destroyed. Among the supplies destroyed was enough rice for thirteen thousand enemy troops for a year.

Another noteworthy event of January, 1967, was the arrival of Maj Gen William Peers to command the 4th Infantry Division, Peers, a veteran of OSS Detachment 101 in Burma, was no stranger to guerrilla warfare in the jungle, and some of that expertise was passed on to the troops of the 4th. Realising that guerrillas must be harassed constantly, Peers tried to keep eighty per cent of the strength of his infantry companies in the field constantly, with two of the three infantry companies of each battalion always deployed. During the early months of the year and almost until the spring, the troops of the 4th Infantry Division were involved in Operation SAM HOUSTON and then FRANCIS MARION along the Cambodian border. Combined, these operations would inflict around two thousand enemy casualties, but the ability of the enemy to flee across the border to safe havens in Cambodia proved frustrating to the 4th and 25th Infantry Divisions.

CEDAR FALLS was followed by JUNCTION CITY with elements

of the 1st, 4th, 9th and 25th Infantry Divisions, the 196th Infantry Brigade (Light), the 173rd Airborne Brigade and the 11th Armored Cavalry Regiment as well as ARVNS and Australians involved to the total of forty five thousand allied troops. The operation was targeted against War Zone C where the VC 9th Division and various NVA battalions had been operating. Once again units cordoned off the area of operations: elements of the 1st Infantry Division, 173rd Airborne Brigade, and 9th Infantry Division sealed the eastern and northern portions of War Zone C, while units from the 4th Infantry Division, 25th Infantry Division, 196th Light Infantry Brigade and 11th Armored Cavalry Regiment sealed the northwestern and northern portions of the AO (area of operations). The southern sector was sealed by elements of the 25th Infantry Division and 11th Armored Cavalry Regiment, though this force also had the mission of acting as the 'hammer' driving north to force the enemy against the 'anvil' of allied troops deployed there.

The operation began on 22 February with airmobile assualts by the 1st Infantry Division and the only major parachute assault of the war by the 173rd Airborne Brigade. As this first phase of the operation progressed on into March little enemy resistance was encountered. More combat would result, though, from the second phase which was aimed at tightening the horseshoe shaped cordon around War Zone C, forcing the enemy to fight. Much of the resulting combat was around fire support bases, generally at night. The 25th Infantry Division, for example, saw heavy fighting around Fire Support Base Gold where one battalion involved – the 2/77th Infantry – was commanded by LTC Jack Vessey, a future Chairman of the Joint Chiefs of Staff. Between 30 March and 1 April, two battalions of the 1st Infantry Division, including Alexander Haig's 1/26, were heavily engaged againt the enemy around Landing Zone George. In the ensuing action, over six hundred of the enemy were killed and the 271st VC Regiment was badly decimated. Among the 1st Infantry Division awards for the action were one DSC, forty eight silver stars, and 121 bronze stars.

The final phase of JUNCTION CITY began on 16 April but was mostly just mopping up of any stray VC/NVA encountered in the area. The final tally of the operation was around three thousand enemy casualties, one hundred base camps destroyed and large numbers of weapons and supplies captured. US casualties were substantial, too, with 282 KIA and over one thousand five hundred wounded.

In the early months of 1967, the 1st Air Cav had been involved in THAYER II a very successful operation in Binh Ding Province

Members of the 173rd Airborne Brigade fire a jeep-mounted 106mm recoilless rifle into an enemy position during a road security operation.

which resulted in over one thousand seven hundred enemy casualties and then PERSHING which continued throughout the year and eventually totaled over five thousand four hundred enemy casualties. More and more the 1st Cav's mobility was enabling it to hit the enemy when other units would have been too slow to respond.

Another operation which began in February was ENTERPRISE involving the 9th Infantry Division and ARVN forces in Long An Province. Well over two thousand enemy casualties resulted from this operation which extended through March 1968. The 9th Infantry Division, like the 1st Air Cav, had a somewhat unique organization to deal with its assignment in the Mekong Delta. The 2nd Brigade was organized in an amphibious role to serve with the MRF (Mobile Riverine Force), while one brigade consisted of two mechanized infantry battalions, and the final one of four foot infantry battalions. The 9th's mission during fall of 1967 was primarily to clear the Rung Sat of the enemy. To accomplish this mission, by summer 1967, between six and eight search and destroy operations were being mounted per month by the OLD RELIABLES. In May, elements of the 9th saw heavy fighting against the 514th VC Battalion. Then, in June, two battalions of the 2nd Brigade began operating with the MRF, Naval Task Force 117 providing the lift element. Throughout the summer and fall, these units jelled and developed their special tactics for the Delta, surprise proving highly critical in an area where rapid movement was often impossible.

Task Force Oregon, formed from the various US infantry brigades in I Corps – including 3rd Brigade, 25th Infantry Division; 1st Brigade, 101st Airborne Division; and 196th Light Infantry Brigade – inflicted about two thousand enemy casualties during Operation WHEELER in September. Once again, however, it was the mobility of the 1st Cav and 173rd Airborne Brigade which allowed these two units to deal the enemy over one thousand five hundred casualties during Operations BOLLING and SHENANDOAH II during the fall of 1967. During the early stages of SHENANDOAH II, the 1st Infantry Division operated along the 'Thunder Road' portion of Highway 13. Pushing towards the Cambodian border, the Big Red One inflicted heavy casualties on the crack VC 272nd Regiment. Beginning in October, the men of the 1st Infantry Division were involved in three major engagements along the Laotian and Cambodian borders. During one of these engagements a battalion of the 1st was ambushed and suffered over one hundred casualties, graphically illustrating that the enemy could still surprise and punish the Americans.

On 25 September 1967, the 23rd (Americal) Division was formed to take over the duties of Task Force Oregon in I Corps. Constituted from units already in Vietnam – the 11th Infantry Brigade,

An infantryman with the AN/PRR-9 helmet-mounted receiver and the AN/PRT-4 hand-held transmitter.

196th Infantry Brigade and the 198th Infantry Brigade – the reputation of the Americal Division was generally bad. It was known for poorer quality troops and officers. Initially, the ad hoc nature of its formation which virtually eliminated any cohesiveness or esprit de corps legislated against its effectiveness. Many of its units, too, were rushed into Vietnam without adequate training on the assumption that there might be an agreement to limit troop strength to that already in country at the end of the year. Problems of the Americal only increased when better quality officers avoided assignment to the division and new recruits assigned picked up the 'traditions' of the veterans – mostly bad.

In late October, it was learned that heavy NVA attacks were planned againt Dak To. As a result, battalions from the 4th Infantry Division and 173rd Airborne Brigade moved into position around the town. From these positions, US troops began mounting aggressive patrols, throughout October and the first two weeks of November heavily engaging the enemy and pulverizing him with artillery and air support. When the 174th NVA Regiment made a stand on Hill 875, two battalions from the 173rd Airborne and one from the 4th Infantry became involved in bitter combat to dislodge the Communists. When they finally captured the hill on Thanksgiving Day, the various border battles around Dak To had accounted for more than one thousand six hundred enemy dead.

Although the buildup in 1967 did not match that during 1966, the Americal Division had been activated in September while the 2nd and 3rd Brigades of the 101st Airborne Division had arrived in November. An important point to bear in mind about the caliber of infantry troops arriving in country in 1967, too, is that large numbers of replacements were coming in for all of the veterans who had come in with their units during 1966. The one year tour of duty was beginning to erode the level of combat experience present in any company. Combat units also suffered from shortages of troops, too, while 'REMF' units always seemed to be overstaffed, thus blunting the teeth and fattening the tail of the US Army in Vietnam. Nevertheless, infantry companies were almost constantly mounting patrols, at this stage of the war maintaining the aggressive stance necessary to keep guerrilla forces from becoming entrenched.

The Infantry During Tet and Its Aftermath

As 1968 began various infantry battalions were involved in operations which had begun late in 1967. These operations continued on through the early months of 1968, and some would actually become adjuncts to operations in the wake of the Tet Offensive which would hit South Vietnam's population centers at the end of January. The 25th Infantry, in particular, had been involved in Operation YELLOWSTONE since late 1967 and on into February of 1968 as well as Operation SARATOGA which began at the same time along the Cambodian border. These two operations would eventually account for over five thousand enemy casualties. The 23rd Infantry (American) Division had also begun an operation in December, 1967 – MUSCATINE – which would continue into June 1968, though only one brigade was heavily involved. This operation would inflict over one thousand one hundred enemy casualties. Finally, the 199th Infantry Brigade had begun Operation UNIONTOWN in Bien Hoa Province on 17 December 1967. Continuing through March 1968, and including fighting during the Tet Offensive, this operation would cost the enemy 922 casualties.

In January 1968 during the weeks preceding Tet, other major operations were launched, especially in I Corps, where the 1st Air Cav's PERSHING II and JEB STUART – the latter aptly named for a 'cav' operation – had kicked off on 22 January. PERSHING II was actually a continuation of operations in II Corps after the bulk of the 1st Cav had begun operating in I Corps and accounted for over six hundred enemy casualties before concluding at the end of February. JEB STUART, on the other hand, was the muscle-flexing initial operation for the 'cav' in northern I Corps and would cost the enemy over three thousand two hundred and fifty casualties by the end of March, though this number includes a substantial percentage inflicted during the counterattacks in the wake of Tet.

Although the Tet Offensive did not actually begin until the early hours of 31 January, the 4th Infantry Division, on alert since 20 January due to rocket attacks against Pleiku, was hit early on the morning of 30 January and saw heavy fighting in defense of Kontum and Pleiku. Then, when the full brunt of the attack was felt the next day, more and more American units became involved, especially as reaction forces for ARVN units. The 1st Infantry Division saw action at Ben Cat, Chau Thanh, Di An, Lai Thieu and Thu Duc. The 1/18 Infantry and A Troop, 1st Squadron/4th Cav saw particularly heavy fighting around Tan Son Nhut during the defense of Saigon and the 1/28 played a critical role in the fighting around An My north of Saigon. By mid-February, so heavily engaged had the 1st Infantry Division been during Tet that in two weeks fighting they had accounted for one thousand five hundred enemy KIA.

The 173rd Airborne Brigade had begun Operation MCLAIN In Bing Thuan Province on 20 and had inflicted well over one thousand

Above left: The 'Blanket' patch of the 1st Air Cavalry was one of the most respected in Vietnam, especially those of the Recon or LRRP units.

Above right: Special Forces beret flash and Recon Team insignia along with the knife produced in Okinawa for issue to members of the Special Forces and irregulars.

Left: Although Vietnam was a modern war, it was often fought with primitive weapons such as this tomahawk, carried by some members of the 101st Airborne and others.

enemy casualties by the time the 'Sky Soldiers' were thrown against the enemy offensive on 31 January. The 4/503 was sent to counterattack at Tuy Hoa where they recaptured Tuy Hoa airfield after vicious close quarters fighting, then moved to clear Tuy Hoa North.

The 25th Infantry Division, which had already been operating around Saigon, played a key role in its defense during Tet, as did the 199th Infantry Brigade. Prior to the offensive being launched, 199th intelligence had indicated the possibility of an attack; hence, battalions of the brigade had been placed nearer the critical Bien Hoa-Long Binh area. At 03.00 hours on 31 January, these precautions proved justified as an attack was launched on Long Binh. Already alert and ready for action, the 199th beat off this attack and went over to the counterattack. The 3/7 saw action in the Cholon section of Saigon where with the help of the mechanised infantry of the 5/60 of the 9th Infantry Division, they had driven out the enemy by 4 February, though it would take to 12 February to clear the last vestiges of the tenacious attackers from this Chinese section of Saigon. Most 9th Infantry Division troops fought in the countryside or at Bien Hoa, My Tho and Ben Tre. Additionally, they played a critical role in keeping Highway 14 open. Members of the battalions assigned to the Mobile Riverine Force helped relieve the important river city of Can Tho.

All told, during the fighting throughout February, approximately twenty thousand enemy troops were killed and somewhere between thirty and forty thousand were wounded. US casualties included about one thousand KIA and four thousand five hundred WIA. Although in terms of breaking the VC, the Tet Offensive would prove to be a major US allied victory, it proved to be a political loss at home since the bulk of the American public remembered only the images of VC sappers in the American Embassy compound or Vietnamese Gen Loan shooting a captured VC on national television. Unfortunately, the image of the US infantryman successfully defending and then counterattacking the enemy with devastating firepower was lost, at least partially through the predisposition of the news media and those opposed to the war to downgrade American successes and inflate Communist ones.

In the wake of the perceived threat posed by the Tet Offensive, the Army commited one-third of its last strategic reserve as the 3rd

Opposite above: Airboat used by the Special Forces for operations in the Mekong Delta.

Opposite below: AN/TRC-90B equipment of the 362nd Signal Detachment.

Brigade of the 82nd Airborne Division was sent to Vietnam in February. The arrival of the 82nd added a few thousand more aggressive light infantrymen just prior to the beginning of massive counterattacks in March to dislodge any Communist troops still holding ground taken during Tet. Shortly afterwards, 8 March also saw the arrival of an interesting general officer as Major Gen Keith L. Ware took command of the 1st Infantry Division. In addition to being a Congressional Medal of Honor winner, Gen Ware was the first draftee to become a general.

On 11 March counterattacks began around Saigon as Operation *QUYET THANG* ('Resolved to Win') began to sweep any remaining VC from the area around the capital. Units taking part were drawn from the US 1st, 9th and 25th Infantry Divisions and 11 Armored Cavalry Regiment as well as various ARVN formations. Following this operation was *TOAN THANG* ('Certain Victory') by forty-two US and thirty-nine Vietnamese infantry and tank battalions in early April to block future attacks against Saigon. Another operation which began on 17 March was *DUONG CUA DAN* ('People's Road') by the 9th Infantry Division to provide security for engineers working on Route 4. Eventually, this operation and its successor would account for 1,251 enemy casualties.

To some extent lost at the time in the massive operations in the wake of Tet was a 16 March sweep by C Company of the 1/20 and B Company of the 4/3, both of the 11th Infantry Brigade of the Americal Division. This operation would later achieve notoriety due to the events at Mai Lai where the troops of C Company would slaughter hundreds of civilians, though the term 'innocent' often applied to the residents of Mai Lai is not entirely applicable since some had a long history of collaboration with the VC. Additional civilians were also killed at My Khe by members of B Company. The 'Mai Lai Massacre' as it came to be known should be indicative of two lessons. First, the poor discipline and lower troop caliber endemic in the Americal Division no doubt contributed to the massacre, though it would be naive to assume this was the only time civilians were slaughtered in Vietnam – war itself is the atrocity and the innocent often die as well as the guilty – indeed frequently *instead* of. However, Mai Lai should also be viewed as a graphic example of the frustration many American infantrymen felt in Vietnam where they often took casualties from an enemy they could not see and where the enemy looked exactly like the peasants who viewed them with dislike. The fact that South Vietnamese troops, with the exception of the Rangers, frequently failed to support American troops on operations and were notorious for not being willing to fight contributed to the view by many Grunts that the enemy was the Vietnamese, all Vietnamese!

Once again through the scare headlines in the American press, most at home believed that Khe Sanh was about to become the US Dien Bien Phu when in actuality, the siege was tying down important NVA/VC assets at a fairly minimal US expenditure of troops and equipment while the rest of South Vietnam was being cleared of Tet attackers. Once the decision to relieve Khe Sanh was taken the operation went quite smoothly, the 1st Air Cav's mobility allowing them to leapfrog ahead of the enemy during Operation PEGASUS to block his escape routes into Laos and inflict additional casualties. Then shortly after the relief of Khe Sanh on 8 April, Operation DELAWARE, involving the 1st Cav, 101st Airborne and 196th Infantry Brigade, began with the objective of clearing the A Shau Valley west of Hue. The 1st Cav air assaulted into the valley while other US and ARVN units swept in on the ground from the east. The US troops met tough opposition throughout April, but by the end of the month, the Communist resistance was broken, though the mopping up portion of the operation would continue until mid-May by which time the enemy had suffered 869 casualties. Additionally, large caches of arms and supplies had been destroyed. The 1st Air Cav followed up this operation with JEB STUART III extending until early November and inflicting over two thousand one hundred casualties along the border of Quang Tri and Thua Thien Provinces.

Between 1 April and 17 May, the airborne troops of the 101st Airborne and the 3rd Brigade, 82nd Airborne swept through the lowlands of Quang Tri and Thua Thien Provinces in conjunction with the ARVN 1st Division, one of the best in the Vietnamese armed forces, inflicting 2,100 enemy casualties. NEVADA EAGLE began when this operation ended and extended through the end of February, 1969, eventually accounting for another 3,300 enemy casualties for the 101st Airborne Division.

In May, elements of the 23rd Infantry Division helped defend the Kham Duc Special Forces Camp from attack, though once again the troops of the Americal Division did not live up to the standards of American infantry, in some cases jumping on evacuation helicopters instead of civilians. The main event in May, however, was the second though smaller, Communist offensive normally known as Mini-Tet. The 199th Infantry Brigade still operating around Saigon was heavily engaged during Mini-Tet especially at Binh Tri Dong. Elements of the 1/4 Cavalry and 1/18 Infantry saw heavy combat near Xam Moi, while the 25th Infantry Division helped counter the

Members of the 196th Infantry Brigade (Light) firing at suspected VC positions during a search and destroy operation.

Communist threat around Saigon. By the time Mini-Tet was over the Communists had once again suffered extremely heavy losses.

In June, the 199th Light Infantry Brigade continued operations around Saigon only now they moved into the 'Pineapple,' an area of swamps and fruit groves west of Saigon filled with booby traps. Still, the 199th patrolled aggressively and on 18 September found a huge enemy supply depot.

With their offensive during the first half of the year unsuccessful, the Communists switched over to stand off rocket attacks against the cities. For the most part, US infantry was tied down then sweeping areas around the populated areas to prevent the Communists from becoming entrenched. More mobility and firepower had been added to US infantry by the arrival in July of the 1st Brigade, 5th Infantry Division (Mechanized).

In late August, the 1/2 of the 1st Infantry Division helped relieve the Special Forces camp at Loc Ninh. Then, in mid-September three battalions of the 1st Infantry Division skirmished with the NVA around Loc Ninh. During this action, Gen Wise, the division CO, was killed when his helicopter was shot down. During the summer and fall, the 173rd Airborne was involved in Operation BOLLING to secure Phu Yen Province. Elements of the 4th Infantry Division along with ARVNs and Montagnard irregulars began sweeping Dak Payour Valley on 22 December to eliminate another Communist safe haven.

The 1st Brigade, 25th Infantry Division had been engaged in heavy fighting at Fire Support Base Buell II and nearby Nui Ba Den Mountain in August, then had to dislodge the VC from Tay Ninh. By 20 September when the enemy was finally cleared from the area, more than two thousand five hundred Communist troops had been killed, though the 25th Infantry Division had taken over one thousand one hundred casualties itself, including 370 KIA. An important tactical innovation to come out of these battles was the 'Force Fed Fire Support' doctrine initiated by Maj Gen Ellas W. Williamson. This tactic assumed that there would normally only be one major contact within a divisional area. Therefore, all divisional fire support would be made available to the commander of the engaged unit. This tactic was in accordance with the evolving US doctrine of using firepower rather than manpower to inflict enemy casualties.

Infantry Battalions in Vietnam Circa 1968

Since virtually all major infantry units which would serve in Vietnam were in country during 1968, a listing of the battalions and their brigade or divisional assignments during their service in Vietnam would be useful at this point to help grasp the extent of the infantry commitment.

In addition to the battalions listed, certain separate companies or platoons served as LRRPs, Rifle Security Units, Combat Tracker Units, Scout Dog Units or on other specialised assignments, including helicopter door gunners. A substantial number of these companies were drawn from the 50th, 51st, 52nd, 54th or 58th Infantry. Then, later, when LRRP units were re-designated Ranger units, the 75th Infantry became the parent unit for the divisional and other Ranger companies.

2nd Battalion, 1st Infantry (Light Infantry)
    assigned 196th Infantry Brigade (light) and American Division
3rd Battalion, 1st Infantry (Light Infantry)
    assigned 11th Infantry Brigade (Light) and American Division

1st Battalion, 2nd Infantry (Infantry)
    assigned 1st Infantry Division
2nd Battalion, 2nd Infantry (Mechanized Infantry)
    assigned 1st Infantry Division

2nd Battalion, 3rd Infantry (Light Infantry)
    assigned 199th Infantry Brigade (Light)
4th Battalion, 3rd Infantry (Light Infantry)
    assigned 11th Infantry Brigade (Light) and American Division

1st Battalion, 5th Infantry (Mechanized Infantry)
    assigned 25th Infantry Division

1st Battalion, 6th Infantry (Light Infantry)
    assigned 198th Infantry Brigade (Light) and American Division

3rd Battalion, 7th Infantry (Light Infantry)
    assigned 199th Infantry Brigade (Light)

1st Battalion, 8th Infantry (Infantry)
    assigned 4th Infantry Division
2nd Battalion, 8th Infantry (Mechanized Infantry)
    assigned 4th Infantry Division
3rd Battalion, 8th Infantry (Infantry)
    assigned 4th Infantry Division

4th Battalion, 9th Infantry (Infantry)
    assigned 25th Infantry Division

1st Battalion, 11th Infantry (Infantry)
    assigned 1st Brigade, 5th Infantry Division (Mechanized)

1st Battalion, 12th Infantry (Infantry)
    assigned 4th Infantry Division
2nd Battalion, 12th Infantry (Infantry)
    assigned 11th Infantry Division and 25th Infantry Division
3rd Battalion, 12th Infantry (Infantry)
    assigned 4th Infantry Division
4th Battalion, 12th Infantry (Light Infantry)
    assigned 199th Infantry Brigade (Light)
5th Battalion, 12th Infantry (Light Infantry)
    assigned 199th Infantry Brigade (Light)

1st Battalion, 14th Infantry (Infantry)
    assigned 4th Infantry Division and 25th Infantry Division
2nd Battalion, 14th Infantry (Infantry)
    assigned 25th Infantry Division

1st Battalion, 16th Infantry (Mechanized Infantry)
    assigned 1st Infantry Division
2nd Battalion, 16th Infantry (Infantry)
    assigned 1st Infantry Division

1st Battalion, 18th Infantry (Infantry)
    assigned 1st Infantry Division
2nd Battalion, 18th Infantry (Infantry)
    assigned 1st Infantry Division

1st Battalion, 20th Infantry (Light Infantry)
    assigned 11th Infantry Brigade (Light) and American Division

3rd Battalion, 21st Infantry (Light Infantry)
    assigned 196th Infantry Brigade (Light) and American Division

4th Battalion, 21st Infantry (Light Infantry)
assigned 11th Infantry Brigade (Light) and American Division

1st Battalion, 22nd Infantry (Infantry)
assigned 4th Infantry Division
2nd Battalion, 22nd Infantry (Mechanized Infantry)
assigned 4th Infantry Division and 25th Infantry Division
3rd Battalion, 22nd Infantry (Infantry)
assigned 4th Infantry Division and 25th Infantry Division

4th Battalion, 23rd Infantry (Mechanized Infantry)
assigned 25th Infantry Division

1st Battalion, 26th Infantry (Infantry)
assigned 1st Infantry Division

1st Battalion, 27th Infantry (Infantry)
assigned 25th Infantry Division
2nd Battalion, 27th Infantry (Infantry)
assigned 25th Infantry Division

1st Battalion, 28th Infantry (Infantry)
assigned 1st Infantry Division
2nd Battalion, 28th Infantry (Infantry)
assigned 1st Infantry Division

4th Battalion, 31st Infantry (Light Infantry)
assigned 196th Infantry Brigade (Light) and American Division
6th Battalion, 31st Infantry (Infantry)
assigned 9th Infantry Division

1st Battalion, 35th Infantry (Infantry)
assigned 4th Infantry Division
2nd Battalion, 35th Infantry (Infantry)
assigned 4th Infantry Division

2nd Battalion, 39th Infantry (Infantry)
assigned 9th Infantry Division
3rd Battalion, 39th Infantry (Infantry)
assigned 9th Infantry Division
4th Battalion, 39th Infantry (Infantry)
assigned 9th Infantry Division

1st Battalion, 46th Infantry (Light Infantry)
assigned 198th Infantry Brigade (Light) and American Division
5th Battalion, 46th Infantry (Light Infantry)
assigned 198th Infantry Brigade (Light) and American Division

2nd Battalion, 47th Infantry (Mechanized)
assigned 9th Infantry Division

3rd Battalion, 47th Infantry (Riverine Infantry)
assigned 9th Infantry Division
4th Battalion, 47th Infantry (Riverine Infantry)
assigned 9th Infantry Division

1st Battalion, 50th Infantry (Mechanized Infantry)
assigned as a general reserve unit under US Army Pacific Command

1st Battalion, 52nd Infantry (Light Infantry)
assigned 198th Infantry Brigade (Light), Americal Division and 11th Infantry Brigade (Light)

2nd Battalion, 60th Infantry (Infantry)
assigned 9th Infantry Division
3rd Battalion, 60th Infantry (Riverine Infantry)
assigned 9th Infantry Division

5th Battalion, 60th Infantry (Mechanized Infantry)
  assigned 9th Infantry Division

1st Battalion, 61st Infantry (Mechanized Infantry)
  assigned 1st Brigade, 5th Infantry Division (Mechanized)

3rd Battalion, 187th Infantry (Airmobile Infantry)
  assigned 101st Airborne Division (Airmobile)

1st Battalion, 327th Infantry (Airborne, later Airmobile Infantry)
  assigned 101st Airborne Division
2nd Battalion, 327th Infantry (Airborne later Airmobile Infantry)
  assigned 101st Airborne Division

1st Battalion, 501st Infantry (Airmobile Infantry)
  assigned 101st Airborne Division (Airmobile)
2nd Battalion, 501st Infantry (Airmobile Infantry)
  assigned 101st Airborne Division (Airmobile)

1st Battalion, 502nd Infantry (Airmobile Infantry)
  assigned 101st Airborne Division (Airmobile)
2nd Battalion, 502nd Infantry (Airborne later Airmobile Infantry)
  assigned 101st Airborne Division

1st Battalion, 503rd Infantry (Airborne Infantry)
  assigned 173rd Airborne Brigade
2nd Battalion, 503rd Infantry (Airborne Infantry)
  assigned 173rd Airborne Brigade
3rd Battalion, 503rd Infantry (Airborne Infantry)
  assigned 173rd Airborne Brigade
4th Battalion, 503rd Infantry (Airborne Infantry)
  assigned 173rd Airborne Brigade

1st Battalion, 505th Infantry (Airborne Infantry)
  assigned 3rd Brigade, 82nd Airborne Division
2nd Battalion, 505th Infantry (Airborne Infantry)
  assigned 3rd Brigade, 82nd Airborne Division

1st Battalion, 506th Infantry (Airmobile Infantry)
  assigned 101st Airborne Division (Airmobile)
2nd Battalion, 506th Infantry (Airmobile Infantry)
  assigned 101st Airborne Division (Airmobile)
3rd Battalion, 506th Infantry (Airmobile Infantry)
  assigned 101st Airborne Division (Airmobile)

1st Battalion, 508th Infantry (Airborne Infantry)
  assigned 3rd Brigade, 82nd Aiborne Division

CAVALRY
2nd Battalion, 5th Cavalry (Airmobile Infantry)
  assigned 1st Cavalry Division (Airmobile)

1st Battalion, 7th Cavalry (Airmobile Infantry)
  assigned 1st Cavalry Division (Airmobile)
2nd Battalion, 7th Cavalry (Airmobile Infantry)
  assigned 1st Cavalry Division (Airmobile)
5th Battalion, 7th Cavalry (Airmobile Infantry)
  assigned 1st Cavalry Division (Airmobile)

1st Battalion, 8th Cavalry (Airborn, later Airmobile Infantry)
  assigned 1st Cavalry Division (Airmobile)

1st Battalion, 12th Cavalry (Airborne, later Airmobile Infantry)
  assigned 1st Cavalry Division (Airmobile)
2nd Battalion, 12th Cavalry (Airmobile Infantry)
  assigned 1st Cavalry Division (Airmobile)

Beginnings of Vietnamization

Under newly elected President Richard Nixon, the process of Vietnamization – turning the war over to the Vietnamese – and the first withdrawals of US troops would become the keynotes of infantry operations during 1969. As it became apparent that the US participation in the war was beginning to fade, so too did any enthusiasm most Grunts felt for endangering themselves in a war they really did not understand. Rather than the large-unit aggressive operations of the previous two years, 1969 became a year where the emphasis was on border security, pacification and city security. Keeping communication lines open resulted in many operations as well, such as road clearing missions by the 1st Infantry Division. I Corps, always critical since it bordered directly North Vietnam, saw commitment of the 101st Airborne Division and the 1st Brigade, 5th Infantry Division (Mechanized) as well as the US Marines. Enemy contact during the first weeks of 1969 remained light, however, for most units. Among the exceptions was the 199th Infantry Brigade (Light) patrolling the approaches to Saigon. The 199th encountered numerous groups of Communist troops attempting to filter back towards the Capital.

In early February, the 101st Airborne moved into the infamous A Shau Valley for Operation MASSACHUSETTS STRIKER followed by Operation APACHE SNOW, the latter including the Battle for 'Hamburger Hill' which became symbolic of the futility of bloody battles for objectives which would be relinquished soon after capture. Even the crack troops of the 101st Airborne became cynical about their leadership after this battle.

In late February, 25th Infantry Division Fire Support Bases along the Cambodian border came under heavy attack. In actions which lasted until April, the 2/27 – part of the highly thought of 'Wolfhounds' battalion – saw particularly heavy fighting. In one action around a fire support base, troops of the 25th Infantry Division accounted for over four hundred enemy dead for a loss of only one American. For the most part, throughout Vietnam during 1969, NVA/VC attacks came against logistical targets as the Communists attempted to slow US operations on the realisation that before too much longer the US troops would be gone.

These attacks were part of the Communist spring offensive, the bulk of which hit in March. Saigon itself had been protected from severe fighting by the presence of the 1st Air Cav blocking NVA infiltration routes, striking at any VC/NVA encountered, and shielding Saigon from attack to the west. Fighting along the

Left: Mortarmen of the 173rd Airborne Brigade fire in support of an operation north of Bien Hoa in May 1965.

Below: During the assault on Hill 875, a member of the 173rd Airborne Brigade assumes the tired, determined look of the archetypal infantryman. Note the 'bug juice' tucked into the rubber band around the helmet.

Cambodian border, particularly, was pitched at times with the 2/5 Cavalry taking the brunt. In further efforts to protect Saigon – efforts it should be noted which were tying down a large proportion of US striking power – elements of the 1st Infantry Division, 11th Armored Cavalry Regiment and 1st Air Cav swept the Michelon rubber plantation northwest of Saigon catching the 7th NVA Division and inflicting more than four hundred casualties. Throughout the war, French executives of Michelon had collaborated with the Communists, allowing them to use the plantation as a refuge, if not actively at least tacitly. Therefore, this operation had long been called for.

On 15 April – income tax day back in the 'World' – the 173rd Airborne Brigade began Operation WASHINGTON GREEN in conjunction with the ARVNs in Bing Ding Province in an attempt to pacify the hamlets. Though such operations did not run up impressive body counts, they were important in preparing the Vietnamese to assume responsibility for the war. The 4th Infantry Division was involved in two major operations during the spring. Between 1 March and 14 April, they took part in WAYNE GREY and then on 22 April began PUTNAM TIGER which would run until September. Combined, these two operations would account for over one thousand one hundred and fifty enemy casualties and help keep the enemy from becoming too aggressive in the Kontum and Pleiku areas. April also saw two brigades of the 1st Air Cav involved in Operation MONTANA RAIDER.

By the summer of 1969, virtually all US infantry units were working more closely with Vietnamese infantry units, carrying out operations down to battalion or lower level with counterpart units as part of a program called 'Dong Thien' (Progress Together). The 1st Infantry Division, for example, worked with the 5th ARVN Division. As the Vietnamization Program progressed, in many cases the only US units in certain areas would be logistical or other support units, prime targets for the Communists from 1969 onwards. As a result, at least some infantrymen found themselves running crash combat training courses for support troops who were now more likely to find themselves in combat.

Although troops of the 9th Infantry Division had begun Operation RICE FARMER jointly with the ARVNs on 1 January 1969, responsibility for the security of the Mekong Delta would soon fall to the ARVNs completely as this was the first area to be handed back when the 1st and 2nd Brigades of the 9th Infantry Division returned to the USA. The first to leave was the 3/60th on 8 July followed by the remainder of the two brigades before the end of August. The 3rd

Brigade continued an aggressive posture throughout the year running aggressive 'Bushmaster' patrols and ambushes under the control of the 25th Infantry Division. When carrying out this type of ambush, a company was inserted into an area just before sundown. Once it was dark, the company split into squads to set smaller ambushes around the area. Then, assuming there had been no contact, they reassembled in the morning to relax under cover throughout the day. Once again, that night they set their ambushes, only in different spots just in case they had been spotted the previous night. Finally, they would be extracted the next morning.

In mid-August, the 2nd Mechanized Infantry Battalion of the 2nd Infantry saw heavy fighting along Highway 13 as the 1st Infantry Division continued aggressive operations along the highways. Also in August, elements of the Americal Division saw fierce fighting in the Hiep Duc Valley.

During later 1969, the 1st Air Cav became an integral part of the Vietnamization Program as they were assigned to work closely with the ARVN airborne forces to prepare them to take over the airmobile role once the 1st Cav and 101st Airborne left the country. Throughout the year, as US units became involved less frequently in large-scale operations, ambushes by small units became the most successful US tactic for hurting the enemy. Once again on these types of operations, the paratroopers of the 173rd Airborne Brigade and the 'Wolfhounds' of the 25th Infantry Division's 27th Infantry proved especially skilled. As 1969 drew to a close the 3rd Brigade, 82nd Airborne Division also left Vietnam to return to Fort Bragg. Although only three infantry brigades had left during 1969, numerous others had received orders for redeployment during 1970.

Into Cambodia

By January 1970, US troop levels were down about 200,00 from their peak. Nevertheless, there remained little serious enemy opposition within most of South Vietnam itself. With the prevention of casualties a priority, most US infantry units were not used as aggressively as in the past either, though there were exceptions. In January for example, the 173rd Airborne Brigade began battling the 8th NVA Battalion for Hill 474, a battle which would last for two months and eventually cost the enemy two thirds of the battalion's strength.

At the end of 1969, the 1st Infantry Division had begun preparing for redeployment to the USA, and by 15 April 1970, the Big Red One was gone, having suffered 20,770 casualties during its years in

Vietnam, more than the division had suffered in World War Two. The 3rd Brigade of the 4th Infantry Division had also been deactivated by 15 April.

Though enemy contacts were less frequent, US units such as the 199th Infantry Brigade were still taking casualties, including Brig Gen William R. Bond, killed by a sniper in April, thus becoming the fifth commander of the brigade either killed or wounded in action. Obviously, leading the 'Redcatchers' was dangerous, but these casualties also illustrate that the brigade commanders were where the action was, in the Infantry School 'Follow Me' tradition.

Despite the fact that South Vietnam was now relatively secure within its own borders, enemy forces and logistics centers just across the border in Cambodia still posed a serious threat to the survival of South Vietnam. As a result, in April, ARVN troops thrust across the border into Cambodia at enemy sanctuaries. On 1 May, US troops followed the ARVNs, with the 1st Air Cav air assaulting into the 'Fishhook' salient followed by a ground push by the 11th Armored Cavalry to link up with the air cavalry. To the north, the 4th Infantry Division pushed across the border and captured an important NVA base camp, while to the south a brigade of the 25th Infantry Division carried out their portion of the 'incursion.' By 13 May, the 4th Infantry Division had already been pulled back across the border to spend the remainder of their time in country patrolling around An Khe. Though the enemy had quickly retreated in the face of the heavy border crossing, within the first week over one thousand Communist troops had been killed and almost five thousand weapons captured, not to mention food, ammunition and other important supplies.

On 7 May, the 3rd Brigade, 9th Infantry Division had pushed into the 'Parrot's Beak,' in some cases using their amphibious mobility to move along the Mekong River. About this time, too, the 1st Cav captured a massive two square mile NVA complex in the 'Fishhook.' Despite the obvious successes of the Cambodia operations, the announcement in the US press that US troops would not penetrate more than 25 miles into Cambodia and would be pulled out by the end of June allowed the enemy to pull back past this limit and await the US withdrawal. Nevertheless, during the operations more than eleven thousand of the enemy were killed for loss of only 337 American dead and 1,524 wounded. Enemy logistics were heavily disrupted, too, forestalling any major offensive against South Vietnam for a year or more.

Throughout the remainder of the year, pullouts continued with the remainder of the 4th Infantry Division gone by December, the

3rd Brigade of the 9th Infantry Division by October, all but the
2nd Brigade of the 25th Infantry Division by December and the
199th Infantry Brigade by October. This left the highly mobile 1st
Cav and 101st Airborne and the questionable Americal Division
along with the 2nd Brigade of the 25th Infantry Division and the
173rd Airborne Brigade as the only major US infantry in country.
The 101st Airborne Division (Airmobile) was used relatively
aggressively in Operation TEXAS STAR from April through
September, but most of the remaining units found themselves
spread thin as they absorbed responsibility for areas formerly under
the control of those units departing. The 173rd Airborne Brigade, for
example, sent the 2/503 to cover an area formerly the responsibility
of a large portion of the 4th Infantry Division, while the 25th
Infantry Division assumed responsibility for areas formerly covered
by the 1st Infantry Division, 9th Infantry Division, and 199th
Infantry Brigade (Light).

As US strength become diluted, fire support bases assumed
greater importance as US units rarely operated now far from their
FSBs. The front line units remaining – mostly tough airborne or
airmobile troops – still offered formidable fighting potential, but the
knowledge that their part of the war was winding down and the
desire to make it home alive resulted in eroding morale even in the
best units. The 1st Air Cav, for example, often considered the best
division in Vietnam, suffered cases of refusals to fight. Even the best
infantrymen by this stage of the war had begun to feel that if their
country was not interested in winning the war why should they be
sacrificed in a futile cause. Individual will in combat often erodes
geometrically in relation to national will and the national will to
fight in Vietnam was about denuded by this point in the war.

The Infantry Departs

Although the US troop commitment to Vietnam would continue to
drop rapidly during 1971, there were still some infantry operations
being carried out. At the end of January, the 1st Brigade, 5th
Infantry Division (Mechanized), for example, launched DEWEY
CANYON II with the objective of establishing a launch point for
LAM SON 719 – the ARVN invasion of Laos – and of opening Route 9
to the border. The actual invasion began on 8 February, though
without American ground forces being involved in the border
crossing. Unfortunately, the ARVN forces did not prove to be ready
to carry out a massive cross border strike and only massive use of US
airpower prevented a total disaster. Some US infantry helped cover

M79 grenadier of the 101st Airborne division.

the ARVN retreat back to South Vietnam, though the US forces remained within South Vietnam.

Generally, the NVA avoided contact with US troops and most US troops avoided contact with the enemy, though the 101st Airborne, still involved in Operation JEFFERSON GLENN until the fall of 1971, was involved in fighting along the western frontiers of South Vietnam. Primarily, however, US Infantry was now used for security around highly critical installations, especially to patrol the areas from which rocket attacks might be launched.

1971 saw the pullout of the two infantry units most closely identified with the war in Vietnam, too, as the 1st and 2nd Brigades of the 1st Cavalry Division (Airmobile) left in March and April, and the 173rd Airborne Brigade left in August. Other units leaving during the year included the 2nd Brigade, 25th Infantry Division in April, the 1st Brigade, 5th Infantry Division (Mechanized) in August (though the brigade had still been engaged in combat as late as June), and all of the American Division except the 196th Infantry Brigade in November. The American Division did not leave without one further incident illustrating the division's problems, however. On 22 March 1971, a battalion of the 196th Infantry Brigade was so slack on defensive procedures that a fire base was overrun resulting in over one hundred US casualties that should have been prevented. Among other officers, the Americal Division commander was reprimanded over this failure.

With only the 3rd Brigade of the 1st Cav, the 196th Infantry Brigade and most of the 101st Airborne Division (Airmobile) remaining of the massive infantry commitment of three years previously, 1972 would mark the final departure of US infantrymen from South Vietnam. In early January 1972, the 3rd Brigade, 1st Cav was involved in skirmishes while securing the 'rocket belt' around the Bien Hoa/Long Binh/Saigon areas, but for the most part US infantry was strictly carrying out 'defensive' operations to protect the US pullout.

During the 1972 Easter Invasion by the NVA, the only US infantrymen who saw action blunting the attack were a few advisors who chose to stay with their ARVN units rather than be evacuated. The 196th Infantry Brigade was sent to reinforce Phu Bai and Tan My but showed that the 'heritage' of the Americal Division was still alive as members of the brigade refused to carry out patrols.

The 101st Airborne had begun its departure from Vietnam in December 1971, and had completed its return to Fort Campbell by

Members of the 503rd Infantry (Airborne) moving across typical rice paddies during a search and destroy operation.

the time the Easter Offensive hit. Then, in late June, the last two brigades of infantry pulled out as the 3rd Brigade, 1st Cav, and 196th Infantry Brigade left. Each did leave one battalion for residual security duties, but these final infantry units – the 3/21 and 1/7th Cavalry – left in August. The US infantry had finally left the rice paddies and highlands of Vietnam either to return to civilian life or to re-orientate themselves for possible ground combat in Korea or Europe as part of the new All-Volunteer Army.

The departure of the last members of the 1st Cav marked the departure of the last of the one hundred and fifty thousand troopers who had served proudly in what was arguably the best division in Vietnam and one of the best in American military history. Other Infantry units had served valiantly as well, however. The killed in action (KIAs) totals for a few selected infantry units, in most cases higher than their World War Two totals, graphically illustrate that, after seven years of combat, the soil of Vietnam was well irrigated with the blood of American infantrymen (see table).

Formation	Killed in Action	Medals of Honor
1st Cavalry Division (Airmobile)	5,444	25
1st Infantry Division	3,146	11
4th Infantry Division	2,531	11
9th Infantry Division	2,624	20
23rd (Americal) Infantry Division	808	11
25th Infantry Division	4,547	21
199th Infantry Brigade (Light)	657	4
173rd Airborne Brigade	1,748	14
101st Airborne Division (Airmobile)	4,011	17

Another indicator of combat intensity is Medals of Honor, as also shown in the table. Though some medals such as the Bronze Star and Air Medal became cheapened by being so readily awarded in Vietnam, the Medal of Honor retained its luster.

The Grunt's War

The grunt, like his World War One predecessor the Doughboy and his World War Two forerunner the Dogface, in general was not interested in the 'Big Picture.' He was interested in surviving until the next day and, in the process, taking such small pleasures as a can of peaches from his C-rations, having a smoke and sleeping somewhere relatively dry and safe. On the average he was the youngest infantryman the United States had ever sent to war and due to the inequalities of the Selective Service System he was likely to be poor, frequently Black or Hispanic, and not particularly well-educated, intelligent or ambitious. Surviving his tour, buying a fast car (often on complicated time plans offered to him through the mail while still in Vietnam), and leaping into bed with a woman with round eyes were generally more important to him than the body count, Vietnamization, or Peace With Honor; Hell, he'd probably seen a lot of fellow grunts – honorable by his standards – in very un-honored pieces bleeding to death in the foul smelling mud of Vietnam.

At times he was concerned with such matters as acquiring an SKS rifle as a souvenir (popular because being semi-automatic rather than full-automatic as the AK-47, he could take it home). If one of his buddies or he had a transistor radio they might listen to Chris Noel or one of the other DJs on Radio Vietnam or wait for the strange adventures of 'Chicken Man' broadcast over the same network. As insane as the adventures of 'Chicken Man' may have seemed, they probably seemed saner than a lot of aspects of the war the grunt was fighting.

For the American infantryman fighting in Southeast Asia perhaps the hardest lesson to learn was that summarised by Chapman in the title of his classic work on jungle warfare – *The Jungle is Neutral* – which, indeed, it is. Even those trained in special operations and jungle warfare found it difficult to adjust to the hell of the realities that was jungle warfare: for conscript 'Eleven Bravos' (infantrymen) it was even worse. For American boys raised in a technological society it was hard to accept that in the jungle American technology had to be supplanted by the grunt with his rifle and sometimes at close quarters with his machete or entrenching tool – both used more than once to shred the flesh of attacking NVA or VC around firebases or in other hand-to-hand encounters. That was assuming the grunt actually saw his enemy; all too often he didn't. He saw his comrades fall prey to boobytraps or snipers or rockets or mortars or, the final insult, 'friendly fire.'

Grunts moved through the jungle single file – 'ranger file' – to minimise the chances of hitting a booby trap. They avoided trails for the same reason, though it made movement far more difficult. The pointman frequently carried a shotgun so that he could sweep the area in front of him should he walk into an enemy patrol or ambush. In some cases, he might have an M79 grenade launcher loaded with a canister round for the same reason. Fear was the grunt's constant companion in the jungle, along with discomfort. The grunt, however had one advantage over the enemy. He knew that for him the key was to survive for minutes until the overwhelming firepower available to back him up could be brought to bear. That is why infantry platoons burdened themselves with extra ammo even though humping it in the jungle was agony.

Humping anything in the jungle eventually became agony as the utilities became filthy and stiff, or during the monsoon sodden and chaffed against the skin. On many patrols the grunt never even got to take his boots off or remove his rucksack for days on end at times. During the monsoon his fingers would become white and wrinkled until they looked themselves like some of the slimy crawling things which called the jungle home. The leeches were the worst. There were the land leeches, which were only about an inch long and which would cling to the skin or clothing as one passed through the bush, but the worst were the green and brown water leeches, which could reach almost a foot in length and looked like bloated cigars when gorged on the grunt's blood. Various other insects joined forces to sting, bite, and otherwise annoy the grunt almost constantly. The insect repellent, often seen in photographs worn tucked into the giant rubber band around the infrantyman's helmet, 'bug juice,' helped but was nasty stuff itself, smelling and tasting much like diesel fuel. As a result of its taste, grunts were reluctant to put it on their lips and around their mouth and, hence, often awakened with badly swollen lips in the morning after a night of acting as the local mess hall for the entomological enemy.

Cleanliness was extemely important in the jungle but was virtually impossible to maintain. As a result, the effect of what back in the 'World' would be minor problems became cumulative. Jungle sores, small cuts and insect bites would not heal and at times, as the grunt watched the jungle rot crawling up his thighs he, no doubt, wondered if there would be any of his body left when his DEROS (Date Eligible for Return from Overseas) arrived. Almost as bad as the leeches, were the ants – a constant, too, always there, always crawling, and always biting; then, as the sweat kept the bites from healing, festering. From the constant filth, pimples also became a problem, and among grunts one was able to tell 'short-timers' by the peroxide baths they began to give their faces in an attempt to clear them up before returning to the 'World.'

In Washington, no doubt, defoliation seemed a great idea to the old men fighting the war from afar in air-conditioned offices; it was not. Even forgetting the problems with Agent Orange which have continued to haunt many, grunts hated moving through defoliated areas. There was no cover, making the infantrymen easy prey for an ambush plus the dead leaves had crumbled into a powder which got into the clothes and chafed the skin until it seemed intolerable, especially since grunts normally could not stop to bathe. The dried creepers in defoliated areas also seemed to reach out to trip or snare the unsuspecting, much like the 'Wait-a-Minute' bush, the thorns of which would entangle the infantryman, especially the newly-arrived 'cherry' who had yet to learn the ways of the bush. The skin between the grunt's fingers and toes which would often become cracked and bleeding, would become especially sensitive to the corrosive powder from the dead flora of the defoliated areas.

In the jungle the smell of death soon became mixed with the smell of stagnant pools, rotting vegetation and unwashed bodies. Normally, even before grunts left on a mission, they avoided washing with soap for a couple of days since the VC had finely developed senses of smell for US soap. Lack of cleanliness affected health and comfort in the jungle but there was, in reality, little comfort, just survival.

Eating was mostly a chore, at best a chance for a slight rest. C-Rations were often known as 'Charlie'-Rats, a pun on the radio code for 'C' and the implication that C-Rats must have been wished upon infantrymen by the enemy. Only someone who has tried to eat a cold can of 'beef slices with potatoes and gravy' with the monsoon rains pouring into the can mixing water with the greasy substance, can appreciate a meal in the jungle. Of course, the rain did drown some of the ants which had crawled into the can. Among the other gourmet selections available in C-Rats were: beef with spiced sauce, sliced pork with juices, beans with frankfurters in tomato sauce, sliced ham with juices, turkey loaf, and others, including the bane of the grunt's gastronomical existence – ham and lima beans. To wash his C-Rats down, he usually had a few swigs of water tasting heavily of the iodine from purification tabs, unless he followed the practice of adding koolaid, which weakened the effect of the iodine but marginally improved the water's taste.

Frequently, the food did not stay around long anyway. Diarrhea was common in the bush, so much so that few infantrymen wore underwear and some even cut holes in their utility trousers.

Sleep in the jungle was, at best, tortured and intermittent unless one virtually collapsed from exhaustion, but that was dangerous, too, since one might have to come awake instantly and engage the enemy somewhere out there in the darkness. To act as an early warning for the platoon, the grunt might be sent out as one of three or four men at an LP (Listening Post), in which case he might get little or no sleep. Or his squad might pull an ambush that night and

A member of the 173rd Airborne Brigade, his M16 at the ready as the sun sets.

have to set up their claymore mines and wait for enemy movement with M16s and grenades at hand and hoping their AN/PRC-25 radio would stay operable should they become involved in a firefight. The infantryman soon picked up certain tricks from the old hands with a few months on the line. The grunt learned to load only eighteen rounds in twenty-round magazines or twenty-seven rounds in thirty-round magazines, for example, with every fifth round a tracer.

The list of problems the grunt encountered fighting in Vietnam could continue: combat units were normally understrength, while rear area units were overstrength; the monsoon rains, even though the temperatures were in the 60s, chilled him after his body had grown used to the tropical heat; at night he got disoriented in the jungle easily; he had constantly to be aware of such dangers as branches pulling the pin on one of his grenades in the undergrowth; before noon the jungle was often shrouded in fog; and during the monsoon, slopes became mudslides which were almost impossible to climb. Then, of course, there were the snakes – pythons, but most of all the kraits, which meant almost instant death. Then, there were the foul-tempered water buffalos or, on night ambushes particularly, tigers or leopards.

As the infantryman has in almost every war throughout history, the grunt had to fight his environment as well as the human enemy. Most grunts who lasted in line units learned to fight and survive in the bush, but just when they were becoming most skillful they were usually rotated home. The one year tour of duty effectively guaranteed that the level of combat experience never reached the hard corps standards of the World War One or World War Two line units. A substantial number of the bodies heli-lifted out of combat areas wrapped in their ponchos were FNGs (Fucking New Guys) who just never had the chance to learn the basics of survival.

Members of the 1st Air Cav assaulting an LZ during Operation OREGON. The man in the foreground carries the M203 version of the M16 with 40mm grenade launcher affixed.

Nevertheless, despite the highly publicised yet relatively infrequent refusals to patrol, the grunts fought well in Vietnam. They fought for their buddies, for those officers and NCOs who earned their respect, and for their country even if not sure why their country wanted them to die in that place.

Tactics

Infantry training during the Vietnam War stressed tactics specifically for the Vietnam combat environment. Infantry training centers in the United States, therefore, had mock Vietnamese villages, rice paddies, bamboo thickets, and so on, where the trainees maneuvered as they learned squad and platoon tactics. At times this resulted in ludicrous situations such as infantry trainees at Fort Lewis, Washington, practicing clearing a Vietnamese village while plowing through snow drifts! On the most basic level, infantry tactics for Vietnam were spelled out in Department of Defense Publication GEN-25 of 10 June 1966, HANDBOOK FOR US FORCES IN VIETNAM. Cautions for patrols, for example were given as follows:

(1) Stay off of roads. trails and dry creek beds: maintain dispersion.
(2) Prevent the VC from predicting the direction of movement by following a zig-zag course.
(3) Dead foliage may be old camouflage over a trap.
(4) Tied down brush may be firing lane for an ambush site.
(5) Avoid moats around villages; they may hide punji traps or booby traps.
(6) Unoccupied huts may have booby traps hidden in the frame or in the roof thatch.
(7) Be cautious of all civilians.
(8) Be cautious in villages where no children are visible or where they are unfriendly.
(9) Do not set a pattern.
(10) Stay alert.

Obviously these cautions are tacitly admitting that the initiative for opening fire was normally with the enemy. Standard Operating Procedures for patrols according to GEN-25 included:

(1) Simultaneous patrol activities by elements of a unit must be closely coordinated and contact maintained when in close proximity in order to save time, protect formations, and maintain security.
(2) Take advantage of inclement weather to conduct patrols; heavy rain will cover noise of ground movement.
(3) In the jungle, trails must be cut through the dense foliage and undergrowth. When practicing dispersion in movement under such conditions lateral contact is very difficult to maintain. Move in multiple columns for added security.

(4) Never return over the same roads.
(5) When patrolling a road lined by heavy undergrowth and dense foliage, reconnaissance by observation should be supplemented by controlled reconnaissance fire.
(6) Use helicopter lift of patrols to expand a zone of operations or to get behind VC units, especially when the VC have concealed routes of withdrawal.
(7) Use stay behind patrols to ambush small groups of VC returning to an area after the departure of the main body of friendly forces.

It is noteworthy that only items 6 and 7 are attempting to take some of the initiative in combat away from the enemy. GEN-25 continues with this theme to say about saturation patrolling:

> **a.** During daylight one of the most successful tactics is saturation patrolling supported by a reaction force. The saturation of an area with squad size patrols allows maximum coverage and fully employs the leadership capabilities of small unit leaders. Saturation patrolling requires detailed planning by the company or higher echelon to coordinate completely all the patrols in the area. Since the VC will not normally engage a superior force, the smaller unit has a better chance of daylight contact with guerrillas. Patrol size will be determined largely by intelligence estimates of enemy strength, disposition and equipment, and by the terrain.
>
> **b.** Conducting night patrols without any prior coordination is dangerous. In certain areas, both Popular and Regional Forces may be patrolling and ambushing. Close liaison and coordination with local forces is imperative to preclude friendly units meeting in the dark and exchanging fire.

The key element of this section on patrolling falls in part 'a' dealing with the use of small patrols, which though normally more effective in Vietnam basically made it a lieutenant's and captain's war rather than a general's and colonel's war, a point field grade officers had some trouble accepting.

GEN-25's comments on '**Sudden Engagements**' with the enemy are succinct but valid:

> Most encounters with the VC while on patrol are sudden meeting engagements. Reaction by the point must be immediate to deliver effective fire at the elusive VC, who has been trained to leap into the brush and slither away on his belly when encountered. Reaction by the remainder of the patrol must be rapid and violent. Immediately bring all available fires to bear on the VC element. Fire low; a ricochet is better than an overshot. After fire superiority is gained, vigorously attack to destroy him. Contact with the VC must be maintained. Pursuit of the VC immediately following an engagement must be aggressive.

GEN-25 offers the following tactics in the section dealing with
'Reaction to Ambush':

    a. When caught in an ambush the friendly unit must immediately
return the fire, gain and maintain fire superiority and vigorously
assault the ambush force. Friendly troops must continue to fire, even
after the VC cease, to prevent his recovering weapons and bodies and
escaping. Once the ambush is overcome, the entire ambush site must be
thoroughly searched and cleared.

    b. Troops moving through suspect areas should carry white
phosphorus (WP) and offensive grenades and, when ambushed,
immediately throw them towards the enemy. Coupled with casualty
producing effects, the WP grenade provides a protective smoke screen.

Section V of GEN-25 offers suggestions on setting ambushes to
inflict maximum enemy casualties:

General
    a. Current service manuals provide squad and detailed guidance on
       the conduct of ambushes. Recent experience with ambushes in
       Vietnam reveals that, all too frequently, ambushes are well laid,
       properly planned and correctly positioned, but fail because of an
       error on the part of a single individual.
    b. Selection of the site is only the first step in the development of a well
       organized ambush. Ambush leaders must be capable and be
       provided with the equipment necessary to successfully carry out
       their assigned mission. Squad leaders must be capable of calling in
       supporting arms, and be proficient in methods of blocking escape
       routes and utilizing booby traps, demolitions and punji traps.

Actions Prior to the Ambush
    a. Make a detailed map study, including use of aerial photos whenever
       possible. Commit to memory the route and terrain – particularly
       those features which will aid navigation. Confirm these terrain
       features as you pass over or near them.
    b. A complete, detailed rehearsal of the ambush must be conducted to
       eliminate errors. Each member of the ambush party must
       thoroughly understand what he is to do.
    c. Arrangements must be made for the employment of all available
       supporting fires.
    d. Movement to the ambush site by concealed routes to avoid detection
       by the VC or VC sympathizers is essential. Contact with civilians
       must be avoided.
    e. Blocking forces must be emplaced in conjunction with mines, booby
       traps and punji stakes along likely avenues of escape in order to
       inflict maximum casualties.
    f. Repeated occupation of the same ambush site must be avoided.
       Using several sites in the same general area insures better coverage
       and more effective results.

Conduct of the Ambush
    a. Maintain light and noise discipline in the ambush site. Do not

permit smoking. Failure to adhere to these basic practices is frequently the cause of an unsuccessful ambush.

    b. Stress the fact that the leader of the ambush is responsible for 'springing' the ambush. 'Springing' the ambush too early or too late leads to failure or to only partial success.

    c. Use a definite, clearly recognizable signal to commence firing. Prearrange and rehearse all signals to be used. Keep signals simple. This eliminates confusion and avoids premature disclosure of the ambush.

    d. Place a heavy and accurate volume of fire in the ambush area, completely covering the killing zone and escape routes.

    e. Fire low to avoid overshooting the target.

    f. Use all supporting fires such as artillery, mortars, tactical air and armed helicopter support.

    g. Pursue by fire when the VC jump into the underbrush opposite the ambush party.

    h. Quickly exploit and search the immediate area for casualties, weapons and documents.

Night Ambush

    a. The night ambush deserves particular emphasis, since most VC operations are conducted at night. Ambushes during the hours of darkness are more difficult to control, but the lack of light or illumination adds to the security of the ambush party and the confusion of those being ambushed.

    b. At night a small ambush party is generally more practical because of greater ease of control and decreased probability of detection. The size of the party will depend on factors such as the size of unit to be ambushed and the estimated VC strength in the area. Some means of illuminating the ambush site after contact must be provided so that the area may be thoroughly searched. Pre-planned artillery and mortar concentrations, hand-held flares or illumination grenades can be used for this purpose.

Special Considerations

    a. The Claymore (M18A1) antipersonnel mine has proved to be highly effective ambush weapon in Vietnam.

    b. 'Stay behind' ambushes can be very successful, since the VC normally follow a unit when it leaves an operational area. Time permitting these ambush patrols should be prepared to remain in the area for several days and use deception tactics to conceal their presence.

GEN-25 goes on to discuss airmobile operations, search and destroy operations, and other types of operations in some detail. The few sections reproduced above are sufficient, however, to make the point that infantry tactics in Vietnam were heavily governed by the fact that except in ambushes or meeting engagements the enemy would normally initiate the combat; infantry tactics were then designed to maximize enemy losses and minimize losses when reacting.

5
SPECIAL OPERATIONS FORCES

As of 1963, when the commitment of US Army Special Forces personnel was growing, the basic Special Forces operational unit was the twelve-man A-detachment. It was organised as follows:

Detachment Commander	Captain (O-3)
Detachment Executive Officer	1st Lieutenant (O-2)
Operations Sergeant	Master Sergeant (E-8)
Heavy Weapons Leader	Sergeant 1st Class (E-7)
Light Weapons Leader	Sergeant 1st Class (E-7)
Intelligence Sergeant	Sergeant 1st Class (E-7)
Medical Specialist	Sergeant 1st Class (E-7)
Radio Operator Supervisor	Sergeant 1st Class (E-7)
Assistant Medical Specialist	Staff Sergeant (E-6)
Demolition/Engineer Sergeant	Staff Sergeant (E-6)
Combat Demolitions/Engineer Specialist	Specialist 5th Class (E-5)
Chief Radio Operator	Sergeant (E-5)

This organisation was frequently modified to fit special needs. For example, when assigned to CIDG advising, the Demolitions/Engineer Specialist was replaced by an Intelligence Specialist, and when serving as MACV Sub-Section Advisors, a team was often expanded to fourteen members with the addition of two psy ops specialists.

The standard Special Forces B-Detachment, which would normally control between four and ten A-Detachments, was comprised of twenty-three men organised circa 1963 as follows:

Detachment Commander	Major (O-4)
Executive Officer	Captain (O-3)
Adjutant	Captain (O-3)
Intelligence Officer	Captain (O-3)
Operations Officer	Captain (O-3)
Supply Officer	Captain (O-3)
Sergeant Major	(E-9)
Intelligence Sergeant	(E-8)
Operations Sergeant	(E-8)
Demolitions/Engineer Sergeant	(E-7)
Heavy Weapons Leader	(E-7)
Light Weapons Leader	(E-7)
Medical Specialist	(E-7)
Radio Operator Supervisor	(E-7)
Supply Sergeant	(E-6)
Administrative Supervisor	(E-6)
Assistant Supply Sergeant	(E-6)

Preventive Medical Specialist   (E-6)
Combat Demolitions/Engineer Specialist   (E-5)
(4x) Chief Radio Operators   (E-5)

It should be noted that some of the administrative officers serving in B-Detachments were not fully Special Forces qualified at times.

By 1965, various modifications had been made to suit B-Detachments for missions in Vietnam. One change within the 5th Special Forces Group (Airborne) was to expand to twenty-four personnel with substantial changes in composition. For example, a Civic Action Officer and a Regional Forces/Popular Forces (RF/PF) Advisor – both captains – were added. Among enlisted personnel, the Combat Demolitions/Engineer Specialist was eliminated, as was one of the Chief Radio Operators and the Preventive Medical Specialist. In their places were added an Assistant Operations Sergeant (E-7), and Intelligence Analyst (E-6) and an Operational Clerk (E-5).

Far more substantial changes were made in B-detachments assigned to special operations in MACV/SOG or the Greek letter projects. Expanded to thirty-nine men, such B-Detachments included a Plans Officer (O-3) instead of an Executive Officer, two Intelligence Sergeants and Operations Sergeants, a Reconnaisance Supervisor (E-8) and sixteen Reconnaisance Team Advisors (E-6).

Controlling between two and five B-detachments and their

US and Vietnamese Ranger officers instructing a class of ARVN Ranger candidates.

attached A-Detachments was the C-Detachments of seventeen men, as follows:

Commanding Officer	Lieutenant Colonel (O-5)
Executive Officer	Major (O-4)
Adjutant, S-1	Captain (O-3)
Intelligence Officer, S-2	Captain (O-3)
Operations Officer, S-3	Captain (O-3)
Supply Officer, S-4	Captain (O-3)
Sergeant Major	(E-9)
Intelligence Sergeant	(E-8)
Operations Sergeant	(E-8)
Assistant Supply Sergeant	(E-7)
Radio Operator Supervisor	(E-7)
Administrative Supervisor	(E-6)
Senior Field Radio Repairman	(E-5)
(4x) Chief Radio Operators	(E-5)

For ease of understanding Special Forces organisation, the C-Detachment can be equated with a company. The Special Forces Group, normally trained specifically for deployment to a certain geographical area, usually comprised three C-Detachments, as well as other specialised aviation, medical, signal and administrative and supply companies or platoons. Although initially members of Special Forces serving in Vietnam were drawn from the 1st Special Forces Group, which had responsibility for the Far East, by the time the US commitment became major, the 5th Special Forces Group had been given responsibility for Vietnam.

Initial Special Forces Missions

Although an involvement in Southeast Asia can be traced back through the OSS which supplied Ho Chi Minh and Vo Nguyen Giap with arms to fight against the Japanese, initial Special Forces involvement in the Indochina Wars is usually traced to a training team from the 77th Special Forces Group (Airborne), which trained Thai Rangers during 1954. During the remainder of the 1950s other training missions from the 14th Special Forces Detachment on Hawaii or the 1st Special Forces Group (Airborne) on Okinawa helped train the special units of the Vietnamese Army, specifically the Joint Observations Battalion (the forerunner to the Viet Special Forces) and the Viet Rangers (the Biet Dong Quan). By the summer of 1960, thirty US Special Forces soldiers were acting as trainers for elements of the South Vietnamese Army.

Actually, the first relatively large-scale Special Forces commitment came in Laos rather than Vietnam. In the spring of

1959, 107 members of the Special Forces under LTC 'Bull' Simons were assigned to FC-3 and sent to train the Laotian Army in counter-insurgency warfare. Broken into twelve Field Training Teams (FTTs), which were really scaled-down A-Detachments of six men, FC-1 'officially' arrived in Laos in July 1959. These teams, drawn from the 77th Special Forces Group (Airborne), rotated into Laos for six months at a time, enjoying limited successes until they helped counter a coup late in 1960. After thus proving their value to the regime, WHITE STAR, as the operation was codenamed, had grown to the point that well over 300 members of Special Forces were involved, though it was not until April, 1961, that their presence was officially acknowledged by allowing them to wear their uniforms and berets. As part of MAAG Laos, the members of WHITE STAR sent in Field Training Teams to various training facilities and as advisors to Laotian Field units. Other FTTs performed the mission they were trained for as they raised and trained Meo and Kha tribal irregulars to fight the Pathet Lao.

By May 1962, six Special Forces teams were working with Meo irregulars, which were formed into 100-man shock companies which ambushed and harassed the Pathet Lao throughout the Laotian highlands. By May 1962, another ten Special Forces teams were assigned to Kha shock companies in southern Laos. Special Forces strength assigned to the WHITE STAR mission peaked in July 1962, at 433.

All foreign military personnel were to be pulled out of Laos as a result of an agreement reached in July 1962. Although the Communists removed few if any of their troops, most of the Special Forces advisors left, though a few continued to work with the Meos in the Chu Porn mountains. In addition to training the Meos and Khas as effective anti-Communist guerrillas, the Special Forces had learned various lessons in Laos which would prove of value in the much larger commitment in the Republic of Vietnam.

The CIDG Program

In November 1961, twenty-eight members of the 1st Special Forces Group (Airborne) had arrived in Vietnam to train the Vietnamese in unconventional warfare. During this early portion of the Special Forces commitment they came under the control of the 'Combined Studies Group.' Forerunners of their comrades who would later be assigned to MACV/SOG, one reinforced A-Detachment was assigned in early 1961 to cross border intelligence operations as well. When it became apparent that Viet Cong influence in the Central Highlands could only be controlled by contesting communist domination of the hamlets, based on their successes with the Meos and Khas, the Special Forces were given the green light in the fall of 1961 to arm and train the Montagnards – the rugged hill people of the Highlands – as irregular militiamen. The fact that the 'Yards' had traditionally been persecuted by the Vietnamese and had no way to defend themselves had made them easy prey for the Viet Cong. The Special Forces had the mission of reversing this trend.

To implement their 'Village Defense Program,' the Special Forces chose the largest tribe in the Highlands – the Rhade. The Rhade village of Buon Enao and its surrounding hamlets in Darlac Province, therefore, received half of Detachment A-113 of the US Army Special Forces as well as an LLDB (Luc Luong Dac Biet) – as the Vietnamese Special Forces were known – detachment in December 1961. Initially, the Special Forces helped primarily with medical and engineering civic action programs to gain the Montagnards' trust, but on 14 February 1962, they actually began training the local militia. A full A-Detachment of the 1st SFG (Abn)

A US Ranger instructor at the Vietnamese Ranger Training Center at Duc My prepares to demonstrate where the Rangers got their nickname 'Snake Eaters' during the survival section of the course.

was assigned to assist the LLDB train the local Defense Forces in basic military skills, including small arms usage, and in building village defenses such as stockades and trenches. As a reaction force to assist villages that came under attack, a central 'Strike Force' received more training and received payment to serve as a full-time unit.

While the CIDG Program was being established, a Special Forces Training Center was established at Hoa Cam under B-110 with three assigned A-Detachments. Various types of irregulars were trained at this camp. The summer of 1962 saw the creation of Border Surveillance Camps under Special Forces auspices. Using Montagnard 'Trail Watchers' these camps along the borders with North Vietnam, Cambodia and Laos acted as bases from which surveillance missions could be launched along communist infiltration routes.

The CIDG Program grew quickly, already having one thousand Village Defense militia and three hundred full-time strikers in existence to defend twenty-eight villages by April 1962. Increasing geometrically, by August 1962, two hundred villages in Darlac Province were protected by the program which now required five full A-Detachments to carry out training and civic action programs. The VC, realising the danger posed by the CIDG Program, launched attacks against various camps, but the Special Forces trained militias proved more than capable of defending themselves. By the end of 1962, in fact, Darlac Province had been declared 'secure.'

HQ US Army Special Forces (Provisional) Vietnam was activated in September 1962, to control the various Special Forces detachments operating in Vietnam. In February 1963, the HQ was established at Nha Trang where it would remain throughout the war. July 1963, also saw Special Forces officially assume control for the CIDG Program under operation SWITCHBACK. As of November 1962, there had been one C-Detachment in Vietnam, controlling three B-Detachments, which controlled twenty-six A-Detachments. Personnel were drawn from the 1st, 5th and 7th Special Forces Groups (Airborne) for six-month temporary duty tours. As of the completion of Operation SWITCHBACK, over fifty thousand hamlet militiamen had been trained bringing almost nine thousand villages under the CIDG Program. Additionally, almost eighteen thousand Strike Force troops, one thousand Trail Watchers and three thousand five hundred Mountain Scouts had been trained. Illustrating the increasing Special Forces commitment by July 1963, 646 Special Forces personnel were in country assigned to one C-Detachment, four B-Detachments and thirty-seven A-Detachments.

Though the CIDG Program had been very successful in its initial aim of allowing hamlets to defend themselves, 1963 saw a shift in its emphasis towards the aggressive use of members of the strike forces for patrolling and ambushes and to harass infiltration routes along the borders. As part of this latter mission, the Trail Watchers established early warning posts and conducted long range patrols and ambushes along the borders. To carry out this mission more effectively, Special Forces camps were established near the borders, eighteen camps with sixty-four CIDG companies assigned having been established by June 1964. As their mission evolved, the Trail Watchers were renamed Border Surveillance Teams, while in the Central Highlands, the Mountain Scouts carried out basically the same mission.

By 1964, CIDG troops initially trained to defend their homes were being uprooted and moved to new homes near the borders where they could act as an interdiction force. During this period, too, the CIDG Program encompassed other minorities as part of the Strategic Hamlet Program. Among those recruited were the Khmer Serei and

A US Ranger instructor examines a leg bandaged by students during the ARVN Ranger course.

Khmer Kampuchea Krom along the Cambodian border and the Hoa
Hao and Cao Dai religious sects. Especially good fighting men were
recruited from among the Nungs, an ethnic Chinese minority, whose
loyalty was so unquestioned that Special Forces used them as body-
guards or to guard detachment compounds.

Seeming to justify the Vietnamese government's suspicions of the
CIDG Program, the Montagnards rebelled in September 1964, but
fortunately Special Forces officers were able to defuse the rebellion
before it became too widespread. It should be noted that the rebellion
was not directed against their Special Forces advisors but against
the Vietnamese from the LLDB.

As camps were established in ever increasing numbers along the
Cambodian and Laotian borders, eighteen Special Forces
A-Detachments and 11,250 irregulars were assigned to border camps
by July 1964. Of course, as Special Forces camps became a bigger
and bigger thorn in the side of the Viet Cong, camps came under
heavier pressure as the threat of VC night infiltration and attack
grew: hence, the importance of the reliable detachments of Nungs.
At one such camp under attack – Nam Dong – Capt Roger Donlon of
the Special Forces earned the first Medal of Honor of the war.

The 5th Special Forces Group Arrives

In October 1964, need for a Group to control the ever increasing
number of Special Forces A-Detachments in Vietnam was
acknowledged with the arrival of the 5th Special Forces Group
(Airborne). The presence of a Group in country meant that members
of Special Forces in many cases now began serving regular one-year
tours rather than TDY tours. As of March 1965, there were 1,465
Special Forces personnel in country assigned to four C-Detachments
(one in each corps tactical zone), twelve B-Detachments and forty-
eight A-Detachments, as well as various special projects.

By this time, regular US ground troops were beginning to arrive to
help stabilise the deteriorating situation. Until US infantry could
take over, however, it was necessary to make use of the lightly-
armed CIDG troops for road and base security, sweeps in 'Indian
Country,' and as reaction forces. In an attempt to win hearts and
minds in the provinces, Special Forces had begun advising local
officials on civil affairs and psy ops in late 1960 as well. Some of the
newly arrived US infantry, particularly the airmobile units, found
the CIDG troops useful adjuncts to act as scouts or to draw
Communist attack, after which the airmobile troops would air
assault in to reinforce them and decimate the enemy. Another way

in which the irregulars worked with the airborne and airmobile troops was by moving in and establishing camps in areas cleared by the 1st Air Cav, 173rd Airborne Brigade or 101st Airborne Division. These same units would then remain available to reinforce Special Forces camps which came under VC attack. One of the bloodiest battles of the war – the Ia Drang Valley – resulted, in fact, from the attack on Plei Mei Special Forces Camp.

Special Forces strength continued to grow throughout 1965, reaching almost one thousand six hundred by the end of the year, with twenty-eight thousand CIDG irregulars plus two thousand three hundred Nungs assigned Special missions under their control and seventy eight SF camps in operation.

The MIKE Forces

To counter the attacks against CIDG camps by VC and NVA regulars, in October 1964, and 'Eagle Flight' had been created at Pleiku with the mission of serving as a reaction force and recon unit. Within a few months, however, this single 'Eagle Flight' had grown

A Special Forces NCO assigned to the 503rd MIKE Force gives parachute instruction to a member of the MIKE Force.

into the Mobile Strike Forces (MIKE Forces for short) consisting of an HQ and three companies with a total strength of about six hundred men. At least a percentage of the MIKE Force members were parachute trained, though they would normally be inserted by helicopter. Although their primary mission theoretically was reinforcement of threatened Special Forces camps, they were used more and more frequently to carry out raids, ambushes, patrols and reconnaissance missions. Because the MIKE Forces were directly under Special Forces control rather than through their 'advisory' relationship with the Vietnamese, the MIKE Forces could be used more aggresively than regular ARVN troops.

Reflecting the growing importance of the MIKE Forces, by June 1965, there were five MIKE Force battalions – one in each corps tactical zone under the control of the corps C-Detachment and one directly under the 5th Special Forces Group (Airborne). (IV Corps MIKE Force was really formed in February 1966.) The five MIKEs were based as follows:

I Corps MIKE Force
 based at DaNang under Detachment A-113
 composed primarily of Montagnards
II Corps MIKE Force
 based at Pleiku under Detachment A-119
 composed primarily of Montagnards
III Corps MIKE Force
 based at Bien Hoa under Detachmant A-302
 composed primarily of Viets, Cambods and Nungs
IV Corps MIKE Force
 based at Don Phuc under Detachment A-430
 composed primarily of Nungs and Cambods
5th Special forces (Airborne) MIKE Force
 based at Nha Trang under Detachment A-503.

Although in December 1966, the MIKE Forces supposedly came under joint Vietnamese/US control, since Detachment B-55 remained in charge of Mobile Strike Force Command they were still fully responsive to Special Forces direction. Used even more aggressively than the MIKE Forces were the Mobile Guerrilla Forces targeted against the VC network within South Vietnam. The Mobile Guerrilla Force normally consisted of a Special Forces A-Detachment, a 150-man MIKE Force Company and a 34-man Combat Recon Platoon. Trained along US Ranger lines, the Mobile Guerrilla Force could operate independently for up to sixty days in remote parts of the country hitting VC logistical sites, ambushing the VC and calling in air strikes on VC concentrations.

The first of the Mobile Guerrilla missions was 'Blackjack 21' in

October, 1966, followed by other 'Blackjack' missions, often initiated by the Mobile Guerrilla Force's own recon platoon making contact and then being reinforced by the MIKE Force company. 'Blackjack' missions might also include ambushing VC tax collectors or couriers, destroying or booby trapping enemy weapons caches and polluting enemy food caches. Inserted via parachute, helicopter or on foot Mobile Guerrilla Forces roamed supposed VC safe areas harassing the enemy wherever possible. As a result, the Mobile Guerrilla Force irregulars become among the most combat worthy indigenous troops in the country, eventually merging with the MIKE Forces in March 1968, when the MIKEs were expanded to multiple battalion Mobile Strike Force Commands.

Special Recon Missions Within South Vietnam

Under the codename 'Leaping Lena,' a special unit was formed in May 1964, to carry out long range recon missions within South Vietnam. Initially, only one Special Forces A-Detachment was assigned, but when this mission evolved into the much more famous 'Project Delta' as many as one hundred Special Forces troops would be assigned. In June 1965, Detachment B-52 was assigned to control 'Project Delta,' which was organised into twelve – later sixteen – recon teams, each consisting of two US Special Forces and eight LLDB. Actually, this team organisation was somewhat flexible

One of the more far out experiments in Vietnam was these boots for Special Forces Recon Teams. Theoretically, the boots would leave the same footprint as barefooted peasants thus keeping the presence of the 'roundeyes' from being obvious. However, the much heavier Americans left deeper footprints. Additionally, these boots were difficult to walk in (*EAGLE Magazine*)

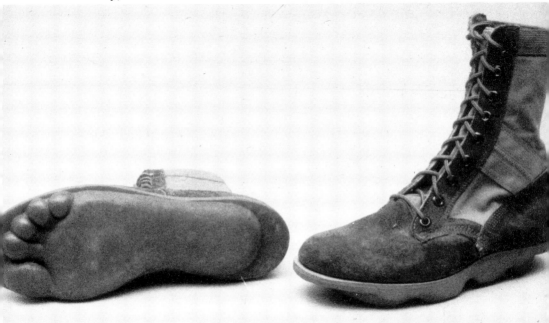

A student learns insertion techniques at the MACV Recondo School during 1968.

varying between two and four US Special Forces and four to eight 'indigs.' Acting as a reaction force of 'Project Delta' was the 91st ARVN Ranger Battalion, while a Nung Security Platoon protected the camp and the 281st Assault Helicopter Company provided lift capability. Of additional interest was the 'Roadrunner' Platoon composed of teams of four 'indigs' who wore VC/NVA uniforms and operated along the enemy trail network.

Although initially formed to gather intelligence, Delta teams were also used to carry out all sorts of unconventional operations from 'snatches' of prominent VC for interrogation to tapping VC communications. Should a Delta team run into a concentration of enemy troops they could call in air strikes or their reaction force to hit them. Often 'Delta' would be assigned to work with a specific US ground unit, such as the 101st Airborne Division during TROJAN HORSE I and II.

Based at Nha Trang along with other special activities, Delta remained operational until June 1970, at its peak having over one thousand two hundred indigenous personnel assigned. To train these personnel, B-52 had helped form the MACV Recondo School in September 1966, which trained not only Delta personnel but long range recon personnel for US and allied units. Among the skills taught were helicopter insertion and extraction techniques, escape and evasion (E&E), survival in enemy territory, communications, photographic intelligence, mapping, long range patrolling, enemy weapons and demolitions.

Other special recon units were formed based on Delta's success. These projects – 'Sigma,' 'Omega' and 'Gamma' – were activated to carry out recon missions in certain parts of South Vietnam. In fact, an ever increasing portion of field combat intelligence was being provided by Special Forces controlled units as camps were established in former VC controlled areas. Increasing commitments, of course, meant the need for an increasing number of Special Forces troops as strength reached 2,627 by July 1966. By October 1966, ninety-seven Special Forces fighting camps were in existence, primarily in key positions to monitor and harass VC infiltration routes.

The Fighting Camps

In the remote areas, it was left to the Special Forces and the CIDG to attempt to exert some government control and to carry out surveillance and patrolling of infiltration routes. Because of the vulnerability of the camps constructed in these remote areas, however, it became necessary to construct them as 'fighting camps' able to withstand concerted enemy attack until relief could arrive. Defended by a combination of claymore mines, phougas, machine guns with interlocking fields of fire, pre- zeroed mortars, barbed wire and strongpoints connected by trenches, these camps used the policy of defense in depth. Designed so that as little as one-fourth of the camp's strength could effectively defend them, the 'fighting camps' placed their most critical facilities – tactical operations center, medical bunker, ammo bunker, 4.2 inch mortars and 105mm howitzers, etc – inside the inner defenses, which were often protected by a specially selected group of Nungs. The lie of the land was also taken into consideration when selecting a camp site so that the most defensible position was chosen.

Above: A rather symmetrical special Forces fighting camp with defense in depth and interlocking fields of fire for automatic weapons.

Below: An interesting Special Forces fighting camp which used a star shape plan popular during the sixteenth and seventeenth century European period of siege warfare because of its ability to allow mutual supporting fire.

By 1967 there were four C-Detachments, twelve B-Detachments and eighty-two A-Detachments assigned to the 5th Special Forces Group (Airborne), while additional Special Forces personnel served on other special missions. Among the B-Detachment assignments of special note were:

B-50   'Project Omega'
B-51   LLDB Training Center
B-52   'Project Delta'
B-53   ARVN Airborne Ranger Training Center
B-55   5th Mobile Strike Force Command
B-56   'Project Sigma'
B-57   'Project Gamma'

Mounting aggressive patrols from the fighting camps, the Special Forces-led irregulars were hurting the VC badly during 1967, resulting in an escalating number of attacks against the camps. In some cases, however, these attacks backfired as the Special Forces and their irregulars turned them into a meatgrinder to decimate the VC. At Loc Ninh, for example, between 31 October and 2 November 1967, over one thousand VC were killed attacking the camp. Fighting camps proved invaluable in the Mekong Delta, too, where patrols using airboats and operating from camps literally built on floating platforms interdicted the VC waterborne supply routes. Requiring only one inch of water to operate, the 'Aircats' skimmed across the flooded delta for patrol, recon, ambush and medevac missions. Operating from Moc Hoa and at least a half dozen other 'floating camps,' the 17-foot airboats became the bane of the VC in the Delta. The 4th Mobile Strike Force Command based in the Mekong Delta added their own 184-man airboat company as well by early 1968 using airboats with .50 machineguns or 106mm recoilless rifles mounted. This increased firepower allowed the 'Green Beret Navy' to sink sampans carrying Communist supplies or infiltrators.

The MIKE Forces continued to grow in both strength and importance, reacting to threats against fighting camps and being used for offensive operations. As a result, during the year between June 1966, and June 1967, MIKE Force strength doubled. Organisation had also become standardised with 185 men organised into three rifle platoons, a weapons platoon and an HQ making up a MIKE Force Company. Armed with rifles, M60 GPMGs, M79 Grenade Launchers and light mortars; the MIKE Forces were still irregular light infantry and not heavily armed enough to be used as conventional infantry. By July 1968, MIKE Force strength had reached more than eleven thousand, divided among the five MIKE Force commands based on local requirements. Directly under the

US Ranger advisors working with the ARVN Rangers on developing patrolling techniques.

5th Special Forces Group (Airborne) were approximately two thousand five hundred troops of 5th Mobile Strike Force Command; under B-16 were about one thousand four hundred and sixty troops of 1st Mobile Strike Force Command; under B-20 were approximately three thousand one hundred and twenty troops of 2nd Mobile Strike Force Command; under B-36 were approximately two thousand and fifteen troops of 3rd Mobile Strike Force Command; and under B-40 were approximately two thousand two hundred troops of 4th Mobile Strike Force Command.

Special Forces Logistics

Particularly noteworthy is the logistics system developed by Special Forces to supply the MIKE Forces, CIDG Program and other Special Forces activities. Due to the corruption in the Vietnamese logistics system and the lack of flexibility within the US system, the 5th Special Forces logistics officers developed a streamlined system using forward supply points in each of the four corps tactical zones, normally along with the C-Detachments. Fighting camps could then be supplied rapidly using C-130s or helicopters. In addition to this rapid supply system, the US Army Counterinsurgency Support Office on Okinawa helped procure special equipment including rucksacks, special rations for irregular troops, 'sterile' weapons which could not be traced to the USA and other items not procurable through normal channels.

Tet

In an attempt to block North Vietnamese incursions, many fighting camps were established in northern I Corps during 1967. However, during the buildup prior to the Tet Offensive of early 1968 and the siege of Khe Sanh, these camps came under extremely heavy pressure, one even having to face NVA tanks. During the Tet Offensive which began on 29 January 1968, Special Forces-led irregulars found themselves committed in the unfamiliar role of fighting in builtup areas, but though their Special Forces advisors took heavy casualties during the fighting, the 'cidgees' showed remarkable courage and tenacity. Once the beaten VC began retreating after the Tet Offensive, the CIDG irregulars harassed them with booby traps and ambushes along their escape routes, decimating them even further. So effective did the CIDG units prove themselves during the Tet fighting, in fact, that they received high priority for armament with the M16 rifle and other more modern small arms and were given much broader responsibility in defending II, III and IV Corps; while regular ARVN units attempted to retake areas of I Corps lost during Tet. Another result was an increase once again in MIKE Force strength to thirty-four companies: five in I Corps based at Da Nang; twelve in II Corps based at Pleiku, Ban Me Thuot, Kontum and Qui Nhon; seven in III Corps based at Lang Hai; and ten in IV Corps based at Dan Phuc, Moc Hoa, To Chau, and Cao Lanh.

This great increase in irregular strength plus other growing Special Forces commitments, however, caused a critical shortage of trained Special Forces NCOs. As a result, experienced NCOs were often asked to do a second tour in Vietnam shortly after completing one and many non-Special Forces trained airborne personnel were assigned directly to Special Forces upon arrival in country. Nevertheless, Special Forces teams throughout the world were denuded of experienced NCOs, and teams in Vietnam often operated under strength. The highly trained medical specialists were in particularly short supply. Still, by the fall of 1968, 5th Special Forces Group (Airborne) strength had reached more than three thousand five hundred.

Vietnamization

Under the Nixon Administration, the priority became preparing the Vietnamese to assume responsiblity for the war, including the various Special Forces programs. Assisting the LLDB became an even higher priority as a result, though Special Forces was still expected to use their assets to provide intelligence and run crossborder operations. CIDG troops were now primarily being used along the western borders of South Vietnam in an attempt to slow down infiltration from Cambodia and Laos. Special Forces strength peaked in 1969 at over four thousand, but Special Forces' role was about to be curtailed. The MACV commander Gen Creighton Abrams was anti-special operations and particularly disliked Special Forces, which he considered sloppy and ill-disciplined. As a result, he pushed for Special Forces to turn many camps over to the Vietnamese before they were ready and thus directly contributed to

A US Ranger advisor to the Vietnamese Rangers observes hand-to-hand combat training in the pit. The US advisor wears a Viet Ranger beret and Viet Ranger pocket patch but carries a personal revolver rather than the issue .45 auto.

their later fall to the VC/NVA. As of the fall of 1969, sixty-three A-Detachments were operating with irregular units along the border interdicting infiltration routes and acting as an early warning system. The camps they operated from were, however, hard to supply since many were under siege for long periods.

By early 1970, the CIDG Program was being phased out with the better CIDG units being incorporated into the South Vietnamese Army, frequently as Ranger units. By the end of 1970, all of the former Special Forces fighting camps had either been closed or converted to ARVN camps. No longer needed in previous numbers, Special Forces strength dropped below three thousand by the end of 1970 as well. Although some CIDG troops and their Special Forces advisors did play an important role in the Cambodia incursion between April and June 1970, by 31 December 1970 all Special Forces participation in the CIDG Program had officially ended.

One other important Special Forces mission in 1970 was the raid on Son Tay Prison on 20/21 November, when sixty-five members of the Special Forces under Col 'Bull' Simons carried out a hard hitting raid deep in North Vietnam, which though meticulously carried out, found the compound empty of POWs.

On 3 March 1971, the 5th Special Forces Group (Airborne) officially departed South Vietnam. At least some residual Special Forces presence remained, however, in advisors assigned to various commands and special operations units.

MACV/SOG

Military Assistance Command Vietnam/Special Operations Group (also known as Studies and Observations Group) was charged with clandestine cross border operations into Cambodia, Laos and North Vietnam. Under the cover of various 'studies groups,' operations spanned intelligence gathering through agent insertions to MIA recovery. Initially activated in January 1964, with contingents of Navy, Marine Corps and Air Force personnel, though Army Special Forces would always be the most prevalent, MACV/SOG worked closely with the CIA on 'Black ops' all over Southeast Asia.

Through the Special Assistant for Counterinsurgency and Special Activities, MACV/SOG came directly under the Joint Chiefs of Staff, though MACV did supervise the unit's activities. When it reached its maximum strength at the height of the US commitment to Vietnam, SOG would have over ten thousand personnel assigned, two thousand of them Americans. Most of those American personnel were from the Special Forces assigned via the paper entity 5th

Special Forces Group (Airborne) Special Operations Augmentation.

SOG's missions took place in Cambodia, Laos, North Vietnam, South Vietnam and China. Among these missions were gathering intelligence about POWs, rescue of POWs, rescue downed aircrews ('Bright Light' missions as these were codenamed), retrieval of sensitive documents from enemy territory, bomb damage assessments, wiretaps, reconnaissance and surveillance, mining and boobytrapping, snatches and assassinations. In some cases agents ('Oodles') were inserted into North Vietnam, while in others false radio stations were operated within North Vietnam. One of the most successful of the SOG 'Black' ops was the insertion of rigged mortar rounds and other ammunition in VC/NVA arms caches. Known as Operation ELDEST SON, this munitions tampering severely eroded enemy confidence in their weapons as they never knew when a grenade or mortar round would explode prematurely or a rifle round would blow up the gun.

Intelligence gathering was carried out by the SOG recon teams, most frequently in Laos. Though the teams often consisted of twelve men, normally only six men (two Americans and four indigs) were inserted on a mission. Missions into Laos were initially known as 'Shining Brass' missions, then 'Prairie Fire' after 1968. Cambodia also received substantial attention from SOG recon teams, missions initially being codenamed 'Daniel Boone' and later 'Salem House.' Missions into the DMZ between North and South Vietnam were codenamed 'Nickel Steel.' To give some idea of the frequency of recon missions across the borders, between 1965 and 1972, 2,675 such missions were launched, resulting in the deaths of 103 US Special Forces.

HQ for MACV/SOG was in Saigon, but missions were 'launched' from Forward Operating Bases at Ban Me Thuot, Kontum, Khe Sanh and Da Nang. Later, three Command and Control sites took over this mission as follows:

Command and Control North (CCN) was located at Da Nang and charged with missions into Laos and north Vietnam, including 'Kit Cat Missions' deep into the North. CCN had launch sites at Hue-Phu Bai, Khe Sanh, Quan Tri and Kham Duc. Normally Recon Teams (RTs) assigned to CCN were codenamed after US states or snakes (i.e. RT Anaconda and RT Kansas.)

Command and Control Central (CCC) was located at Kontum and charged with missions into the Tri-Borders Region where South Vietnam, Cambodia and Laos meet. CCC Recon Teams were named primarily after US states.

Command and Control South (CCS) was located at Ban Thuot and charged with missions into Cambodia. CCS Recon Teams were named after implements and facets of the weather (i.e. RT Fork and RT Lightning.)

MACV/SOG Recon Team equipped for a recon mission. (Society of Vietnamese Rangers)

RTs normally were composed of three US Special Forces and nine indigenous troops, usually Nungs or Montagnards. Such teams were known as 'Spike Recon Teams.' At SOG's peak there were about seventy such teams, though at any time perhaps only fifty per cent would be ready for operations due to heavy casualties or personnel turnover. Should a larger force be needed, SOG had its 'Hatchet Forces' of five USSF and thirty indigs. These units were frequently used to set ambushes for NVA or VC infiltrating into South Vietnam. If two or more 'Hatchet Forces' were combined for a mission they were known as 'Havoc Forces.' Finally, full SOG companies were available for major operations. These were known as SLAM (Search-Locate-Annihilate-Monitor) Companies.

After the C&C units were shut down in March 1971, a reduced SOG presence continued in what was called 'Task Force Advisory Elements.' Special Mission Advisory Groups (SMAG) had also come into existence in February 1971, to train the South Vietnamese

Special Mission Service to take over SOG operations. However, many members of SF continued to carry out missions with the Special Mission Service. During the 1972 Easter Offensive from the North, many of these remaining Special Forces troops helped call in airstrikes and acted as recon elements for ARVN divisions operating against the NVA. The final 'officially unofficial' SOG presence was with Technical Directorate Assistance Team 158, which theoretically was created in May 1972 to help with US military assistance but which continued to carry out clandestine missions until March 1973 when it was deactivated.

How Effective Was Special Forces?

The 'Green Beret' myth grew during the Vietnam War to the point where it was difficult to determine fact from fiction. However, certainly, in many ways the Special Forces proved the most effective US Army personnel in Vietnam. During the period before the massive US troop buildup particularly, the CIDG Program was working very well as Special Forces performed their primary mission of training and working on civic action. As the war progressed the ability of members of Special Forces to operate as light irregular infantry, to confront the enemy in his own territory effectively, and to move quickly and without being detected dictated that they were used more and more in support of US conventional ground troops who could not do these things.

Though Special Forces still proved extremely effective, the irregulars they had initially trained to defend their homes had now become mercenary soldiers fighting for the Americans rather than the South Vietnamese. As a result, when their Special Forces advisors left, a substantial portion of their will to fight departed as well. Versatility is one of the strengths of Special Forces and its members carried out their missions very effectively; many of those missions just were not the ones for which SF had been created.

PSY OPS

Civil Affairs and Psychological Operations Units fell under the blanket of 'Special Warfare' just as Special Forces did. Psychological Operations units in most basic terms ran propaganda operations against the North Vietnamese and the Viet Cong. Missions included

Special Forces officer serving with irregulars wears Tiger Stripe camouflage and boony hat. (*Larry Dring*)

propaganda leaflet printing and distribution, provision of loud-speakers for propaganda broadcasts (often by 'ralliers'), production of radio and television shows designed to influence public opinion and perceptions, and operations of mobile radio facilities. Provision of psy ops advice to the South Vietnamese was also an important mission as well.

Initially, the 7th Psychological Operations Group on Okinawa provided Psy Ops control for Vietnam, but as of 1 December 1967, the 4th Pyschological Operations Group was established in Vietnam and took over responsibility, remaining until 2 October 1971. Additionally, one psy ops battalion was assigned to control operations in each corps tactical zone as follows:

I Corps	7th Psy Ops Battalion based at Nha Trang, later at Da Nang
II Corps	8th Psy Ops Battalion based at Nha Trang, later Pleiku
III Corps	6th Psy Ops Battalion based at Tan Son Nhut, later Bien Hoa
IV Corps	10th Psy Ops Battalion based at Can Tho

Four Psy Ops companies – the 19th, 244th, 245th and 246th – served in Vietnam between February 1966 and January 1968, as well. The 2nd Civil Affairs, 29th Civil Affairs, and 41st Civil Affairs companies also served at various times between December 1965 and December 1971, providing assistance and advice to Vietnamese regional officials.

LRRPS and Rangers

At the beginning of the war, there was no standard organisation for Long Range Reconnaissance Patrols, though a directive on LRRPs had first been published in 1961, and Field Manual 31-18 published on 18 June 1962 dealt with Long Range Patrols. Nevertheless, LRRPs were not in existence when US infantry units began deploying to Vietnam. The nature of the Vietnam conflict where locating the enemy was so difficult, however, gave impetus to the formation of small reconnaissance units responsible to the brigade or division commander. As it evolved in Vietnam, the LRRP/Ranger company

Opposite above: A very useful weapon in certain night ambush situations in Vietnam was the M16 rifle with the starlight scope mounted.

Opposite below: A member of the Special Forces trains CIDG troops in the use of the M79 grenade launcher.

was comprised of 118 men, normally three or four officers and the remainder enlisted personnel. There was usually a company HQ section, a company communications section, a company operations section, and two patrol platoons. Each patrol platoon had one officer and forty-three enlisted men assigned. The basic operational unit was the six-man team, of which each platoon had seven. The team was composed of the team leader, usually an E-5 or E-6; the assistant team leader; the senior scout observor (normally the point man); the junior scout observor (normally the 'tailgunner' who acted as rear guard); and two radio operators. As with any theoretical table of organisation, in combat these numbers were often reduced, some companies maybe only having half or three-quarters the specified number of teams available and some teams operating with only four or five men.

Among the missions assigned to the LRRPs were: gather intelligence on enemy strength, equipment, disposition, organisation and movement; locate enemy reserves, command posts and key facilities; carry out surveillance of enemy routes, bases, etc; locate targets for air strikes, artillery or ground attack; carry out bomb or artillery damage assessments on the ground; carry out ambushes, combat patrols, or raids against assigned enemy targets; take enemy prisoners for interrogation; emplace and monitor sensors; tap enemy communications; recover downed aircrews and equipment; reconnoiter possible landing zones for airmobile operations; advise and train other units in recon operations; perform other missions as assigned. Although the LRRPs within a division might be assigned to the G-2 or G-3 section or to divisional cavalry, frequently it was the G-2 officer who assigned the LRRPs their missions. Within the LRRP company, each team had a designation based on a two digit system. The first digit identified the platoon and the second digit the team. Therefore, Team 14 would be the fourth team of the first platoon.

The first major US Army combat unit committed to the Vietnam War was the 173rd Airborne Brigade, which was also the first unit to form Long Range Reconnaissance Patrols. Shortly thereafter the 101st Airborne Division, which had trained divisional recon elements known as 'Recondos' in the past, also saw the need for small divisional units to gather timely local combat intelligence, to scout and to carry out ambushes against the enemy. Initially, most LRRPs did not have special training, though some were graduates of the Ranger course at Fort Benning. Volunteers who had proven themselves able at bushcraft and able to work as part of small teams formed the nucleus of these initial provisional LRRP units.

Although infantry brigades and divisions normally saw the usefulness of LRRPs shortly after arriving in country and formed such units, the practice was not formalised until 8 July 1966 when Gen Westmoreland issued an order covering the formation of LRRPs.

Among the various infantry divisions, the 4th Infantry Division made some of the most extensive use of LRRPs, assigning four LRRP platoons to each brigade, one for each battalion and one for the HQ Company. Among the noteworthy successes of 4th Infantry Division LRRPs was the enemy sighting which led to Operation 'Junction City,' one of the most successful of the war.

Initially LRRPs received little special training or were put through a divisional or brigade training course given by graduates of the Ranger school or by experienced LRRPs. In September, 1966, however, the MACV Recondo School was established at Nha Trang to train Project Delta personnel but also to train LRRPs. Included were practical skills useful for carrying out patrols in enemy territory such as: survival, field medicine, land navigation, silent movement, photography, communications, helicopter insertions and extractions, and escape and evasion. Even after training either at the divisional level or the Recondo School, however, a LRRP still had to prove himself in the field before being fully accepted onto a team.

LRRP tactics reflected a combination of Ranger patrolling skills and SOPs (Standard Operating Procedures) developed to fit the specific environment the LRRPs were operating in. The six-man LRRP team was too small to engage in pitched combat so stealth was their most important weapon along with constant alertness. While on an operation which usually lasted about a week, the LRRPs normally got little sleep, and that while still wearing equipment ready to depart instantly. Whenever the team stopped they assumed 360 degree defensive positions. So important was silence that communications were by hand signals or hand written notes when operational. If it was necessary to speak, a whisper directly in the ear was used. Radio communications were often via coded clicks on the radio's talk button rather than by voice. Equipment was taped and checked to make sure it did not rattle. Faces and equipment were also camouflaged.

Unless sent on an ambush, hunter/killer or snatch mission; LRRPs normally tried to avoid contact with the enemy. If they discovered the enemy they tried to remain hidden and call in helicopter gunships, artillery fire, airmobile infantry or jets to deliver the firepower. If they did have to fight, the LRRPs operated on the principle of hitting hard and fast and then getting out of the area

A LRRP of the 9th Infantry Division does a commo check with his survival radio. He wears the black beret sometimes worn by the LRRPs and MACV Recondo School pocket patch.

rapidly. On some ambushes, however, they operated as stay-behinds, hiding near an abandoned position to ambush VC or NVA scavenging for discarded equipment. Using interlocking fields of fire, claymore mines, detonating cord in trenches where the enemy could take cover and any other edge they could get, the LRRPs wreaked havoc in many of their ambushes, becoming some of the most feared of American troops. Many LRRPs also received sniper training and would use their long-range shooting skill to decimate the enemy.

Although the LRRPs used basically the same equipment as other infantrymen they often supplemented or altered their weapons and equipment to fit their missions. One innovation designed primarily for the LRRPs was the special freeze-dried LRRP rations, which were much easier to carry on long patrols than traditional C-Rations.

One of the keys to the success of the LRRPs was the sense of team unity which developed, often resulting in LRRPs serving multiple tours, thus granting them a far higher level of combat experience than was normally found in conventional Army units. Although some LRRPs were from rural backgrounds, many were also from cities. Among ethnic minorities well represented were American Indians and Americans of Oriental descent who, if only glimpsed through the jungle, might pass as the enemy.

Versatility was an important trait among the LRRPs who had to adjust to their environment. LRRPs from the 9th Infantry Division and the 199th Infantry Brigade, for example, operated in the Mekong Delta and, hence, had to learn to use small boats, while LRRPs from the 1st Air Cav would often be dropped off to set an ambush around an LZ from which other airmobile troopers were being pulled out.

By 1967, the LRRPs were termed LRPs (Long Range Patrols) and had become much more standard in their organisation. Assigned to the divisions in country at the time were the following LRP Companies:

1st Cavalry Division (Airmobile)
    Company E, 52nd Infantry (LRP)
1st Infantry Division
    Company F, 52nd Infantry (LRP)
4th Infantry Division
    Company E, 20th Infantry (LRP)
    Company E, 58th Infantry (LRP)
9th Infantry Division
    Company E, 50th Infantry (LRP)
23rd Infantry Division
    Company E, 51st Infantry (LRP)
25th Infantry Division
    Company F, 50th Infantry (LRP)
101st Airborne Division
    Company F, 58th Infantry (LRP)

Additional LRP units circa 1967 were Company F, 51st Infantry (LRP) assigned to the 199th Infantry Brigade and sixty-one-man LRP detachments assigned to the 11th Infantry Brigade and 173rd Airborne Brigade, while two such detachments were assigned to US Army Vietnam. Company D, 151st Infantry (LRP) was assigned directly to the 2nd Field Force HQ. This unit is of special interest since it was an Indiana National Guard unit activated and sent to Vietnam, though it should be noted the unit had been raised and trained as an airborne/Long Range Patrol company and, hence, was among the most qualified in the Army/National Guard reserve system.

A LRRP of the 75th Infantry (Ranger) moves quietly through the jungle as he scouts for the enemy. He wears a 'boony hat' rather than the more cumbersome and noisy steel helmet.

LRRPs Become Rangers

Although LRRP companies had been operating in the traditional Ranger role, frequently had Ranger qualified officers, and used the Ranger manual as their guide, it was not until 1 January 1969 that the LRRPs officially became designated as Rangers when the 75th Infantry (Ranger) was reactivated (it had previously been the World War Two Merrill's Marauders) to consolidate the long range patrol assets in Vietnam. Although now designated as Rangers, however, only those members of the 75th Infantry (Ranger) who had completed the Fort Benning Ranger course were authorised to wear the Ranger tab. Company organisation remained basically the same, though three officers and 115 enlisted men, divided into an HQ staffed by the company commander and seventeen enlisted men and two fifty-man LRRP platoons, each divided into an HQ of one officer and one NCO and eight six-man patrols became relatively standardised. Ranger companies were assigned as follows:

1st Cavalry Division (Airmobile)
    Company H, 75th Infantry Division
1st Infantry Division
    Company I, 75th Infantry (Ranger)
4th Infantry Division
    Company K, 75th Infantry (Ranger)

1st Brigade, 5th Infantry Division (Mechanized)
    Company P, 75th Infantry (Ranger)
9th Infantry Division
    Company E, 75th Infantry (Ranger)
23rd Infantry Division
    Company G, 75th Infantry (Ranger)
25th Infantry Division
    Company F, 75th Infantry (Ranger)
3rd Brigade, 82nd Airborne Division
    Company O, 75th Infantry (Ranger)
101st Airborne Division
    Company L, 75th Infantry (Ranger)
173rd Airborne Brigade
    Company N, 75th Infantry (Ranger)
199th Light Infantry Brigade
    Company M, 75th Infantry (Ranger)
I Field Force
    Company C, 75th Infantry (Ranger)
II Field Force
    Company D, 75th Infantry (Ranger)

Of these units, Companies E. F, G, I, K and L basically had the authorised strength of 118. Companies C, D and H, were overstrength C, normally, having 230 men and D and H normally 198 men. Companies M, N, O and P were basically half-strength companies with sixty-one men. Though reorganised as Rangers, the companies of the 75th Infantry carried out the same basic long range patrol function in addition to acting as a brigade or divisional reaction/special mission force.

During the war it is estimated that somewhere over twenty-three thousand Long Range Reconnaissance Patrols were carried out, of which about two-thirds resulted in enemy sightings. Somewhere around ten thousand enemy killed in action were accounted for by the LRRPs, some through ambush or sniping but many more through calling in air strikes or artillery fire. Despite operating under dangerous conditions, LRRPs suffered a lower percentage of killed in action than normal line infantry units due to their high state of training, motivation, and professionalism.

Ranger Advisors

Although some graduates of the Ranger course served with the LRRPs, approximately two thousand acted as advisors to the Biet Dong Quan (the Vietnamese Rangers). In addition to helping establish the Ranger training centers at Trung Lap, Tet Son and Duc My, many of these advisors served in the field with the BDQs, hundreds giving their lives in the process.

6
ARMY AVIATION

If World War One can be termed the war of the machine gun and World War Two the war of the tank and airplane, Vietnam can be termed the war of the helicopter. Not only did Army Aviation come into its own during the Vietnam War, but it assumed a primacy which has continued until today.

According to TOE 1-75G, the Infantry Division Aviation Battalion circa 1967 had thirty-seven officers, fifty-seven warrant officers and 273 enlisted men with four OH-6A observation helicopters, six UH-1B armed helicopters and twenty-seven UH-1D utility/transport helicopters. This battalion was subdivided into an HQ and HQ Detachment, an Airmobile Company (Light) and an Aviation Ground Support Company. Normally, this battalion would be supplemented by separate assault helicopter companies to augment it. There was also a divisional Air Cavalry Troop consisting of twelve officers, thirty-three warrant officers and 124 enlisted men with five OH-6A observation helicopters, seven UH-1B armed helicopters and six UH-1D utility/transport helicopters.

In Vietnam, the separate Assault Helicopter Company normally consisted of nineteen officers, twenty warrant officers and 219 enlisted men. Aircraft typically consisted of eight UH-1C armed utility helicopters and twenty-three UH-1D utility/transport helicopters. The Medium Helicopter Company (also known as the Assault Support Helicopter Company) usually consisted of fifteen officers, twenty-six warrant officers and 228 enlisted men. Aircraft included two OH-6A observation helicopters and sixteen CH-47 cargo helicopters. Frequently, various mixes of helicopter companies or platoons would be assigned to a division, brigade or battalion for a specific operation. This mix might include armed UH-1B or UH-1C Hueys or later AH-1G Cobras, UH-1Ds for troop transports and CH-47s for supply and artillery movement.

The airmobile division was a separate entity with far greater internal helicopter support. According to TOE 1-100T, it had its own aviation group with 218 officers, 347 warrant officers, and 1,427 enlisted men. In addition, there was an air cavalry squadron with seventy-eight officers, ninety-six warrant officers and 596 enlisted men, and an aerial rocket artillery battalion assigned to the divisional artillery. In total, the divisional TOE called for 428 helicopters of various types and six fixed wing aircraft. The Aviation Group was broken into an HQ and HQ Company, a Ground Support HQ Aviation Company, two Helicopter Battalions and an Assault Support Battalion. The Assault Helicopter Battalion was further subdivided into an HQ and HQ Company, an Aerial Weapons Company and three Assault Helicopter Companies. The divisional artillery had a total of fifty-nine helicopters assigned, including thirty-six 2.75-inch rocket firing UH-1Bs and sixteen armed OH-6s with the XM-7 system.

Since specific aircraft are already being mentioned and will continue to be throughout this chapter, at this point a discussion of aircraft types used by the Army in Vietnam would probably be useful.

Army Aircraft Types

Utility/Transport Helicopters
Utility helicopters, especially the Huey 'slicks,' delivered the airmobile warrior to battle and extracted him from combat. As a result, there were never enough transport helicopters in Vietnam.

By far the most ubiquitous helicopter of the war was the **UH-1D Iroquois**. With a crew of betweeen two and four (pilot, co-pilot, crew chief, door gunner) and capable of carrying up to eleven passengers, the Huey, as the UH-1D was commonly known, could cruise at about

A CH-47 Chinook lifts a Hawk surface-to-air missile into position.

100 miles per hour with a range over 300 miles. By the end of 1966, over three thousand Hueys had been ordered from Bell Helicopter. Although not armed for the offensive role, the UH-1D was equipped with M-60 door guns to give suppressive fire around an LZ. The UH-1H was a version of the Huey with an engine giving enhanced performance, though nowhere near as many saw service as the UH-1D. UH-1s also did yeoman service as medical evacuation helicopters ('dustoffs'). By the peak of US involvement, 116 were serving as flying ambulances.

The **Ch-47 Chinook** was the medium helicopter workhorse in Vietnam. Though capable of transporting up to thirty-three troops, its primary value was as a cargo mover, it being capable of lifting over 22,000lbs externally. Chinooks were especially useful in recovering other helicopters which had been shot down, being credited with lifting out 11,500 disabled aircraft, mostly Hueys. Chinooks also proved invaluable in lifting artillery into position at firebases and for 'artillery raids.'

Sikorsky's **CH-54 Tarhe** was known as the 'Flying Crane' because of its ability to lift such items as armored vehicles, heavy artillery or downed aircraft. Using a detachable pod, the CH-54 could also lift eighty-seven troops, though it was rarely used in this role.

The **OH-6A Cayuse**, often known as the 'Loach,' was the principal observation/scout helicopter used in Vietnam. In addition to its two crew members, the OH-6 could carry up to four passengers and was occasionally used to insert small teams or to carry commanders for visual observation of an area of operations. The OH-6 could also be armed with 7.62mm machine guns or a mini-gun to function as a light attack helicopter.

Helicopter Gunships
The first gunship used in any quantity in Vietnam was the **UH-1B** followed by the **UH-1C**. Armament included the two M-60 door-mounted machine guns found on other Hueys plus an M-5 40mm grenade launcher, 2.75 inch rocket pods and quad 7.62mm machine guns. The UH-1C was also armed at times with a minigun. The first purpose-designed gunship, however, was the **AH-1G** Huey Cobra, which was first deployed to Vietnam in November 1967. Very fast, with a maximum speed of 219 mph, and very heavily armed with a GAU-2B/A minigun (later two XM-28 miniguns) and/or 40mm grenade launchers and up to seventy-six 2.75 inch rockets on its stub wings the Cobra proved a devastating weapon in support of the infantry or operating with an OH-6 on hunter/killer operations as part of a 'Pink Team.'

Fixed Wing Aircraft

The **O-1 Bird Dog** was by far the most widely used fixed wing aircraft, performing the forward air control (FAC) and artillery spotting function. Capable of carrying the pilot and one passenger at a speed of a little over 100 mph, the O-1 also functioned as a scout aircraft along roads and around installations vulnerable to attack.

For carrying passengers and cargo, the Army also had available the following aircraft in Vietnam:

U-1 Otter	ten passengers
U-6 Beaver	five passengers
U-8 Seminole	four passengers
C-7 Caribou	thirty-two passengers or 5,000lb of cargo
OV-1 Mohawk	primarily used for reconnaissance
U-021 Ute	ten passengers or 1,600lb of cargo

The Growth of the Airmobility Concept in Vietnam

On 11 December 1961, the 57th Transportation Company (Light Helicopter) and 8th Transportation Company (Light Helicopter) arrived in Saigon with their thirty-two helicopters. In less than two weeks they were flying combat missions for the South Vietnamese. The next month, the 93rd Transportation Company (Light Helicopter) and the 18th Aviation Company (U-1A Otter) joined them, the latter primarily to deliver replacement parts to keep the H-2ls flying.

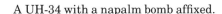

A UH-34 with a napalm bomb affixed.

Although initially the helicopter companies were loosely controlled by MACV, as more aviation assets arrived in country the necessity for a controlling formation became obvious. Hence, the 45th Transportation Battalion was sent to assume command of the various aviation units. Throughout 1962 other units continued to arrive, including the 57th Medical Detachment (Helicopter Ambulance) with the first Hueys sent to Vietnam and the 23rd Special Warfare Aviation Detachment to provide visual and photo recon using the OV-1 Mohawk.

The Howze Board

As the realisation that airmobility was going to play a key part in Vietnam and future conflicts dawned among senior Army officers, the Howze Board was formed in April 1962, to study Army aviation requirements. The board consisted of thirteen general officers and five civilians, who submitted their final report on 20 August 1962. The primary innovation which resulted from this report was the air assault division, which would have 459 aircraft assigned as opposed to the approximately one hundred assigned to a normal division. To provide part of the artillery for this new type of division would be twenty-four armed Mohawks and thirty-six armed Hueys.

The board also recommended the formation of an air cavalry brigade which, using 316 aircraft, would function in the classic cavalry role – screening, reconnoitering and carrying out actions. It was envisioned that Caribous and Chinooks would be used to supply forward air assault units.

Obviously, if implemented, the Howze Board's recommendations would establish the need for far more Army aviators – 8,900 by 1963 and 20,000 by 1968. To help meet this demand it was recommended that warrant officers should be trained for many of these slots.

Learning on the Job

While the first Army aviators deployed to Vietnam were perfecting the tactics which the thousands who would follow them would use, they were also helping to train Vietnamese pilots in the use of the helicopter. At the same time they were carrying out the earliest experiments with armed helicopters, the first fifteen armed Hueys deploying to Vietnam in September 1962. These initial 'gunships' were followed by eleven UH-1B armed helicopters which after their arrival in November 1962, were assigned to the Utility Tactical Transport Helicopter Company at Tan Son Nhut. It soon became apparent that the armed helicopters played an important role in cutting transport helicopter losses. Tactics began to evolve, too, for the armed helicopters. For example, they usually engaged targets at their maximum range, making their gun or rocket run one after the other. However, by late 1964 it was already becoming apparent that a much faster armed helicopter was needed which could range ahead of the slicks.

Air assault tactics developing during 1963 were predicated on the lack of enemy air defense capability. Most frequently, the 'V' formation at 1,500 feet was used with an armed recon element of two, three or four helicopters preceding the slicks by between one and five minutes. Routes to and from the landing zones (LZs) were varied and upon arrival at the LZ troops were unloaded as rapidly as possible to cut the time the helicopter was immobile and hence a better target. Whenever possible, it was attempted to have all helicopters in a flight on the ground simultaneously and departing simultaneously. In case an LZ was found to be heavily defended upon arrival, an alternative would have already been decided upon. To make missions easier, the 'Eagle Flight,' consisting of an armed Huey as a Command and Control helicopter, seven unarmed troop transport Hueys, five armed escort Hueys and one medevac Huey had been developed. Such 'Eagle Flights' were available for immediate action and proved so worthwhile that by November 1960, all helicopter companies in Vietnam were using them.

By September, 1964, the Army had the following aircraft in Vietnam: 33 O-1 (Bird Dog), 20 U-6A (Beaver), 8 U-8 (Seminole), 6 OV-1 (Mohawk), 32 CV-2 (Caribou), 27 OH-1 (Otter), 250 UH-1 (Iroquois), and 9 CH-37 (Mohave). To keep this assortment of almost 400 aircraft flying, there were 3,755 Army aviation personnel in the country. Late in 1964, these aviation assets were organized as follows:

13th Aviation Battalion (based at Can Tho) assigned to the support of IV Corps with three Huey companies and one Bird Dog platoon.

145th Aviation Battalion (based at Saigon) assigned to support III Corps with two Huey companies and an armed helicopter company.

52nd Aviation Battalion (based at Pleiku) assigned to support I and II Corps with two Huey companies, one Bird Dog platoon, and one Caribou platoon.

14th Aviation Battalion (based at Nha Trang) assigned to support all of the Republic of Vietnam and Thailand with a maintenance company, an Otter company, and Bird Dog platoon.

765th Transportation Battalion (based at Vung Tau) assigned to support all aviation companies with three maintenance companies, one Caribou company, and one special warfare Mohawk detachment. This latter detachment – the 23rd Special Warfare Aviation Detachment – had six armed OV-1 Mohawks which provided photos, visual recon, artillery spotting, and could provide their own .50 defensive fire.

The 1st and 61st Aviation Companies flying Caribous proved especially useful because of the aircraft's STOL (Short Take Off and Landing) characteristics. Isolated Special Forces camps, for example, were often supplied by Caribous.

Throughout the era of the Howze Board, the 11th Air Assault Division (created from the re-activated 11th Airborne Division of World War Two Pacific Theater fame) had been experimenting with the airmobile concept in cooperation with the 10th Air Transport Brigade. However, in July 1965, the 11th was replaced as the US air assault division by the re-activated 1st Cavalry (Air Assault) Division, which as deployed to Vietnam, would have its own aviation group with 434 aircraft.

The first US Army ground unit to see action in Vietnam in the airmobile role, however, was the 173rd Airborne Brigade, which was supported by the 145th Aviation Battalion. A concept which proved particularly worthwhile was the co-location of one aviation company with the brigade. The fact most of the helicopter crews were already experienced operating in the country also made the 173rd's transition much easier.

The helicopters themselves needed more preparation than the men. When the 1st Cavalry Division prepared to deploy to Vietnam, for example, their Chinooks needed 1,334 modifications to prepare them, while the Hueys needed nearly two thousand.

With US infantrymen arriving by the tens of thousands, already by the end of 1965 it was apparent that there were not going to be enough helicopters to go around. As a result, helicopters received excessive use, resulting in a maintenance problem by 1966. Since each chopper needed approximately ten hours of maintenance per hour of flight, crews were forced to work throughout the night so that aircraft would be ready for flight the next day.

Maintenance Support

In an attempt to alleviate some of the maintenance problems, on 17 January 1966, the 34th General Support Group was formed to provide separate aircraft maintenance and supply. To allow it to carry out effectively its mission countrywide, the group was not placed under the 1st Aviation Brigade, nor the 1st Logistical Command, but directly under US Army Vietnam. The most unique unit assigned to the 34th was the USNS *Corpus Christi Bay*, also known as the 1st Transportation Corps Battalion (Depot) (Seaborne). In actuality, this was a floating aircraft maintenance facility which arrived on 12 April 1966 carrying 370 Army maintenance personnel and 130 civilian crewmen. Thirty-seven maintenance functions were consolidated aboard this ship, allowing it to function as a depot level repair facility capable of doing complete overhaul and of fabricating components. Additionally, it carried a library of 180,000 engineering drawings on film and could broadcast over closed circuit TV drawings to satellite maintenance facilities. Originally, the *Corpus Christi Bay* had been docked at Cam Ranh Bay but was later moved to Qui Nhon where it was nearer the 1st Air Cavalry.

The 1st Aviation Brigade

The 1st Air Cav had brought a CH-47 Chinook battalion and there was also the separate 147th Medium Helicopter Company with Chinooks. Both quickly proved their value for emplacing artillery batteries and other heavy transport chores. However, with the Chinooks as with other choppers, the crews had to work at educating the troopers not to overload them.

Based on the early experiences of the 173rd Airborne Brigade, except for the 1st Air Cav, each brigade had one assault helicopter company allotted. The large number of assault helicopter companies this necessitated, however, indicated a need for an aviation brigade to control those assets not directly assigned to the 1st Air Cav or other units. Hence, on 1 March 1966, the 1st Aviation Brigade was

The OH-58 Kiowa was used for command and control and light transport in Vietnam.

formed under the command of Brig Gen George P. Sereff. One of the first – and extremely important – steps taken by the new brigade was the publication of basic manuals standardizing operational procedures, training schools, safety regulations, etc. The 1st Aviation Brigade also instituted systematic experiments in conjunction with the 1st Infantry Division to determine the best methods for supporting line divisions. As a result, one combat aviation battalion HQ was assigned directly to support each infantry division.

In April 1966, the Army gave up the Caribou to the Air Force, thus granting them fixed-wing tactical airlift responsibility as part of the trade off necessary to allow the Army to have armed attack helicopters.

Shortage of Aviators Becomes a Problem

1966 saw the shortage of Army aviators becoming critical as it became necessary to send helicopter pilots back for a second tour in Vietnam even as soon as a year after completing a previous tour. The expected shortfall by the end of 1966 was five thousand aviators and by the end of 1967 nine thousand. In an attempt to fill the shortage on 29 March 1966, the Secretary of Defense gave the go-ahead to raise from 120 to 410 the number of aviators graduating from training each month, though in actuality it would take until mid-1967 to reach this rate. To fill the short-term need, an attempt was made to get some of the two thousand reserve Army aviators to volunteer for service in Vietnam, but only sixty responded. Other commands were denuded of aviators in an attempt to keep the choppers flying in Vietnam, at one point only 250 aviators being left for Europe and thirty-four for Korea.

At Fort Rucker, where Army aviators were trained, the thirty-two-week course was designed especially to prepare pilots for service in Vietnam. To get more helicopter pilots, the Army started training a large number of warrant officers as well, thus opening flight school to non-college graduates with a strong desire to fly.

Once they had graduated from Fort Rucker and arrived in Vietnam, new pilots – no matter what their rank – were given a flight check, then twenty-five hours of non-combat flying before

Opposite above: CH-54 Tarhe helicopter lifting in a 155 mm howitzer to a fire support base for Battery C, 16th Artillery, 41st Artillery Group, 173rd Airborne Brigade.

Opposite below: Members of the 1st Battalion, 9th Cavalry, 1st Cavalry division (Airmobile) prepare for extraction on a UH-1D Huey.

moving into the right seat to fly as co-pilot on combat missions. Once they were deemed experienced enough, they took over their own chopper. Although ninety hours of flying per month was considered the maximum desirable, once operational pilots flew up to one hundred hours almost as a norm and in some cases over one hundred and ten hours per month.

Shortages did not just occur in pilots but in qualified crew chiefs and mechanics as well. Crew chiefs and mechanics were especially good examples of the problems caused by the one year tour of duty in Vietnam as they were normally rotated out when they had reached their peak of efficiency.

Supporting heli-lifted infantry with artillery caused some special problems on airmobile operations. Aerial rocket artillery in the 1st Air Cav proved quite efficient, but on most airmobile operations conventional artillery support was also available and, as a result, careful plans had to be made to keep helicopters from flying into the zones into which tube artillery was firing. Normally, the aerial rocket artillery waited on the ground ready for immediate takeoff to support ground operations. To get tube artillery closer to where it was needed, the CH-54 could be used to lift 155mm howitzers, while the CH-47 proved highly efficient at emplacing 105mm howitzers.

The Huey Cobra Arrives

On 1 September 1967, the first Huey Cobra (AH-1G) purpose-designed gunships arrived. The first six in country were assigned to the 1st Aviation Brigade where they could be used to train pilots to fly them. Just a few months later armed helicopters would prove invaluable during the Tet Offensive. For example, armed helicopters of the 120th Assault Helicopter Company were airborne and counterattacking the VC within three minutes of the alert at Tan Son Nhut, while others at Bien Hoa responded almost as quickly. As a result of the rapid response of the gunships neither base was overrun and large numbers of enemy attackers died. Later, during the post-Tet Offensive period when lost ground was being regained, the 1st Air Cav's mobility made it a key unit in regaining control of large portions of I Corps and in relieving Khe Sanh.

Normally, armed helicopters such as the Cobra were assigned to

Opposite above: Battery A, 3rd Battalion, 34th Artillery (Riverine) assigned to the 9th Infantry Division prepare their 105mm howitzer for action.

Opposite below: 155mm self-propelled howitzer of 2nd Battalion, 138th Artillery.

The door gunner on an AH-1G gunship of the 7th Squadron, 1st Air Cav scans the ground for a target for his mini-gun.

one of five types of units; assault helicopter companies; attack helicopter companies; general support helicopter companies; aerial rocket artillery battalions (in the airmobile divisions); and air cavalry troops. There were also five primary categories of mission for armed helicopters; armed escort of aircraft, vehicles or personnel; security for observation helicopters; direct fire support; aerial rocket artillery support; and hunter-killer teams.

The 101st Becomes Airmobile

On 28 June 1968, General Order 325 called for the reorganization of the 101st Airborne Division into an airmobile division. The conversion was to be carried out in three phases; the first of these, running from 1 July to 1 December 1968, would incorporate the activation and organization of the 160th Aviation Group to support the division and the reorganization of the division base. The second phase, which would run from 1 December 1968 to 1 June 1969, would include the conversion of the division's armored cavalry squadron to air cavalry. The third phase would encompass the activation of an aerial rocket artillery battalion.

Throughout the reorganization, the 101st Airborne remained in combat. Although in most ways, the reorganization of the 101st was based on the TO&E of the 1st Air Cavalry Division, the 101st's maintenance organization was very different as it used a more cellular, decentralized organization. This system was to prove so effective that the 1st Cavalry would reorganize along similar lines.

Although in July 1968, the 308th Aviation Battalion was reassigned to the 101st Airborne from the 1st Aviation Brigade, this still left the 1st Aviation Brigade as the largest Army Aviation command in the world with 25,181 men assigned as of 31 July 1968. When one considers that this is larger than the authorised strength for most infantry divisions in Vietnam, this figure is even more impressive.

Among the units assigned to the 1st Aviation Brigade at this time were four Combat Aviation Groups – the 12th, 16th, 17th and 164th. Subsidiary to these four groups were twelve combat avaiation battalions and two combat support aviation battalions, each with various assault helicopter companies, reconnaissance airplane companies, surveillance airplane companies, corps aviation companies, utility airplane companies, assault support helicopter companies and heavy helicopter companies assigned. Additionally, each of the Combat Aviation Groups, with the exception of the 16th, had an air cavalry squadron directly assigned. Assigned directly to the 1st Aviation Brigade were the 478th Heavy Helicopter Company, the 58th Aviation Battalion, the 16th Signal Company and the 125th Air Traffic control Detachment. At its peak strength in material, the 1st Aviation Brigade had under its control 641 fixed wing aircraft of various types, 441 Cobra AH-1G gunships, 311 CH-47 transport helicopters, 635 OH-6A observation helicopters and 2,202 Huey UH-1 transport helicopters.

In addition to its flying duties, the 1st Aviation Brigade was operating schools to train Vietnamese, Korean, Thai, Australian and US personnel to fly the Huey. As new aircraft arrived these schools would train crews in the new equipment. For example, when the Huey Cobras arrived, pilots from the 334th assault Helicopter Company were trained to take them into combat.

The Air Cavalry Troop

Since the air cavalry troop has been mentioned in various contexts, at this point it would be worthwhile to clarify its structure and mission. Normally, one air cavalry troop was organic to each armored cavalry squadron and three were organic to the air cavalry squadron of the airmobile division. According to TOE 17-98T, the Air Cavalry Troop as assigned to an airmobile division had a strength of 18 officers, 30 warrant officers and 104 enlisted men. A captain commanded the troop, which was broken into a troop HQ, an

A member of the 1st Air Cav guides in a slick during operations in January 1968.

aviation section, a maintenance section, a scout platoon, an aero rifle platoon and a weapons platoon. The scout platoon flew five OH-6 observation helicopters armed with an XM-7 weapons system. The aero rifle platoon had four nine-man rifle squads supported by five UH-1 utility helicopters in an organic lift section. The weapons platoon had five UH-1B armed helicopters and later AH-1 Huey Cobras.

Air Cavalry Troops were normally used for one of three major types of mission as follows:

> **Intelligence**   Visual reconnaissance of roads, areas, targets; bomb damage assessment; LZ reconnaissance and selection; target acquisition; prisoner snatch operations; Ranger/LRRP support.
> **Security**   Providing early warning of impending attack; screening ops; first-and-last-light reconnaissance of areas; protection for convoys or downed aircraft.
> **Economy-of-Force Missions**   Artillery raids; combat assaults and ambushes; delaying actions; sustained security for construction of fire bases; base defense reaction force operations.

Normally, depending on the operation, various color-coded teams from the air cavalry troop would be assigned. The RED TEAM consisted of two gunships used for offensive operations. The WHITE TEAM consisted of two light OH-6 observation helicopters armed with 7.62mm miniguns used to carry out reconnaissance of areas, normally with one flying high to provide cover, radio relay and navigation and one flying low to observe. The PINK TEAM consisted of a mixture of red and white with one OH-6 observation helicopter flying low over the area, while an AH-1 or other gunship circled to provide suppressive fire and radio relay. BLUE TEAMS consisted of UH-1s with their aero rifle platoon embarked to carry out ground intelligence or security operations. Normally, the most commonly encountered team was the PINK TEAM.

One of the best illustrations of the use of an air cavalry troop's assets would be during fire base construction. Initially, the troop's aero rifle platoon would be inserted to provide security for the selected LZ. Then an engineer team would come in and clear enough space for a chopper to land additional engineering equipment to be used to clear the area of the entire fire base. While this clearing was taking place the aero rifle platoon would carry out ground reconnaissance around the area while a PINK TEAM overhead provided reconnaissance and firepower.

Lam Son 719

During Lam Son 719, the move against VC/NVA logistical and base areas in Laos, US aviators flew missions in support of the Vietnamese, though US ground forces were prohibited from taking part by Congress. The aviation task force for this operation was based on the 101st Airborne's aviation assets supplemented by additional units. Air cavalry units provided very effective recon on the flanks of the advance and in front of ground operations and also provided reconnaissance and security around landing zones. The Huey Cobra got its first test against tanks, too, during Lam Son 719 when it went up against PT-76 armored vehicles. Between 8 February 1971 and 24 March 1971, sixty-six tanks were sighted, with six of them being destroyed and eight immobilised. However, the enemy anti-aircraft fire was heavier than expected, which caused heavier helicopter losses than anticipated.

While US ground units had been pulling out throughout 1970–72, a large proportion of aviation units remained to provide airmobility to the ARVNs. However, in preparation for the departure of the 1st Aviation Brigade in late March, 1973, most of the final US Army aviation units pulled out during early March, 1973.

During the war, 1,018 Army pilots died in action or in crashes, as did 2,041 members of Army air crews. Over 36,000,000 helicopter sorties were flown during the war and over 4,600 helicopters were shot down, though it should be remembered that many of these helicopters were salvaged and repaired, and hence, a substantial portion of this number returned to service. At least 100 Army aviation companies served in Vietnam, many doing two or even three tours, seeing action in virtually every battle from the DMZ to the Delta. Perhaps the best indicator of the niche carved out by the Army aviators in Vietnam is that when the first Army aviation elements arrived they were viewed, in effect, as aerial truck drivers, but by the end of the war, Army aviation had assumed its place as a combat arm alongside the infantry, armor and artillery.

7
ARTILLERY

Gunners and infantrymen have always made jokes at each other's expense: in Vietnam, for example, artillerymen especially liked the locally-made versions of the Infantry School patch, which instead of the sword with the motto 'Follow Me' bore a male organ with the words 'Swallow Me.' However, in combat both have always realised their mutual need. In Vietnam particularly, the grunts needed the devastating hail of metal the artillery forward observer could call down in their support, while the gunners needed the infantry to help defend their firebases in a war with no front lines.

By 1967, the standard infantry divisional artillery consisted of 208 officers, 28 warrant officers and 2,553 enlisted men equipped with fifty-four 105mm towed howitzers, eighteen 155mm towed howitzers and four 8 inch self-propelled howitzers. The 8 inch and 155mm howitzers were normally in one battalion and the 105mm howitzers were split between three battalions. In addition, divisional artillery would have enough (if there is ever enough of any equipment in combat) trucks, ammunition carriers, and so on, to support their guns. Divisional artillery normally had its own aviation contingent as well, consisting of nine OH-6A Cayuse observation helicopters and two UH-1B Huey helicopters. Each 105mm battalion normally consisted of forty officers, three warrant officers and 488 enlisted men. The battalion's eighteen howitzers were assigned six each to three batteries. Frequently, in Vietnam, however, especially after 1968, each battalion was modified to have four batteries, each of six guns. This increased battalion strength to fifty-two officers, three warrant officers and 582 enlisted men. The extra battery gave more versatility when the battalion was split, as frequently happened in Vietnam to allow support for dispersed infantry maneuver battalions. The extra battery also offered more potential for augmenting another battery's fire.

Artillery Weapons Used in Vietnam

The basic artillery weapon was the 105mm towed howitzer, which was normally used in the direct support role. Light in weight and dependable, its high rate of fire made it extremely useful in supporting maneuver battalions.

Initially, artillery units in Vietnam were equipped with the **M101A1**, virtually the same howitzer in use with US forces since World War Two. Weighing 2,220kg, the M101 had a maximum range of 11,200m and could fire eight rounds per minute. Among the ammunition available for it were HE (High Explosive), HEAT (High Explosive Anti-Tank), Smoke, WP (White Phosphorous), Chemical, and Illumination.

In 1966, the improved version of the M101, the **M102**, was first issued to the 1st Battalion, 21st Field Artillery in March. Over the next four years the M102 replaced the M101 throughout the Field Artillery in Vietnam. At 1,470kg in weight, the M102 was almost a ton lighter than its predecessor, a definite advantage in an environment where artillery portability was especially important. The M102's rated range was slightly greater as well at 14,000m due to a barrel which is twelve per cent longer. A full 360 degree traverse was easier with the M102 as well, an important consideration in Vietnam where fire might have to be delivered in any direction. The same basic ammunition types were used in the M102, plus the 'Beehive' flechette round which proved devastatingly lethal in fire base defense.

Artillerymen were ambivalent about the new gun. The M101 had had a waist-high breech which made it easier to load and had had high ground clearance. The M102, on the other hand, was lighter and thus more air portable, making it easier to heli-lift with more ammunition. Its ability to traverse a full 360 degrees and its lower silhouette, making it a harder target for the enemy, were also definite advantages.

The **M108** 105mm self-propelled howitzer saw very limited service in Vietnam – two artillery battalions were equipped with it – and proved poorly suited to the environment. Weighing 22,452kg, the M108 was not transportable by helicopter yet lacked sufficient range to counter its limitations.

The **M114A1** 155mm towed howitzer was widely used in Vietnam for augmentation of the 105s with heavier guns. Another World War Two era design, the M114 weighed 5,800kg and could be heli-lifted into position. Its range, however, was only 14,600m somewhat short for its weight. Its normal rate of fire was two rounds per minute of HE, Smoke, WP, Illuminating or Chemical/Gas. The traverse limits of the M114 were only 53 degrees as well, though field expedient steps were sometimes taken to increase this.

The **M109** self-propelled 155mm howitzer was used in direct support with the 1st Brigade, 5th Mechanized Division in Vietnam, but normally was used in the area support role or to augment the

105s. At 20,500kg this weapon was actually lighter than the M108, though it still had to be moved into position via road.

The **M107** self-propelled 175mm gun proved a useful heavy adjunct to the direct support 105s in Vietnam. Capable of hurling its 174lb projectile out to 32,700m, the M107 would prove especially useful in support of the crossings into Laos and Cambodia when it could be positioned just inside the South Vietnamese border and still give far-ranging fire support to operations across the border. Initially the very short tube life (about three hundred rounds) of the M107 proved a problem, but a tube with a life about four times as long was developed to replace it.

Sharing the same carriage with the M107 was the **M110** self-propelled gun. Capable of firing its 200lb projectile out to 16,800m, the M110's forte was its great accuracy. Frequently, artillery units would have both 175mm and 8 inch tubes available and would switch them back and forth on their carriage to suit the mission.

Other artillery weapons which saw at least limited deployment to Vietnam included the **M42A1** twin 40mm self-propelled anti-aircraft gun, which was used in the ground support role as well. Due to lack of radar, the M42 was not particularly effective as an anti-aircraft gun, but its cyclic rate of 120 rounds of 40mm per minute made it very effective in the close support or base defense role.

Another weapon which saw limited though effective use was the **M55** quad .50 caliber machine gun system which was used mounted on trucks or APCs in the convoy escort role and for base defense. The **Hawk** surface to air missile air defense system was also deployed to Vietnam. Hawk (Homing All the Way Killer) was very mobile and could counter supersonic aircraft flying anywhere between 100m and 15,000m away. It also had its own radar for acquiring targets. Since there was little North Vietnamese air threat in the South, deployment of the Hawk was mostly precautionary.

Of growing importance as the war progressed was the Aerial Rocket Artillery, which proved invaluable in support of the airmobile divisions and of airmobile operations. Originally, such support came from UH-1B or UH-1C helicopters armed with forty-eight 2.75-inch rockets, but, in early 1968 the first purpose-designed gun ship, the AH-1G Huey Cobra, which carried seventy-six rockets and was 30 knots faster, began coming into service. In 1970, the designation for helicopter gun ships functioning as artillery changed to Aerial Field Artillery. Characteristics of the aerial artillery are covered more thoroughly in the chapter on Army Aviation.

Target Acquisition was of extreme importance in Vietnam due to the heavy jungle canopy in some places and due to the likelihood of

AN/MPQ-4 radar unit installed on a rooftop in Saigon by artillerymen from the 40th Artillery for use in directing counter mortar fire.

friendly civilians being present near hostilities. As a result, three Target Acquisition Batteries were deployed to Vietnam: Battery F, 2nd Target Acquisition Battery, 26th Artillery; HQ Battery, 8th Target Acquisition Battalion, 26th Artillery; and HQ Battery, 8th Target Acquisition Battalion, 25th Artillery. Each of these batteries was assigned to one of the Field Force headquarters. Battery F established bases to monitor the DMZ, including some sound ranging equipment.

Two radars were deployed to aid in target acquisition – the AN/MPQ-4 and the AN/TPS-25. The AN/MPQ-4 got mixed reviews from its users as it had two disadvantages. Intended as a countermortar radar, it scanned too small a sector and could not locate low-trajectory weapons such as rockets, a favorite NVA/VC weapon. The AN/TPS-25, a surveillance radar, on the other hand, was considered extremely effective.

Acoustic, seismic and other types of sensors saw substantial use after 1967 as well, in some cases proving very useful in alerting firebases of impending attack. Sensors proved particularly useful during the defense of Khe Sanh when they would alert defenders of potential enemy buildups, buildups which would then be saturated with ordnance.

Artillerymen in Vietnam

In the early 1960s, the first US artillerymen arrived in Vietnam as advisors to the Vietnamese. Teams were assigned at corps, division, brigade and battalion level. The most basic advisory team usually consisted of one US artillery officer and one US artillery NCO working at the battalion level. In conjunction with this program, promising Vietnamese officers were identified and sent to Fort Sill for advanced training. One of the first problems encountered by the advisory teams was the defensive philosophy left over from the French era. By 1965, however, the Vietnamese were learning to use artillery in support of offensive operations; this was one of the more important accomplishments of the advisory teams. The advisors also found great deficiencies in fire direction techniques and had to work closely with their Viet counterparts to improve their techniques of directing fire.

These early advisors learned while they taught. One lesson they absorbed quickly was that light, mobile artillery was invaluable in Vietnam since it could be moved quickly via helicopter lift. As a result, the 105mm howitzer was quickly identified as the most useful weapon.

The advisors' experiences were relayed back to Fort Sill and would prove of immense value as the US troop buildup in Vietnam began during 1965. Eventually, a total of seventy US artillery battalions would be deployed to Vietnam, and each would find its task at least slightly easier due to lessons passed on by the early advisors. Perhaps the most important of these lessons was the need for breaking down artillery support into components assigned directly to maneuver battalions. Prior to the Vietnam War, divisional artillery was the primary module, though the divisional artillery was designed to be broken down into battalions and batteries if desired. Doctrine called for the divisional artillery to support the maneuver unit – infantry, armor, cavalry – while any other artillery units available would be in general support. Generally, each of the three artillery battalions within divisional artillery would be assigned in support of a brigade. Rarely, however, had the artillery been broken into individual batteries for support missions. The fluid nature of the counterinsurgency war in Vietnam, on the other hand, a war with no 'rear areas,' necessitated a change in doctrine. The infantry or other maneuver units being supported were widely

Special Forces Camp Bu Nard manned by SF Detachment A-344 and CIDG irregulars. The camp is designed with multiple layers of defensive works with the Special Forces team located within the inner cordon. Two artillery pieces can be seen in 360-degree traverse emplacements at the top end of the camp, able to give all-round fire. Two undeployed pieces can be seen at the left.

dispersed, often being shuttled into and out of combat by helicopter. As a result, each maneuver battalion was assigned an artillery battery in support, a battery that was often heli-lifted into a fire support base near its maneuver battalion's area of operations. So closely associated were the light (105mm) battalions with their brigades that the battalion would often be deployed to and from Vietnam with its brigade rather than as a divisional element.

With support likely to be called for in any direction, these supporting batteries had to be positioned for 360 degree fire as well and had to maintain their own decentralized fire direction capability. Obviously, logistics for artillery units became much more of a headache than when the artillery was concentrated into divisional artillery. In fact, field grade artillery officers often found themselves spending most of their time working out complex logistical difficulties.

Extremely important in Vietnam were the Artillery Forward

Observers assigned to infantry companies. These Forward Observers kept the supporting battery informed via radio of the unit's position and called in supporting fire as needed.

Divisional medium and heavy artillery – the 155mm and 8 inch guns – normally remained under the divisional artillery commander's control. The divisional artillery commander, normally a brigadier, also had to coordinate aerial fire support, etc. Divisional artillery was often sited to protect important US or Vietnamese government installations. Additionally, it would support with augmentation fire any friendly forces within range. Field Force Artillery (what would normally be considered corps artillery) almost always was assigned the area protection and support mission. To coordinate fire support, there was normally present at all maneuver HQs above company level an Artillery Fire Support Coordinator in charge of coordinating field artillery, helicopter gunships, tactical air, naval gunfire and any other type of fire support. This coordinator had to choose the type of support best suited to his assigned unit's mission plus get clearance to expend ordnance due to the possible danger to civilians or other units in the area and coordinate with aircraft to prevent them flying into a firing area.

Perhaps the single greatest tactical innovation of the Vietnam War was the development of large-scale airmobile maneuver forces. To support the air cavalry and airmobile infantry, artillery, too, had to be airmobile. The 105mm howitzer battery with a basic load of ammunition could be moved in eleven CH-47A sorties. As a result, rarely did infantry operate outside of the range of artillery support. Because of the fluid 'lines' in Vietnam, however, this artillery being leap-frogged around the country could be very vulnerable to attack. This led to the development of the Fire Support Base concept.

The Fire Support Base contained both infantry and artillery. Chosen for security and potential for allowing fire in any direction in support of the maneuver elements in the area, the base usually contained a single battery supported by a company of infantry. Generally, the six-gun battery would be positioned with five guns on the points of a star and the sixth gun in the middle. At night, the center gun would fire illuminating rounds while the others would give direct fire support. The infantry would establish a perimeter and dig in around it. Barbed wire, claymore mines, trip flares, phougas, spikes and other defensive measures were set up around the perimeter to inhibit enemy infiltration. Close fire support in defense of the base would be provided by M60 GPMGs, .50 MGs 81mm mortars and 4.2 inch mortars. Aggressive patrols were also launched around the base.

If the Fire Support Base came under attack the artillery would frequently use direct defensive fire with the XM546 'Beehive' round. Loaded with over eight thousand flechettes, the Beehive was a devastating anti-personnel round. It was first used on 7 November 1966 when one round killed nine enemy attackers. The 105s defending their own base might also fire air bursts over the enemy.

Should a fire base come under attack from enemy artillery, counterbattery fire would immediately be brought down. Since Fire Support Bases were sited to allow mutual support when one base came under attack, fire support from other bases would immediately be called in, often on pre-sited coordinates. So important was mutual fire support considered that if no other bases were within range, batteries would frequently be split to establish two mutually supporting fire bases.

Artillery was considered so critical in base defense that frequently large base camps would have their defense assigned to the senior artillery officer.

Those artillery units assigned to the Mekong Delta encountered special problems caused by the high water table. One solution was the development of the 'airborne platform,' 22 square feet in size with four adjustable legs to distribute the weight. The platform could be lifted by Chinook and emplaced; then another Chinook could bring in an M102 howitzer and ammunition and emplace them directly onto the platform. Alternatively, a CH-54 Sky Crane could lift both together. Another development for use in the Mekong Delta was floating barges, which had armor plate around the sides, ammunition storage at both ends and troop accommodations in the middle. Each barge carried two 105mm howitzers mounted on special plates allowing 360 degree traverse. A normal riverine battery consisted of three barges carrying the guns and five LCM-8s, three LCMs as push boats for the barges, one LCM as a command post and fire direction center and one LCM as an ammunition carrier. One such unit was the 1st Battalion, 7th Artillery which provided support for the 2nd Brigade, 9th Infantry Division.

The first US Army artillery unit deployed to Vietnam arrived in May 1965, when Battery C, 3rd Battalion, 319th Artillery came in with the 173rd Airborne Brigade. On 31 May 1965, this battery took part in an air assault as part of Task Force Surut. Within three hours of landing, Battery C's 105s were firing preparation fire in support of the infantry landings. A few days later, the airborne artillerymen were firing in support again, this time of South Vietnamese troops. 27 June saw a much more intensive commitment as Battery C provided fire support for the 173rd Airborne during its penetration

Artillerymen of the 3rd Battalion, 319th Artillery, 173rd Airborne Brigade firing their artillery at near maximum elevation.

into War Zone D. Over the next four days, nearly five thousand rounds were fired in support, during which many important lessons about fire support in combat were learned. During the next months, in fact, the 3rd Battalion of the 319th Artillery became somewhat of a test unit for Fort Sill, sending back reports on the lessons learned in Vietnam so that they could be incorporated into the training curriculum.

In July 1965, other artillery units started arriving in support of brigade or divisional-sized units being deployed to Vietnam. So fast was the buildup, in fact, that by March 1966, I and II Field Force Artillery, each under a brigadier, had been formed to control all non-divisional artillery.

Although the artillery assigned to the 173rd Airborne had already been employed on airmobile ops, it was the arrival of the 1st Cavalry Division (Airmobile) in September 1965, that really marked the dawn of a new type of warfare. Organised specifically around the helicopter, the 1st Air Cav would require extreme mobility on the part of its supporting artillery. In the Ia Drang Valley campaign, for example, seventy-nine tactical moves were required of the artillery, sixty-seven of them by air. Quickly learning the lessons through OJT (On the Job Training) at Fire Bases, the Air Cav gunners fired over forty thousand artillery rounds and aerial rockets during the push into the Ia Drang. Flying artillery (helicopter gunships), of which the 1st Cav had a battalion, also began to prove its worth in close support during this campaign.

The arrival of new artillery units kept pace with the buildup of maneuver units in country so that by the end of 1966, there were four artillery HQs and thirty-nine artillery battalions of various types, including the one aerial rocket battalion assigned to the 1st Cav. The larger the operations, the more important was artillery support. During MASHER/WHITE WING in early 1966, for example, 141,712 rounds were fired in support. Larger operations, of course, entailed more and more detailed planning and coordination in artillery movement, employment and logistics. Operation BIRMINGHAM as an example involved the displacement of seven Field Artillery Battalions, but even that number seems small compared to Operation JUNCTION CITY in February 1967, which involved seventeen artillery battalions or their equivalent.

To retain the element of surprise as much as possible during JUNCTION CITY instead of carrying out the normal artillery area surveys, photogrammetic surveys using aerial reconnaissance photos were used. JUNCTION CITY also taught the artillerymen other useful lessons: high-angle fire was more effective in penetrating the jungle canopy, and within certain parameters, the AN/MPQ-4A radar was very useful in directing counterbattery fire. One other noteworthy aspect of the operation was that Battery A, 3rd Battalion, 319th Artillery airborne artillerymen jumped with the 173rd Airborne on 22 February 1967, marking the most recent combat jump by US airborne artillerymen.

One of the first shortages, and a most critical one, to occur as a result of the rapid buildup was in well-trained Artillery Forward Observers. Although the slot was meant to be filled by an artillery lieutenant, frequently NCOs had to serve as Forward Observers. The need for more dispersed fire control centers also meant that fire direction centers were normally understaffed when an operation was necessary. To make sure the large influx of artillerymen arriving in country were prepared, by 1967 orientation courses had been established in country to teach methods and tactics used in Vietnam and to orient allied personnel.

During the Tet Offensive which struck at the Chinese New Year in 1968, US artillery helped turn back the VC drive in many places. During the re-taking of Hue, for example, a single artillery preparation on the night of 23/24 February killed 161 of the enemy. In III Corps, the most heavily populated part of the country, the 1st Infantry Division estimated that artillery accounted for as many as seventy per cent of the more than one thousand enemy killed by the division. Although the siege of Khe Sanh continued after most of the Communist gains during the Tet Offensive had been regained, it offered another example of the effectiveness of artillery. There were five Marine artillery battalions within the base, but these were supplemented by four Army 175mm batteries – one north and three east of the base – which gave augmentation fire. About 160,000 rounds were fired against enemy positions around the base, probably accounting for thousands of VC/NVA killed. During the siege, the technique of using artillery bombardment in conjunction with bomb runs to increase enemy casualties proved especially effective, though fire coordination was particularly critical. Although Khe Sanh at the time was often compared to the French situation at Dien Bien Phu, in reality US counterbattery fire was so successful that Khe Sanh was actually viewed by many senior US officers as an 'anvil' against which to smash much of the NVA's offensive potential.

During the relief of Khe Sanh, the artillery of the 1st Air Cav proved particularly valuable as it did when the airmobile troops moved into the A Shau Valley in April 1968. Prior to the second operation into the A Shau in July 1968, by the 101st Airborne Division, fire bases were established at critical locations and eight batteries were moved in. Each 105mm battery had three thousand rounds stockpiled and each 155mm battery had two thousand rounds stockpiled.

In many cases during 1968 and 1969, enemy attacks on fire support bases were turned into mini-'Khe Sanhs' as pre-planned fire support and the use of 'Beehive' rounds heavily decimated the attackers. 1968 also saw the first National Guard artillery unit deployed to Vietnam as artillery strength grew towards its peak in 1968.

As of January 1968, shortly before strength peaked, artillery organisation in Vietnam is shown in the accompanying table.

US Artillery in Vietnam January 1968

I Field Force Artillery

41st Artillery Group
7th Battalion, 3rd Artillery, 105mm towed
7th Battalion, 15th Artillery, 8 inch/175mm
2nd Battalion, 17th Artillery, 105/155mm towed
1st Battalion, 30th Artillery, 155mm towed

52nd Artillery Group
5th Battalion, 6th Artillery, 105mm self-propelled

6th Battalion, 14th Artillery, 8 inch/175mm
5th Battalion, 22nd Artillery, 8 inch/175mm
1st Battalion, 92nd Artillery, 155mm towed
5th Battalion, 27th Artillery, 105mm Towed
6th Battalion, 32nd Artillery, 8 inch/175mm

II Field Force Artillery

23rd Artillery Group
2nd Battalion, 11th Artillery, 155mm towed
2nd battalion, 13th Artillery, 105mm
1st Battalion, 27th Artillery, 155mm self-propelled
6th Battalion, 27th Artillery, 8 inch/175mm
2nd Battalion, 32nd Artillery, 8 inch/175mm

54th Artillery Group
7th Battalion, 8th Artillery, 8 inch/175mm
7th Battalion, 9th Artillery, 105mm towed
2nd Battalion, 35th Artillery, 155mm self-propelled
1st Battalion, 83rd Artillery, 8 inch/175mm
6th Battalion, 77th Artillery, 105mm towed
    attached to 25th Infantry Division
6th Battalion, 15th Artillery, 105mm towed
    attached to 1st Infantry Division

108th Artillery Group
1st Battalion, 40th Artillery, 105mm self-propelled
8th Battalion, 4th Artillery, 8 inch/175mm
2nd Battalion, 94th Artillery, 175mm

Divisional Artillery
1st Infantry Division
1st Battalion, 5th Artillery, 105mm towed
1st Battalion, 7th Artillery, 105mm towed
2nd Battalion, 33rd Artillery, 105mm towed
8th Battalion, 6th Artillery, 155mm/8 inch self-propelled

25th Infantry Division
1st Battalion, 8th Artillery, 105mm towed
7th Battalion, 11th Artillery, 105mm towed
2nd Battalion, 77th Artillery, 105mm towed
3rd Battalion, 13th Artillery, 155mm/8 inch self-propelled

1st Cavalry Division
2nd Battalion, 9th Artillery, 105mm towed
1st Battalion, 77th Artillery, 105mm towed
1st Battalion, 21st Artillery, 105mm towed
2nd Battalion, 20th Artillery, Aerial Rocket Artillery

4th Infantry Division
6th Battalion, 29th Artillery, 105mm towed
4th Battalion, 42nd Artillery, 105mm towed
2nd Battalion, 9th Artillery, 105mm towed
5th Battalion, 16th Artillery, 155mm/8 inch self-propelled

23rd Infantry Division
  6th Battalion, 11th Artillery, 11th Infantry Brigade,
    105mm towed
  1st Battalion, 14th Artillery, 198th Infantry Brigade,
    105mm towed
  3rd Battalion, 82nd Artillery, 196th Infantry Brigade
    105mm towed
  3rd Battalion, 18th Artillery, 8 inch/175mm
  3rd Battalion, 16th Artillery, 155mm towed
101st Airborne Division
  2nd Battalion, 319th Artillery, 105mm towed
  2nd Battalion, 320th Artillery, 105mm towed
  1st Battalion, 321st Artillery, 105mm towed

9th Infantry Division
  2nd Battalion, 4th Artillery, 105mm towed
  1st Battalion, 11th Artillery, 105mm towed
  3rd Battalion, 34th Artillery, 105mm towed
  1st Battalion, 84th Artillery, 155mm/8 inch self-propelled

Brigade or Regimental Artillery
173rd Airborne Brigade
  3rd Battalion, 319th Artillery

199th Light Infantry Brigade
  2nd Battalion, 40th Artillery, 105mm towed

11th Armored Cavalry Regiment
  3rd Squadron Howitzer Batteries, 155mm self-propelled

Innovations of Note

Among the more unique artillery organisations in Vietnam was Battery D, 2nd Battalion, 13th Artillery, which was organised on a rather ad hoc basis as a combined 105mm and 155mm battery for special purposes, such as supporting the 3rd Mobile Strike force on operations. When so organised, Battery D would be comprised of three 105s and three 155s. The 105mm howitzers were better for close in fire and had a high rate of fire, while the 155mm howitzers were better in punching through the heavy jungle canopy.

The 'artillery raid' was a concept which, as it evolved in Vietnam, allowed artillery to be used in a very aggressive manner for offensive operations. In a raid, artillery would be heli-lifted or occasionally towed to a remote location from whence it would then mass fire on enemy concentrations, then quickly pull out.

One of the more controversial artillery tactics developed in Vietnam was 'Harassing and Interdiction fire' placed on areas of suspected enemy occupation. Some thought this technique interdicted VC/NVA infiltration routes, while others felt that all it did was waste ammunition. In truth, there is some validity to both claims. When such fire was based on sound intelligence information or against areas known as enemy refuges, it was occasionally very effective. Most of the time, however, such fire was really just wasteful.

Vietnamization

In 1967, assistance and liaison with the Vietnamese artillery began on a limited basis, but after 1969 the Vietnamization process really shifted into high gear. Americans still found that the Viets needed the most assistance with fire control and target survey methods. During the changeover to Vietnamese control of the war, while Viet artillery units were coming up to strength and skill, US artillery units frequently continued to provide support for Vietnamese maneuver units. Though Vietnamization was well under way, in May/June 1970 during the Cambodian invasion, US artillery units were heavily involved. Between US and Vietnamese units, almost 850,000 rounds were fired in support of this operation. The January 1971 invasion of Laos, LAM SON 719, also saw substantial US support from heavy artillery units positioned just inside Vietnam. After the Easter Offensive of 1972, when Vietnamese troops encountered heavy NVA artillery support for the first time, it became apparent that the ARVN artillerymen needed more training in counterbattery fire so teams were sent to Fort Sill for extensive training. By this time, however, except for advisors, the involvement of US artillerymen in the war was virtually over.

The Lessons

Certain important conclusions and lessons can be taken from the experience of the artillerymen who served in Vietnam. First, the importance of the forward observer actually on the ground with the infantrymen was once again proven to be immense. Forward observers had to learn to cope with very difficult conditions and far greater responsibility than they had been led to expect, yet they responded very well. The problem of heavy cover, especially, forced them to learn tricks such as using spotting rounds to determine their location, adjusting fire with smoke rounds before HE to help insure the safety of the infantrymen they were supporting, to adjust by sound in dense cover and to make use of any vantage point available – trees, hills, rocks, etc. The forward observer's map reading skills often meant he was the only one with a company who really knew where they were, too; hence, he often acted as his unit's navigator.

The complex nature of the various types of support available made the job of the fire support coordinator an especially important one in Vietnam as well, a point that was noted for future US operations. As did the rest of the US Army in Vietnam, the artillerymen had to learn the importance of airmobility and to adjust their tactics accordingly. As a result, the fire support base was established and became a vital weapon in area denial operations. The rapid helicopter movement of guns also necessitated the development of 'combat loading' doctrine so that when artillery was heli-lifted to a fire base or for a raid, everything needed to commence firing was readily available.

Just as artillerymen on the Napoleonic battlefield knew the importance of chain shot or grapeshot in decimating the enemy, artillerymen in Vietnam learned how devastating the flechette-loaded 'Beehive' round could be on enemy personnel. Most of all the artillerymen found themselves in the position that gunners of the Napoleonic or American Civil War had often found themselves in of having to defend their guns. As a result, when choosing a battery site supporting fire and other defensive considerations as well as 360 degree fire capability became very important. The key word in summing up the US artillery experience in Vietnam is 'learn,' for the artillerymen did learn how to cope with a guerrilla war even though it was a type of war not ideally suited for the traditional employment of artillery.

Infantry Division Artillery

Mission

To provide direct and general artillery support for the Infantry division, Armored Division or Infantry Division (Mechanized).

Assignment

Organic to Infantry Division, Infantry Division (Mechanized), or Armored Division.

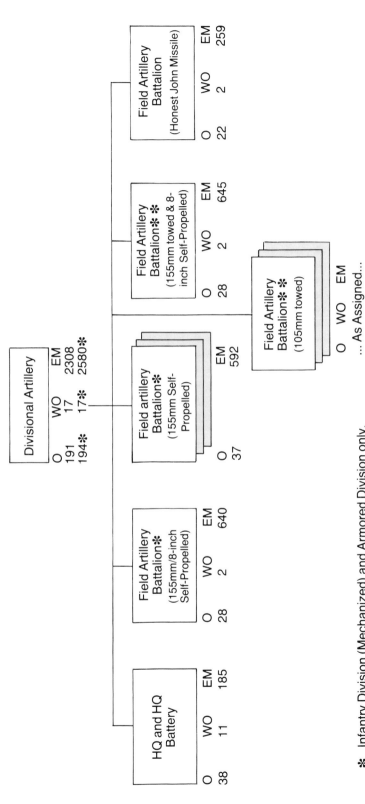

Divisional Artillery

O	WO	EM
191	17	2308
194✱	17✱	2580✱

HQ and HQ Battery

O	WO	EM
38	11	185

Field Artillery Battalion✱
(155mm/8-inch Self-Propelled)

O	WO	EM
28	2	640

Field artillery Battalion✱
(155mm Self-Propelled)

O	WO	EM
37		592

Field Artillery Battalion✱✱
(105mm towed)

O	WO	EM
		... As Assigned...

Field Artillery Battalion✱
(155mm towed & 8-inch Self-Propelled)

O	WO	EM
28	2	645

Field Artillery Battalion
(Honest John Missile)

O	WO	EM
22	2	259

✱ Infantry Division (Mechanized) and Armored Division only.

✱✱ Infantry Division only.

8
ARMOR

Vietnam is generally considered a 'grunt's' war rather than a tanker's war, and this view is justified since the infantryman carried most of the combat burden in Vietnam. The mobility of armored cavalry formations, however, made them extremely valuable in Vietnam, especially during the later phases of the war when the lessening number of combat troops made mobility highly critical. Early in the war, the upper echelons of the US command structure actually believed that most of Vietnam was unsuitable for the use of armor, while armor officers themselves continued to think in terms of a classical tank war on the German plain against their Russian counterparts. The deployment of tanks and armored personnel carriers to Vietnam would help dispel both these reservations and this tactical mindset on the part of those who actually served in Southeast Asia with cavalry units, though the bulk of US armored hardware and doctrine remained oriented towards a war in Europe.

In Vietnam, the typical armored battalion organisation was generally modified to thirty-seven officers, three warrant officers and 532 enlisted men equipped with fifty-four M48 tanks, four M106 4.2-inch mortar carriers, fourteen M113 Armored Personnel Carriers, two Armored Vehicle Bridge Layers, five M88 Recovery Vehicles and various trucks. The Vietnam tank company would normally consist of five officers and eighty-seven enlisted men equipped with seventeen M48 tanks, one M113 APC and one M88 Recovery Vehicle. For comparison, the standard TO&E for 1967 showed a tank company with virtually an identical organisation, though it did show only eighty-five enlisted personnel.

There were, however, substantial differences between the Armored Cavalry Squadron standard TO&E and the typical Armored Cavalry Squadron serving in Vietnam. According to the TO&E, the squadron would have forty-five officers, thirty-six warrant officers (primarily helicopter pilots) and 824 enlisted men equipped with twenty-seven M41 Tanks, seventy-five M113 APCs, six M577 Communication Carriers, five Recovery Vehicles and nine OH-6A, eleven UH-1B and six UH-10 helicopters. In Vietnam, however, due to the heavy combat load placed on the armored cavalry squadrons, they evolved into a somewhat more powerful formation with fifty officers, thirty-six warrant officers and 963 enlisted men equipped with twenty-seven M48 tanks, nine M125 81mm mortar carriers, seventy-three M113 APCs (often modified to 'ACAVs'), four M132 flamethrower carriers, six M577 Communication Carriers, five M88 Recovery Vehicles and nine AH-1G, nine OH-6A, two UH-1B and six UH-1D helicopters, plus various types of trucks. The normal Armored Cavalry Troop consisted of five officers and 192 enlisted men with nine M48 tanks, three M125 mortar carriers, twenty-one M113 APCs and one M88 recovery vehicle.

Armored and Cavalry Equipment

The **M48A3** was the preferred tank for service in Vietnam since it was fitted with a diesel engine giving better performance and greater crew safety from fire. Weighing over 50 tons and capable of speeds up to 30mph, the M48 was equipped with a 90mm main gun plus a .50 and a .30 MG. The **M48A1** and **M48A2**, also saw service in Vietnam but were considered less desirable by the troops: both have gasoline engines, though the latter is an improved one with fuel injection. Variations of the M48 used included the **M48 Armored Vehicle Launched Bridge**, which has a scissors bridge which can cover gaps of up to 60 feet, and the **M88 Recovery Vehicle**.

The **M551** Armored Reconnaissance Assault Vehicle or light tank began to see service in cavalry squadrons after 1969. Weighing about one-third what the M48 did, the M551 could perform better in the marshy areas of Vietnam, its ground pressure per square inch being about half that of the M48. It could also achieve speeds of up to 45mph and had substantially greater range than the M48. Armament was a 152mm gun/missile launcher, though in Vietnam the gun only was normally used. This gun used caseless ammunition, which had a somewhat bad reputation in Vietnam for catching fire should the M551 take a hit. A .50 and a .30 MG were also affixed. The aluminum hull was also more susceptible to mine damage which, combined with the flammability of the caseless ammunition, caused M551 crew members initially to dislike the tank. However, its sophisticated night vision equipment did win it some admirers after it proved itself in night operations.

The **M113** Armored Personnel Carrier was used in many guises in Vietnam. Weighing about 12 tons and with a road speed of about 42mph, the M113 proved very versatile in Vietnam and was often used as an assault vehicle since the enemy only rarely employed armor. With added machineguns and armor shields for the machinegunners the M113 was known as the Armored Cavalry Assault Vehicle (ACAV). The basic armament was only a single .50

A member of the 11th Armored Cavalry Regiment checks the air filter on an M-113 APC.

MG, but this was generally upgunned. Variations of the M113 included the **M577** Command and Communications version, the **M125** 81mm mortar carrier, the **M132A1** flamethrower model, the **M806A1** recovery vehicle and the **M548** cargo carrier.

US Armor Advisors

When the first US advisors arrived in Vietnam, the Vietnamese Army had some armor deployed one regiment per military region. These regiments were primarily equipped with M8 Armored Cars, M3 Half Tracks, M3 Scout Cars, M24 Tanks and M8 Towed Howitzers. In June 1955, one US armor officer was sent as an advisor to the Vietnamese Armor School, then in 1956, selected Vietnamese officers began attending the US Armor School at Fort Knox. Under this US influence, the Vietnamese re-organized their armored forces into armored cavalry regiments. Late in the 1950s, the first US advisors were actually assigned to Viet field armored units, though in the past there had been more than a dozen assigned to MACV.

In 1962, more advisors arrived and were assigned to armored Cavalry regiments and squadrons. In addition to working with the Vietnamese to improve training and tactics, these advisors also began to scout the country for the possibility of employing US armored units there; unlike many of their superiors in MACV who felt that armor was poorly suited for operations in Vietnam, these advisors in the field saw great possibilities for the use of armor, especially in quick-moving armored cavalry squadrons.

By 1965, each Viet armored cavalry regiment had a major assigned as an advisor and another officer, normally a captain, and two NCOs assigned to each squadron. These advisors provided advice and assisted their counterparts with their access to American fire support, communications and medical evacuation. In addition, they reported to their superiors on Vietnamese armored operations and any lessons learned. When paired with willing counterparts, these advisors proved especially useful at building skill and confidence in the Vietnamese armored officers and senior NCOs. However, they found it hard to overcome the defensive mentality the Viets had inherited from the French. One aid to building aggressiveness in the Vietnamese armored cavalry formations was the arrival in 1962 of M113 armored personnel carriers, which gave the Viets broader ability to move off roads. As new companies were formed and equipped with M113s, they were assigned US advisors as well.

With the increased US assistance both in material and advisors, Vietnamese armored formations grew towards the goal of an armored cavalry regiment with each Vietnamese division. However, despite the efforts of advisors and the improved tr..ining of Vietnamese armored crewmen, the armored units continued to be used in the 'palace guard' mode of many third world countries. Assigned primarily to secure various headquarters, the Vietnamese armor was known for being very political, especially under the Diem regime.

The US Cavalry Arrives

Although the first US armored unit arrived in country on 9 March 1965 when the 3rd Platoon, Company B, 3rd Marine Tank Battalion ground ashore, initially, the Army had little inclination to deploy tanks. When consideration was being given to deploying the 1st Infantry Division, in fact, it was planned to leave the division's two tank battalions behind and to convert its mechanised infantry to regular 'grunts.' Among the reasons offered for this reluctance to deploy the armored/mechanised units was the danger of mines, the unsuitability of the terrain, and the need for large numbers of support troops to keep the vehicles running. Finally, it was decided that only one armored unit – the divisional cavalry (1st Squadron, 4th Cavalry) – would deploy with its M48A3s, to some extent as an experiment. Because some M114s, which had been used by the Vietnamese had performed poorly, it was decided that all M114s in the 1st Squadron would be replaced with M113s. Once the 1st Infantry Division had arrived in country, the 1st Cavalry Squadron was split into troops, one assigned to each brigade to offer some mechanized recon capability when the division was split. Since Gen Westmoreland believed that tanks absolutely could not operate in the jungle, they were withdrawn from the cavalry troops, however, and held in reserve at the squadron base at Phu Loi. This left only the squadron's air cavalry troop under the control of the squadron headquarters.

As more US units were deployed to Vietnam, armored units did begin to 'infiltrate' the US order of battle, though perhaps not quite as easily as the Communists were infiltrating Vietnam. Late in 1965, however, Gen Westmoreland began to see the usefulness of highly mobile and hard-hitting ground cavalry and requested the deployment of the 11th Armored Cavalry Regiment and the 25th Infantry Division, the latter with all of its armored and mechanised units intact. Even with the arrival of more ground cavalry units, though, it became apparent that air cavalry had taken over many of the scouting tasks formerly the domain of ground cavalry.

The first major engagement involving US armor was by Troop A, 1st Squadron, 4th Cavalry in the battle of Ap Bau Bang. Minus their nine tanks which had not been returned to them, Troop A plus three rifle companies and a recon platoon were sweeping along Highway 13. On 11 November 1965, Troop A, along with an artillery battery, the command group and a rifle company, moved into a defensive position. At about dawn this position came under attack, but fortunately the APCs had been used the night before to clear fields of fire and the Troop A commander had called for a dawn 'stand to' in anticipation of a possible attack. As a result, the M113s were in position to mount a counterattack with their .50 MGs and help break the enemy assault, though two M113s and three M106 mortar carriers were destroyed in the process.

Partially based on the successes of the 1st Squadron, 4th Cavalry, even minus its tanks, and in response to Gen Westmoreland's request for more armored units, in early 1966, the 25th Infantry division deployed to Vietnam with its armored and mechanised units. Based on 1st Squadron experiences and the recommendations of advisors who had been serving with ARVN cavalry units the APCs were equipped with gun shields and extra machine guns. The M48A2C gasoline-powered tanks were also exchanged for M48A3 diesel-powered tanks. In addition to suggesting changes in M113 armament better to suit them for employment in Vietnam, other experiences of the advisors to the Vietnamese armored cavalry were incorporated into an orientation packet for arriving US armored units which discussed the terrain to be encountered, made suggestions for modifying equipment (such as adding the machineguns and shields to the M113s), likely enemy weapons and tactics to be encountered and suggested tactics for US cavalry units.

A few weeks after their arrival in country, units of the 25th Infantry Division took part in the first multi-battalion US armored operation during CIRCLE PINES in the jungle and rubber plantations twenty klicks north of Saigon. During this eight-day operation, more than fifty enemy were killed and a substantial number of enemy arms and supplies were captured. More importantly, the Viet Cong had notice served that previous safe areas were no longer tenable.

Modifications of US Cavalry Tactics

Though the fears that armored units were completely unsuited for operations in Vietnam definitely proved unfounded, cavalry units did have to modify and improvise tactics and techniques in Vietnam. This was especially true in countering ambushes where the swift use of firepower was critical. Soon, however, US commanders learned to use armor as a jack hammer to tear the enemy free from his sanctuaries. The rapid insertion of airmobile infantry behind enemy units being pushed by armor frequently resulted in the creation of a killing zone from which few enemy escaped. Mechanised infantry proved very useful, too, on 'mounted' search and destroy operations. During June 1966, for example, the 1st Battalion, 5th Infantry (Mechanized) proved it could effectively carry out search and destroy missions even during the wet season.

During the early years of US armored commitment, the use of tanks and APCs was avoided at night, but as experience was gained US cavalry became very skilled at night operations. One type of night operation which evolved was the 'Thunder Run' which employed armored vehicles along roads firing their machine guns along the roadsides to trigger ambushes and discourage mining.

In September 1966, the 11th Armored Cavalry Regiment, the

M551 Airborne Armored Reconnaissance vehicles and M113 APC of the 11th Armored Cavalry Regiment conducting a sweep around Long Binh.

largest US armored unit to be deployed to Vietnam, arrived in country, though some of its tanks had been replaced with M113s. With an authorized strength of 3,672 men, the 11th Armored Cavalry brought with it fifty-one M48A3 tanks, 296 M113 APCs, eighteen self-propelled howitzers, nine M132 flamethrower vehicles and forty-eight helicopters, giving it a formidable array of firepower.

Separately, the 2nd Battalion, 34th Armor arrived in country at about the same time and was attached to II Field Force. Soon, however, its tank companies were parcelled out since armor was in such short supply.

Countering Enemy Ambushes and Mines

The 11th Armored Cavalry Regiment was initially used to secure the roads and provinces around Saigon, though elements of the unit frequently operated off the roads as well. The enemy attempted to decimate the armored units through ambushes, but the 11th ACR developed standard operating procedures for dealing with ambushes. Using their heavy firepower, they would fight clear of an ambush while protecting any vehicles they were escorting. Once clear of the killing zone, the cavalry would re-group and hit the enemy while reinforcements were rushed to hit the enemy on the flanks and tactical air and artillery support would be called down on enemy concentrations.

One tactic which proved particularly effective against ambushes was the 'herringbone' in which the armored vehicles turned alternatively to the sides of their direction of march, thus placing their heaviest armor and main armament towards the flanks.

Within the center, unarmored vehicles could take refuge or continue to move clear of the ambush. The use of 90mm canister rounds – each loaded with 1,280 shot or 5,600 to 10,000 flechettes – gave the tanks a meatgrinding counterambush capability which proved itself again and again.

Finding a solution to the vulnerability of tanks and APCs to mines was much more difficult, especially since the Viet Cong used 'random mining' – not placing conventional mine fields but perhaps just one or two mines along likely traveled paths or roads. One of the greatest lessons learned about mines by US forces, in fact, was that in a land war in Europe random mining could prove very effective against Soviet armor. About seventy-five per cent of all tank and APC losses in Vietnam were to mines. Just in the period June 1969– June 1970, for example, the 11th Armored Cavalry Regiment encountered over one thousand one hundred mines. The 'Thunder Road' and similar 'Roadrunner' missions were, therefore, very important in limiting VC access to roads for mining. Cavalry troops took other precautions to protect themselves including always wearing their helmets and flak jackets while mounted, even in the high heat and humidity of Vietnam, and riding on top of their vehicles. However, to counter the latter, the VC started emplacing mines or booby traps fired by trip wires in the tree tops.

After 1969, M113s and Sheridan MM551s had supplemental belly armor, which helped limit mine damage somewhat. Another attempt in Fall 1969, however, was less successful; front 'mine rollers' for M48 tanks were tested then but proved only marginally effective and were not used extensively.

Despite the threat of ambushes and mines, however, the value of armor had been proven and by early 1967, the US Army had one armored cavalry regiment, six mechanised infantry battalions, four armored cavalry squadrons and two tank battalions in country. With this many mounted units in country it was becoming increasingly apparent that cavalry units, especially those equipped with ACAVs (the modified M113s with gun shields and more machineguns) were extremely effective in conjunction with airmobile infantry. Also used ahead of the groundpounding grunts, the M113s proved useful at breaking trail and as assault vehicles.

By 1967, US forces along with allied forces were ready to take a more aggressive stance against the VC and NVA within South Vietnam by moving into areas previously considered VC safe areas and cleaning out the enemy. In one such operation, CEDAR FALLS, armored units helped seal off the 'Iron Triangle' by establishing blocking points west of the Saigon River. During this same

M56 self-propelled 90mm anti-tank gun saw only limited use in Vietnam.

operation, tanks proved useful for interdicting night VC river traffic as they would detect enemy movement with their searchlights and direct fire against the VC craft. Mechanized infantry proved valuable as well during CEDAR FALLS as they carried out search and destroy operations within the 'Iron Triangle.'

Almost as soon as CEDAR FALLS was completed, its sister operation JUNCTION CITY absorbed many of the armored and mechanized units for road security, convoy escort, search and clear and reaction force duties. Many of the combined arms tactics using infantry and mechanized forces were perfected during JUNCTION CITY and would be used again and again in the future. Cavalry units got a chance to carry out a more traditional armored mission, too, during JUNCTION CITY when they launched a rapid relief of 'Firebase Gold' which was under extreme enemy pressure.

Despite initial worries about the capability of cavalry units to operate in large parts of Vietnam, mechanized units even proved successful in the Mekong Delta where the 2nd Battalion, 47th Infantry (Mechanized) and the 3rd Battalion, 60th Infantry (Mechanized) of the 9th Infantry Division found the flooded paddies difficult but not impossible to traverse.

No matter what other missions they were assigned, throughout Vietnam, armored units carried out road security and convoy escort. Though extremely boring and tedious these missions could also be among the most dangerous due to the likelihood of ambush and mines.

US Armor in the Tet Offensive

Just prior to the Tet Offensive, intelligence reports indicated enemy buildups along the borders so armored units had been shifted to block possible infiltration routes. When the Tet Offensive actually struck, though, armor proved valuable in breaking it, especially due to their ability to move rapidly. US armor proved valuable in the defense of Pleiku and Kontum, but it proved most important in the battles in III Corps around Saigon, particularly at An My and Ben Cat. It is probable, too, that cavalry and mechanized infantry fighting in Saigon's suburbs played a decisive role in saving the city. Key installations at Tan Son Nhut and Bien Hoa were special VC targets outside Saigon. The 3rd Squadron, 4th Cavalry was sent to reinforce the defenders at Tan Son Nhut and upon arrival drove a wedge between the attackers but then came under heavy attack themselves. Reinforced by other cavalrymen, they managed to pin six hundred or more VC between the cavalry and artillery and gunship support, resulting in over three hundred enemy killed. The cavalrymen continued to assist in the defense of Tan Son Nhut by carrying out sweeps around the area over the next few days.

The even more important air base area at Long Binh-Bien Hoa came under heavy attack as well. The 2nd Battalion, 47th Infantry (Mechanized) was committed as a reaction force on the night of 30 January, then on early 31 January reinforced part of the complex under attack and helped clear enemy sappers from the ammunition depot. Especially impressive was the drive by the 11th Armored Cavalry Regiment over 103 klicks in eight hours to Bien Hoa, after which the cavalrymen moved into positions surrounding the base. For the next month, the 11th remained in the area providing security.

As a result of the Tet Offensive, US armored units were widely dispersed, having been committed piecemeal to stabilize the situation in various parts of the country. Equipment losses had been rather heavy, too, as units had been committed frequently where the fighting was heaviest. Still, when a second smaller offensive hit the Saigon area in May 1968, the armored units responded to the challenge. A third 1968 offensive began in August, this time directed against US troops in an attempt to inflict casualties which the American people would find unacceptable.

By then, however, US armor had regained the initiative. Armored elements of the 1st Brigade, 25th Infantry Division used their mobility and firepower as part of combined arms teams decimating VC and NVA units in III Corps. Also in I Corps, the 1st Squadron, 1st Cavalry, 23rd Infantry Division saw heavy fighting blocking NVA units advancing towards Tam Ky City. NVA units in I Corps were, in fact, not used to facing US armored cavalry and, as a result, the newly deployed 1st Brigade, 5th Infantry Division (Mechanized) had great initial successes.

In the wake of Tet with much of the VC strength decimated, mechanised units proved invaluable in using the cordon and search of villages for VC remnants during 1968 and 1969. In carrying out cordon and search and destroy operations the cavalry units developed the technique of just before dark dropping off four-man ambush teams from moving M113s so the VC/NVA could not be sure where the teams were deployed. The M113s would then laager for the night but remained on alert to act as a reaction force for the ambush teams should they encounter the enemy. So quick was their response that the longest recorded time to reinforce an ambush team was under four minutes from the time the first round was fired. Of course, as anyone who has been in combat can attest, four minutes can seem awfully long!

As of the end of 1968, US armored/cavalry/mechanised infantry strength peaked in the Republic of Vietnam, so it would be useful at this point to enumerate in a table units in country at that time. Note that various air cavalry units are not included, although the 2nd Squadron, 17th Cavalry is included (*), though beginning in December 1968, this unit was assigned to the 101st Airborne Division, and began converting from ground cavalry to air cavalry.

US Army Armored Units in Vietnam December 1968

Armored Units
    2nd Battalion, 34th Armor
    1st Battalion, 69th Armor
    1st Battalion, 77th Armor

Armored Cavalry
    1st Squadron, 1st Cavalry
    2nd Squadron, 1st Cavalry
    Troop E, 1st Cavalry (Reconnaissance)
    1st Squadron, 4th Cavalry (Division Reconnaissance)

3rd Squadron, 4th Cavalry (Division reconnaissance)
3rd Squadron, 5th Cavalry (Division Reconnaissance)
1st Squadron, 10th Cavalry (Division Reconnaissance)
11th Armored Cavalry Regiment
Troop A, 4th Squadron, 12th Cavalry (Reconnaissance)
Troop G, 15th Cavalry (Armored Cavalry)
Troop B, 1st Squadron, 17th Cavalry (Reconnaissance)
2nd Squadron, 17th Cavalry (Division Reconnaissance)*
Troop D, 17th Cavalry (Reconnaissance)
Troop E, 17th Cavalry (Reconnaissance)
Troop F, 17th Cavalry (Reconnaissance)
Troop H, 17th Cavalry (Reconnaissance)

Mechanized Infantry
2nd Battalion, 2nd Infantry (Mechanized)
1st Battalion, 5th Infantry (Mechanized)
2nd Battalion, 8th Infantry (Mechanized)
1st Battalion, 16th Infantry (Mechanized)
2nd Battalion, 22nd Infantry (Mechanized)
4th Battalion, 23rd Infantry (Mechanized)
2nd Battalion, 47th Infantry (Mechanized)
1st Battalion, 50th Infantry (Mechanized)
5th Battalion, 60th Infantry (Mechanized)
1st Battalion, 61st Infantry (Mechanized)

The M551 Arrives

The first Sheridan M551 light tanks arrived in Vietnam during
1969. The M551 was intended to replace the M48s in divisional
cavalry squadrons and the ACAV platoons in regimental cavalry
squadrons. However, the regimental squadrons of the 11th Armored
cavalry kept their M48 tanks. The first units to receive M551s were
the 3rd Squadron, 4th Cavalry and the 1st Squadron, 11th Armored
Cavalry Regiment.

When one of the first crews issued an M551 struck a mine which
ruptured the hull and ignited the caseless ammunition, many crews
lost confidence in the new system. However, the effectiveness of the
vehicle's night vision devices and the deadliness of its 152mm
canister round helped restore confidence. By late 1970, over two
hundred M551s were in country, though even at this late date, they
retained a tendency to have electrical problems and problems with
the caseless ammunition.

Using Mobility to Seal the Borders

1968 saw the perfection of 'Pile-On' tactics whereby mechanised or
cavalry units would quickly reinforce any engaged unit. As large
areas of jungle were cleared with 'Rome Plows' to deny sanctuary to

An M551 Sheridan tank of A Troop, 1st Battalion, 1st Cavalry Regiment, Americal Division on operations in March 1970.

the enemy, armored units were assigned the task of protecting the engineer units.

Early in 1969, the only combat between US and Communist armored vehicles occurred at Ben Het. The Special Forces camp at Ben Het was a key position overlooking the Ho Chi Minh Trail and thus a prime target for the VC/NVA. Early in 1969, tanks from the 1st Battalion, 69th Armor had been sent to Ben Het to beef up the camp's defenses, and in February had seen use for counterbattery fire as the enemy shelled the camp heavily. Then, on 3 March 1969, the enemy attacked with PT76 tanks. American M48s replied with HEAT rounds, knocking out two PT76s and an enemy troop carrier.

In addition to helping clear jungle areas, armored forces played a more active role in disrupting the enemy logistics system in operations such as REMAGEN and MONTANA RAIDER during which supply bases within South Vietnam were eliminated. By 1970, armored units, having helped clear the bulk of the enemy from within the country, had switched over to helping secure the borders where their mobility allowed them to cover large sections and rapidly respond to incursions.

During 1969 and 1970, too, the stress on Vietnamization of the war resulted in an increased advisory and assistance effort with the South Vietnamese armored forces. As the actual US withdrawals began, however, the armored units found themselves among the last to go as their mobility made them invaluable in projecting force with the minimum number of US troops. In some cases, even when their division was redeployed to the USA, cavalry squadrons remained behind in Vietnam.

One operation which called upon the assets of many of these remaining units was the move into Cambodia in May–June, 1970, as the 2nd Battalion, 34th Armor; 2nd Battalion, 47th Infantry (Mechanized); and 11th Armored Cavalry Regiment were all committed. After crossing the border the armored units helped secure LZs for infantry to come in via helicopter. The 11th Armored Cavalry pushed into Cambodia and seized key objectives such as the city of Snual, the hub of a large Communist logistics network. In addition to inflicting enemy casualties, the armoured units contributed especially to the capture of large numbers of enemy supplies in Cambodia.

By 30 June 1970, all US armored units had pulled back into South Vietnam, though some Viet armor continued to operate across the border. One thing that became very apparent was that the move into Cambodia had put great strain on the logistics system for the mechanized and armored units. Most of the logistics centers were located near the Vietnamese coasts, which stretched re-supply lines for critical spares well past the point of efficiency. Even the 11th Armored Cavalry Regiment, which had some repair crews assigned directly to the combat units, had problems because they lacked spare parts to carry out needed repairs. As a result, far too many vehicles had to be towed back into Vietnam from Cambodia. It had been becoming particularly obvious that armored units needed maintenance and logistics supply units based much further forward than was the practice in Vietnam; Cambodia emphasised the problem even more.

The next cross border operation, LAM SON 719, was carried out entirely by the Vietnamese as US troops were banned by Congress from carrying out any other cross border operations. Still, US armored units did cover the Vietnamese logistics routes inside Vietnam leading to the Laotian border and covered the Vietnamese withdrawal back to Vietnam after the completion of the operation.

So important were the armored units considered during the final phases of US combat involvement that by 1970 armored units (including air cavalry, which was classified with ground cavalry) accounted for almost fifty per cent of US combat units remaining in country, and by 1971, this figure had risen to more than fifty per cent. Since they were performing reconnaissance, security and reaction duties, the armored and mechanized units saw a large portion of the combat during this period as well.

The last US ground cavalry unit to conduct operations was Troop F, 17th Cavalry, which left on April 1971. However, some air cavalry units remained until 1973, many taking part in operations during the 1972 Communist Easter Offensive.

The Lessons

Although at any given time only a relatively small percentage of US armored, mechanized or cavalry units were serving in Vietnam, they made a significant contribution in both mobility and firepower. They also helped a new generation of armor officers and NCOs to learn some of the lessons that can only be learned while facing a real live enemy who shoots back.

Among those lessons, one of the most important was the value of the air cavalry as scouts for the ground cavalry. Before the Vietnam War much of the doctrine regarding air cavalry was theoretical, but Vietnam proved the concepts and honed a formidable new weapon. Too often in Vietnam, tank or cavalry units were tied down on rear area security or on road security rather than being employed properly for reconnaissance or in combined arms teams. However, it should be borne in mind that normally the absence of large enemy formations in most cases legislated against proper employment of the armored forces. The necessity of moving maintenance and logistics units supporting armored units further forward was an important lesson. It should have been learned from the shortages experienced by Gen Patton during his drives across Europe during World War Two (experiences, no doubt, his son George S. Patton, Jr empathised with while commanding the 11th Armored Cavalry Regiment in Vietnam). Nevertheless, this remained one of the biggest problems faced by mounted troops in Vietnam.

As with any war, some of the lessons learned have been incorporated into US armor doctorine and some have been forgotten and will probably have to be relearned if US armor takes to the battlefield again. Vietnam was not really a tanker's war, but the tankers who were there were blooded, and those lieutenants and captains are now the colonels and generals commanding US armored battalions and divisions.

9
INTELLIGENCE

Because of the nature of the counterinsurgency war in Vietnam where it was difficult to identify the enemy, intelligence played a highly critical role, yet the effectiveness of the US intelligence effort in Vietnam remains highly controversial to this day, even to the extent of generating a network television documentary on the subject which resulted in a complex and lengthy lawsuit against the network by Gen William Westmoreland. In actuality, considering the fact that US intelligence personnel operating in Vietnam – just by the fact they were primarily Caucasians operating in an Oriental environment – had to rely heavily on their Vietnamese counterparts for much of their raw data, they did a very competent job. The fact that field commanders and Department of Defense bureaucrats often made their decisions based on the political situation in the United States rather than the intelligence provided them, makes it difficult to judge how effective the intelligence provided was. As is frequently the case in the intelligence world, too, the failures in Vietnam were apparent while many of the successes have remained classified.

The intelligence war in Vietnam concerned many agencies including the Central Intelligence Agency, the National Security Agency, the Defense Intelligence Agency and the State Department. This chapter will deal primarily with Army Intelligence and the Army Security Agency, though other branch intelligence units and the civilian agencies will be mentioned from time to time.

The infantry division TO&E called for a G-2 Section staffed by six officers and nine enlisted men, with a LTC serving as the G-2. In addition, each division would normally have a military intelligence detachment assigned provisionally. Such detachments had a strength of approximately one hundred men. The one assigned to the American Division, for example, was comprised of eighteen officers, five warrant officers and seventy-three enlisted men. These MI Detachments were generally broken down into four sections – counterintelligence, imagery interpretation, interrogation and order of battle. The interrogation section was usually the largest section since a line division was likely to take a substantial number of prisoners. In addition, the infantry divisional commander would have available certain assets for gathering his own local intelligence including Long Range Reconnaissance Patrols (LRRPs).

The biggest single problem faced by intelligence units in Vietnam was locating the enemy. Secondary to this objective were such other considerations as the military, paramilitary, logistical and political organisations of the enemy; the location of enemy logistical and base areas; the trails, waterways and other infiltration routes used for supplying enemy fighting units; and the extent and type of military supplies coming from China, the Soviet Union and other Warsaw Pact countries. Once the US troop buildup began in 1965, it became apparent as well that US intelligence officers needed to be able to brief senior US officers on enemy capabilities and vulnerabilities. To carry out this mission effectively, it was necessary to establish order of battle information, including enemy composition, disposition, strength, training status, morale, tactics, logistics, combat effectiveness, important personalities and identification of uniforms and insignia.

Raw intelligence was received from advisors, operations with Viet intelligence agencies, the 5th Special Forces Group (Airborne); airborne radio intercepts; photographic reconnaissance; radar reconnaissance; agents and various other sources. As of 1965 when the buildup began, the J-2 (Intelligence) staff for MACV (Military Assistance Command Vietnam) included the following divisions: Reconnaissance and Photo Intelligence, Intelligence Production, Collection, Counterintelligence and Security, J-2 High Command, Current Intelligence and Indications and Target Research and Analysis. This organisation evolved to include a Weather Office and then by October 1965, combined and streamlined the other departments into five main divisions: Intelligence, Plans and Training, Intelligence Operations, Central Intelligence and Management.

Under the Intelligence Division fell the Combined Intelligence Center, with seven primary teams, one for each of the four corps tactical zones and one each for Laos, Cambodia and North Vietnam. Under the Intelligence Operations Division fell the Combined Military Interrogation Center, the Combined Document Exploitation Center and the Combined Material Exploitation Center.

Arriving in November 1965 was the 525th Military Intelligence Group, which provided overall control for the various Army Intelligence assets in country. Among the units assigned to the 525th were a signal company, an aviation detachment, the 135th MI Detachment (Counterintelligence), the 149th MI Group (Collection), the 1st Battalion (Air Reconnaissance Support) and the 519th MI Battalion (Consolidated). This latter unit was responsible for US

Army personnel assigned to the Combined Military Interrogation Center, the Combined Document Exploitation Center and the Combined Exploitation Center. The 135th MI Detachment, which handled counterintelligence, was organised into six regional sub-units, normally co-located with the Viet Military Security Service, which handled counterintelligence for the Vietnamese.

When the sudden buildup of US forces began, intelligence resources with a knowledge of Southeast Asia and of the local languages were stretched exceedingly thin. However, rapid expansion took place. Just on the MACV J-2 staff, for example, by May 1967, the staff had grown about fifty per cent to 467. As of July 1965, in country were the 704th Intelligence Corps Detachment; Detachment I, 500th Intelligence Corps Group; and 218 intelligence advisors with the Vietnamese. Additionally, the 704th Counterintelligence Detachment had forty-six men to carry out the counterintelligence mission. These numbers would burgeon by June 1967 to 2,466 troops assigned to US intelligence units and another 622 assigned as advisors.

In working with the Vietnamese intelligence services, US money, equipment, manpower and organisational know-how were all important, but the shortages of trained linguists made close cooperation with the Viets an absolute necessity. The fact that US intelligence personnel normally rotated home after a one-year tour, while Viet intelligence personnel remained, also legislated in favor of close cooperation; hence, the various aspects of Combined Intelligence. One of these which paid dividends in the field was the assignment of US intelligence detachments to Vietnamese divisions and of Viet intelligence detachments to US corps level commands. Additionally, US advisors were assigned to the Vietnamese intelligence school at Cho Lon where they shared their expertise in intelligence tradecraft and organisation.

Although intelligence cooperation was stressed at all levels, it seemed to receive special stress in combined interrogation. US Army interrogators were trained at the military language school at Monterey and were then assigned to the Combined Military Interrogation Center in Saigon. This center was staffed by both US and Viet groups, each with a director of equal rank. Normally, the results of interrogations carried out were reproduced in 350 copies which were distributed to eighty-two facilities around the world. It should be understood that CMIC would not have been able to carry out all interrogations. Initial interrogation was carried out at lower echelons and if the detainees proved of interest they were forwarded to the CMIC. Additionally, there were teams from CMIC with each corps throughout Vietnam backed up by 'Go Teams' at the CMIC center who were ready to be sent on short notice anywhere an unusually large number of prisoners were taken.

Among other CMIC duties was the handling of *Hoi Chanhs*, also known as 'ralliers,' who had come over from the Viet Cong. CMIC also gave interrogation training to troops from all over the country, including an orientation on the Geneva Convention.

Despite the great importance of documents from an intelligence point of view, at first it proved difficult to convince Vietnamese troops to bring in captured papers. US troops, however, had been better conditioned in this aspect of intelligence work. The Combined Document Exploitation Center generated intelligence from those documents brought in and deemed of sufficient importance to be forwarded to it. Opened in October 1966, the CDEC had over three hundred US and Viet Military personnel assigned, plus a number of trained Viet civilians.

Documents captured by maneuver units were usually sent first to their brigade headquarters (which frequently had a thirty-two-man intelligence detachment assigned) for a quick screening for intelligence of immediate importance. Then, documents would be passed to division, then on to the CDEC. Some field units had facilities for duplicating documents so they they could keep a copy and send the original on rapidly to the CDEC.

The CDEC was broken into five primary branches: storage and retrieval, operations, evaluation, translation and administration. Between July 1966 and May 1967, three million pages of documents were received by the CDEC, about ten per cent of which were deemed sufficiently important to translate and distribute. Upon receipt of a document, it was initially screened by Viet civilians in the evaluation branch who divided the documents into five categories:

ALPHA   documents requiring immediate processing, such as an enemy plan to ambush a maneuver unit; immediate contact with the affected unit would normally be made via the 'hot line.'

BRAVO   documents containing information of strategic importance such as order of battle information; such documents were quickly summarised into English.

CHARLIE   documents of marginal intelligence value; these were normally not translated and not processed further.

DELTA   usually propaganda items or foreign currencies: the former were funneled to psy war agencies and the currency was sent to storage for possible use (i.e. 'Black operations', agents, etc.).

ECHO   crypto or other communications intelligence; such data was funneled to ASA/NSA immediately.

ALPHA and BRAVO documents of sufficient importance were routed for full translation.

By 1967, the CDEC was generating 1,400lb of reports every day. Once those documents of importance were translated, they were microfilmed, filed and indexed on a computer system using an IBM 1401.

The primary source of technical intelligence was the Combined Material Exploitation Center which carried out the examination, identification, analysis, evaluation and dissemination of intelligence on enemy equipment. The CMEC was broken into two primary divisions – Administration and Support (graphics, receiving and shipping, laboratory) and Exploitation (communications and electronics, weapons and munitions, mobility, general supplies and equipment, medical). In addition, there were five field coordination teams which helped keep captured equipment flowing back to the CMEC and evaluated items which could not be returned to the center.

Lists of equipment especially wanted for analysis were made up and distributed to maneuver units. At times to help counter soldiers' love of souvenirs, passes or other incentives were offered for the capture of especially desirable items. Screening of captured items usually took place at division or corps level. Once it was forwarded to the CMEC, equipment was evaluated to determine its threats, capabilities and limitations. The information so produced was used to develop countermeasures. In the case of the discovery of large amounts of material, such as a large VC supply dump, 'Go Teams' were available.

Combined Intelligence Center

The Combined Intelligence Center was the primary intelligence production facility. This center evolved from the Target Research and Analysis Center which had been created in January 1965, primarily to identify B-52 targets for 'Arc Light' missions. At first, there was a vast shortage of US personnel at the CIC. Then as the number of US personnel increased, the facility quickly proved too small so the intelligence personnel had to carry on amidst some confusion while their new building was being completed. This building, opened in January 1967, would eventually house over five hundred US intelligence personnel drawn from all services as well as over a hundred Vietnamese. The CIC was organised into six main sections: order of battle, area analysis, imagery interpretation, technical intelligence, research and analysis and targets. Using the J-2 teletype, the CIC would rapidly communicate with all major US commanders in Vietnam, thus giving it the capability of disseminating critical information quickly.

Because of the need to understand enemy capabilities – particularly in country – the Order of Battle Branch was considered of primary importance. The Order of Battle Branch produced information on enemy ground order of battle, order of battle studies and political order of battle. The Ground Order of Battle Section had five teams, one for each corps tactical zone and one for North Vietnam, Laos and Cambodia. The Order of Battle Studies Section was broken into a strength, composition and disposition team; a combat effectiveness team; a tactics and training team; and a logistics team. The Political Order of Battle Section was broken down by the VC military regions and produced intelligence on the boundaries, locations, structure, strength, personalities and activities of the VC organisation within South Vietnam.

Each corps area OB Team would gather data from captured documents, interrogations, agent reports, situation reports, etc. OB information was disseminated to field units through the MONTHLY ORDER OF BATTLE SUMMARY and was updated daily via cable. Additional OP information was distributed through the MACV J-2 Periodic Intelligence Report which was also published monthly.

The Area Analysis Branch of the CIC was broken into five sections: Lines of Communication (with teams for highways, railways and waterways), Entry Zones (with teams for airfields, helicopter landing zones [LZs], parachute drop zones [DZs], beaches, and ports), Cultural Features (with teams for telecommunications, urban areas, etc), Terrain (with teams for landforms, vegetation, drainage, soils, etc), and Weather. Among other duties, the Area Analysis Branch working with a topographical company supporting the CIC produced specialised maps containing intelligence information of use to maneuver units. Some of these maps were especially useful for Special Forces teams operating in VC-controlled areas. The branch also produced a gazetteer with 127 1:100,000 Communist map sheets of South Vietnam with VC/NVA names for places. This gazetteer proved invaluable during interrogations and document analysis.

The Technical Intelligence Branch had seven technical specialty sections manned by the following detachments: Chemical – 18th Chemical Detachment; Ordnance – 528th Ordnance Detachment; Engineer – 571st Engineer Detachment; Quartermaster – 590th Quatermaster Detachment; Medical – 521st Medical Detachment; Signals – 18th Signal Detachment; and Transportation – 30th Transportation Detachment. From the point of view of the average grunt, by far the most important product of the Technical

Intelligence Branch was a manual on enemy booby traps which saved many lives and limbs in Vietnam.

The Imagery Interpretation Branch was aided by such equipment as the Ar85 viewer, computers, Itek rear-projection viewers, CAF Model 910 Ozalid Printmaster, Map-O-Graph, micro densitometer, photo rectifier and multi-sensor take-up table. Using this equipment, this branch produced 1:50,000 aerial photographs of the entire country to aid maneuver units.

Another important service of the CIC was the Combined Intelligence School with US and Vietnamese instructors. The school offered a four-day course for Vietnamese sector S-2s and their US advisors. These forty-four US sector advisors were extremely important in gathering data and in operating local agents.

In November 1966, the Combined Intelligence Staff came into existence primarily to provide information on the Viet Cong infrastructure within Military Region IV. The pilot program would evolve into the ICEX Program and then the Phoenix Program (which will be discussed in detail later in this chapter) designed to destroy the VC infrastructure within South Vietnam.

The 1st Military Intelligence Battalion (Air Reconnaissance Support) at Tan Son Nhut was in charge of disseminating aerial reconnaissance information to Army maneuver units in a usable form. As a result, this unit worked closely with the Air Force which controlled most of the aerial recon assets. One of the first steps taken by the 1st MI Battalion was the preparation of a handbook for Army personnel on how to effectively use aerial recon. To supplement information from the Air Force, the 1st MI Battalion also worked with Army OV-1 pilots on doing some basic photo recon in conjunction with other missions.

In addition to aerial reconnaissance photos, seismic and other sensors, people sniffers mounted on helicopters and planes and other advanced technical information gathering systems were used. On the more basic people level, divisional or corps LRRPs were available to gather intelligence, while strategic or broader tactical intelligence could be gained through the use of Special Forces reconnaissance elements such as MACV/SOG and Projects 'Delta,' 'Sigma' and 'Omega.' To keep track of the information flowing in from diverse sources, the J-2 developed a Collection Management System using computers.

Among various intelligence exploitation efforts, one of the most effective was the *Chieu Hoi* program, in which former Communists who had come over were used for intelligence and psychological warfare purposes. *Chieu Hoi* were also used in the Kit Carson

Scouts, who acted as guides for US units and oriented them in VC methods. Later some *Chieu Hoi* would serve very effectively as the 'teeth' of the Phoenix Program in the Provincial Reconnaisance Units (PRUs).

Certain operations throughout the war proved particular intelligence bonanzas. Among the first was CEDAR FALLS in January 1967, which resulted in the capture of about five hundred thousand pages of documents, including the complete VC 1966-67 campaign plan and 1,500 pages of crypto and signal intelligence. JUNCTION CITY which followed CEDAR FALLS in February 1967, proved another windfall as large quantities of film were captured which allowed the identification of various members of the Viet Cong hierarchy.

Intelligence Production

After all of the intelligence collection had taken place, it was still necessary to process the information and present it in usable form for making tactical and strategic decisions. This mission fell to the intelligence analysts, mostly young lieutenants recently graduated from the US Army Intelligence School at Fort Holabird, Maryland. The 'production' of intelligence came under the Intelligence Division of J-2, Military Assistance Command.

The Intelligence Division was broken into four main branches. The Current Intelligence and Indications Branch provided MACV with daily briefings on current intelligence, published the J-2 Intelligence Summary and Weekly Watch Report, and produced certain sensitive studies and reports access to which was limited to US personnel (normally carrying the classification NOFORN indicating no foreign distribution). The Order of Battle Branch took the information from the Combined Intelligence Center and other sources and produced information for MACV on enemy strength; OB Branch also published manuals and a MACV Order of Battle Summary which was considered highly reliable and which received distribution of 425 copies. The Estimates Branch briefed MACV on enemy capabilities and vulnerabilities and the Strategic Resources Branch briefed MACV on the political situation within Vietnam.

From the point of view of both the historian and the average line officer or grunt in Vietnam, the Intelligence Division's most useful contribution was a large array of studies of enemy tactics. Among the more useful were: *Ambush Tactics, Antiairborne and Antiairmobile Operations, Employment of Snipers, Defense Against Armor,* and *Viet Cong Structures and Field Fortifications.*

These and dozens more prepared US maneuver troops to counter enemy tactics.

Counterintelligence

Counterintelligence personnel advised the South Vietnamese Military Security Service as well as carrying out their own investigations. As of August 1965, the Counterintelligence Division had three branches – Personnel Security, Counterintelligence and Security of Military Information. To cope with the increasing load of security checks and other Counterintelligence missions, by September 1966, the 135th Military Intelligence Group had assumed responsibilities for MACV counterintelligence.

Counterintelligence teams were sent to every province in Vietnam, normally located with the local Vietnamese Military Security Service detachment. Among other duties, the counterintelligence teams oriented US personnel about security and enemy espionage and worked on methods for protecting US installations against enemy espionage. It was the counterintelligence teams, too, which established guidelines for NOFORN information and arranged security for classified documents. Initially, their mission also included keeping files on American personnel missing in action (MIA) or known captured, however, as the number of POW/MIA grew, this task was turned over to the Defense Intelligence Agency. Working with the Army Security Agency, the Counterintelligence Teams issued directives about communications security.

US Intelligence Order of Battle 1967

As of 1967, the controlling command for the various intelligence assets in Vietnam was the 525th Military Intelligence Group, which included the 135th MI Group, the 149th MI Group, the 519th MI Group, the 1st MI Battalion (Air Reconnaissance Support) and the various Military Intelligence Advisors. Separate under J-2 MACV was the 509th Radio Research Unit Group, the cover designation for the command controlling the various Army Security Agency units in country. Assigned directly to divisons were MI companies and Army Security Agency (ASA) companies as follows:

1st Infantry Division
    1st MI Company and 337th ASA Company
4th Infantry Division
    4th MI Company and 374th ASA Company

9th Infantry Division
    9th MI Company and 335th ASA Company
25th Infantry Division
    25th MI Company and 372nd ASA Company
101st Airborne Division
    191st MI Company and 371st ASA Company
23rd Americal Infantry Division
    635th MI Company and 328th ASA Company
        Note: the 328th ASA Company did not arrive in country until late 1968.

Additionally, there were certain other independent MI or ASA Companies operating in country by 1967 including: the 45th, 184th, and 185th MI Companies engaged in image interpretation and other collection missions; and the 1st, 101st, 138th, 144th, 146th, 156th, 175th and 330th ASA Companies assigned various missions.

Army Security Agency

The ASA, under the cover designation Radio Research Units, monitored enemy communications, working with the Vietnamese Special Security Technical Branch. The first ASA troops had been sent to assist the Vietnamese in this mission during April 1961. In addition to monitoring enemy communications, ASA units located VC transmitters and thus provided intelligence about the location of enemy units and gave warning of increased radio traffic possibly indicating an upcoming operation. The controlling ASA command, the 509th Radio Research Group, included among its assets the 303rd Radio Research Battalion, 313th Radio Research Battalion, 8th Field Station, 224th Aviation Battalion and 101st Radio Research Group, the latter in charge of communications security.

Military Intelligence and the Tet Offensive

To a large extent the intelligence agencies have received a bad rap in regards to the Tet Offensive. Admittedly, the offensive caught both the US and Vietnamese command structure by surprise, but this was not from lack of intelligence. In fact, a document captured by the 101st Airborne Division on 19 November 1967 indicated that the VC believed that final victory was near. This document was not only translated and circulated but was even publicized in a news release. Nevertheless, it was not taken to indicate a massive offensive on the scale of the Tet Offensive. Interrogations also indicated that the VC expected the country to be liberated by Tet. Rather than being caught by surprise, MACV J-2 had been warning Gen Westmoreland of an impending offensive since late in 1967. However, few believed the offensive would be countrywide. Instead, it was foreseen that Khe Sanh and other border posts might come under attack.

It should also be noted that since MACV and the American government wanted the American people to believe the war was going well and that the VC strength in the country had been severely weakened, intelligence officers who predicted an offensive on the massive scale that actually took place would not have been viewed kindly by high-ranking superiors. Traditionally, intelligence officers have had to fight a tendency to interpret raw data the way their superiors would like to see it interpreted.

The Tet Offensive itself offered somewhat of a minor intelligence bonanza as at least some documents – frequently the diaries kept by VC cadremen – were captured and a substantial number of prisoners were taken for interrogation. On the negative side, what was actually a great victory over the VC was viewed by the American people as a great defeat since a few VC made it into the embassy compound. Gen Loan, one of the most effective of the Vietnamese officers working with American Intelligence personnel, was also somewhat compromised in his effectiveness by the newsreel footage of him shooting a VC suspect in the head. The suspect, it should be noted, had just helped execute in cold blood the families of some Vietnamese policemen.

As Vietnamization began, intelligence personnel were among those who would remain in country the longest, though, of course, many of those assigned directly to divisions left with their parent unit. Among the first to leave would be the 135th Military Intelligence Group (Counterintelligence) and the 149th Military Intelligence Group (Collection) which left Vietnam in September 1969. Six provisional military intelligence battalions had been formed in November and December 1967, to operate in specific areas of the country, thus decentralizing the US intelligence effort to some extent. Although one of the battalions only remained operational until the fall of 1968, the remainder continued to operate until July 1970. The 1st Military Intelligence Battalion (Air Reconnaissance Support) would leave in April 1971, while the 519th Military Intelligence Battalion (Consolidated), which was responsible for the Combined Intelligence Center, the Combined Document Exploitation Center, the Combined Military Interrogation Center and the Combined Material Exploitation Center remained in Saigon until October 1972. The 525th Military Intelligence Group did not leave Tan Son Nhut until March 1973, making it one of the last US Army units to be pulled out of Vietnam.

Because of the important role they played in monitoring enemy intent, the various Army Security Agency contingents also remained until very late before leaving Vietnam. The US Army Security Agency Group, Vietnam, the 8th US Army Security Agency Field Station and the 224th US Army Security Agency Battalion (Aviation) all remained until late February or early March 1973. Two battalions, however – the 303rd and 313th ASA Battalions – left in June 1971, while various ASA Companies were redeployed during 1970–72.

Before leaving, however, both the MI and ASA units still had great contributions to make during the last years of the war. Although the Vietnamese were beginning to assume a greater portion of the combat burden, this only increased the need for timely intelligence to allow the limited ARVN resources to be used most effectively. The operations in Cambodia between April and June 1970, proved to be an intelligence boon, both in terms of documents and equipment. The move into Laos by the Vietnamese during January–April 1971, also resulted in some valuable intelligence; however, US intelligence estimates of the number of Communist anti-aircraft guns available may have fallen somewhat short, thus allowing US helicopter strength to be severely denuded during the operation.

The Phoenix Program

Arguably the most effective, but also the most misunderstood US intelligence operation of the war was the Phoenix Program. Phoenix (from the Vietnamese *Phung Hiang*) evolved from the ICEX Program which was mentioned earlier. Though Phoenix had been in the planning stages late in 1967, the real impetus that got it rolling was the Tet Offensive. As a result, in July 1968, the program was really launched. The Viet Cong infrastructure within South Vietnam was Phoenix's target, and it proved very effective at combating this target. With Province Intelligence Operations Coordination Teams at the province level and District Intelligence Operations Coordination Teams at the district level, Phoenix was well decentralized and thus much more efficient at locating the local VC cadre and neutralizing it. Although heavily staffed with Vietnamese personnel, the Phoenix Program also had four to five hundred junior military intelligence officers assigned. Other US military personnel from the Special Forces and SEALs worked closely with the Provincial Reconnaissance Units and the National Police Field force, which acted as the 'teeth' of the Phoenix.

The first mission of the Phoenix Program was to identify the approximately sixty-five to eighty thousand members of the VC infrastructure. To quote the *Phung Hoang* advisor's handbook:

> The mission of an Intelligence and Operations Coordinating Center is to neutralize the Viet Cong infrastructure. In order to effectively do so, it is axiomatic that first you know the enemy. Therefore, files and procedures are necessary for *Phung Hoang* Centers. Once a suspect VCI is identified (name and VCI position are known) two index cards are prepared and catalogued both in alphabetical and village/hamlet files. The next step is to develop a VCI Target Folder on the individual: . . .

These files became invaluable in identifying the VC leaders and cadre members, who were then captured and interrogated, then turned if possible. Failing this, they were ambushed by PRUs and eliminated or, occasionally, assassinated by special teams, though this later aspect received undue publicity when the Phoenix Program came under fire. To fight a counterinsurgency, waging a successful war against the infrastructure is an absolute necessity; Phoenix was extremely successful, virtually wiping out VC capability in much of South Vietnam. The very fact that the Easter Offensive of 1972 and the final offensive were almost entirely carried out by the NVA rather than the decimated VC is a tacit admission of the success of the Phoenix Program.

Issues of morality aside, those involved in the Phoenix Program were intelligence professionals who realised that in most cases captured VC were more valuable than dead ones for interrogation purposes. US intelligence personnel assigned to the Phoenix Program received in country training at the *Phung Hoang* Advisors Orientation course at Vung Tau.

A good insight into the day-to-day job of the MI officers assigned to the Phoenix Program can be gained from an examination of the Operational Planning Guide which was included in the advisors' handbook:

I. **General:**
1. NP [National Police]. PSB [Police Special Branch], MSS [Military Security Service], PRU [Provincial Recon Units], S-2, RD (as appropriate) can establish informant networks throughout the area of responsibility.
2. Situation section develop a current counterintelligence estimate for the area (Province or District).
3. Prepare a counterintelligence collection worksheet listing all intelligence resources.
4. Develop a list of the VCI methods of operation in the area, i.e., tax collecting, proselyting, armed propaganda, terrorism in order of the VCI priority.
5. Levy specific intelligence collection requirements on specific agencies. (*See* Case Officer Operations.)

II. Analyze the intelligence available
1. Determine VCI patterns of activity.
2. Determine VCI routes used.
3. Determine VCI commo-liaison activity.
4. Determine VCI support activities.
5. Determine VCI probable courses of action.

III. Assign Case Officers to specific areas of interest, for example:
1. VCI village organizations and activities.
2. VCI district organizations and activities.
3. VCI province organizations and activities.
4. Commo-liaison activities.
5. Terrorist activities.
6. Specific individuals.

IV. Case Officers Build Intelligence:
1. VCI personality targets are assigned to case officers.
2. All available information reports, captured documents and interrogation reports on the individual are assembled in the VCI Target Folder.
3. 'VCI Target Personality Data Forms' (*See* SOP 3, Annex 7) and 'Short Form Offender Dossiers' (*See* MOI Cir 2212) are initiated. (These forms are securely attached to the VCI Target Folders.)
4. VCI Target Folders are reviewed daily by case officers who levy Information Requirement Forms (*See* SOP 3, Annex 14) to fill the gaps on the VCI Target Personality Data Form and in the Short Form Offender Dossier.
5. Source reports, responses to Information Requirement Forms, Captured Documents, Chieu Hoi debriefings, interrogation reports, etc are received by case officers who extract the relevant information to be posted to the 'VCI Target Personality Data Forms' and Short Form Offender Dossiers.' These reports are filed in the dossier or an Information Summary (SOP 3, Annex 8) is prepared.
6. Recommendation for an operation against the target is made when data base will ensure a reasonable chance of apprehension and conviction before the Province Security Committee.

V. Case Officers prepare initial Operations Plans to be provided the action agency. Consider following factors:
1. The target.
2. The results required.
3. The support required from member agencies.
4. The forces available.
5. Operational security.

VI. Approval of action agency Operations Plan by PIOCC or DIOCC Chief.

VII. Conduct special training, briefings, and/or rehearsals required.

VIII. Execute the Operation.

IX.   Exploit the operation and conduct critique.

X.   Add intelligence to the Local Data Bank.

Although the number of military intelligence officers assigned to the Phoenix Program was relatively small comparatively, they accomplished very real results and gathered invaluable intelligence. Although the Phoenix Program later had many critics within the US Congress and within the Press, it is difficult to find a critic who actually worked in the program and saw its effectiveness first hand.

The Final Military Intelligence Assignments

After the pullout of the 525th MI Group, any residual military intelligence capability within South Vietnam was in the Defense Attache's Office, which was in charge of administering American military assistance. However, within the DAO was a relatively large intelligence section, though there was a much larger contingent of CIA and DIA agents than MI personnel. Included within the intelligence section was a Current Intelligence Section, which tried to keep track of the military situation within South Vietnam. In addition to the few active duty MI officers this section contained a reasonable number of former MI officers or NCOs. This section spotted the North Vietnamese buildup which preceded their invasion of the South, though there was little possibility of the US doing anything militarily to halt the buildup.

A few members of Military Intelligence also worked on resolving the MIA (Missing in Action) question, negotiating with the North Vietnamese for the return of remains and for information on missing US personnel. In this they worked with the Joint Casualty Resolution Center (JCRC) which was staffed by a number of Special Forces personnel as well as some MI and others. During the final evacuation of Saigon, the last remaining American MI personnel attempted to help get those Vietnamese who had worked for the CIC, the Phoenix Program and other sensitive operations evacuated, though a few personnel did get left behind. One of the very last Americans to be evacuated, in fact, was an MI officer attempting to get a final group of Vietnamese on a helicopter.

10
COMBAT SUPPORT AND SERVICE UNITS

Backing up the combat effort of the US Army in Vietnam were those units giving direct support and those giving indirect support by supplying the services and supplies needed to keep the Army operating. Among the service units particularly, though their contribution was absolutely necessary, there was a tendency for officers and senior NCOs to establish their own little fiefdoms – often overstrength fiefdoms – with more concern for paperwork than for the grunts fighting the war. As a result, at times the black markets in Saigon were frequently better equipped than some line units. The money to be made on the black market also seduced more than one supply officer or sergeant, who might come home a millionaire but rarely came home in handcuffs.

Combat Support

Intelligence, Engineer, Signals and Military Police are normally considered the combat support branches. As intelligence has been discussed in its own chapter, only the latter three branches will be covered here.

Engineer
When the US armed forces began deploying to the Republic of Vietnam in substantial numbers they found a country incapable of supporting a modern Army such as that possessed by the United States. Roads, ports, bridges, airfields, pipelines and bases would have to be constructed if large numbers of US troops were going to serve in Vietnam. This job would fall primarily to the Army engineers, though in I Corps USMC engineers and Navy Seabees would carry out much of the construction.

The engineer battalion supporting an infantry division during the Vietnam War, according to TOE 5–155G, had a strength of forty-four officers, two warrant officers and 951 enlisted men. Commanded by an Engineer lieutenant colonel (LTC), this battalion would be broken down into a 219-man HQ and HQ company, three 154-man combat engineer companies and a 162-man bridge company. Among

One example of a Special Forces fighting camp.

the types of equipment available to an engineer battalion would be: eighteen fifteen-man inflatable assault boats, twenty-eight three-man inflatable reconnaissance boats; eight aluminium bridge erection boats; six C160 60-ft armored vehicle launched scissors bridges; various types of aluminium floating bridge sections; three shovel mounted cranes; four road graders; twelve scoop loaders; fifty-eight 5-ton 6x6 dump trucks; six 400-gallon water trucks; and hundreds of other trucks, trailers, and other vehicles, including four full-tracked combat engineer vehicles.

On 1 December 1966, the US Army Engineer Command, Vietnam, was established provisionally; then merged with the US Army Engineer Command staff of USARV in March 1968. US Army Engineer Command, Vietnam, was re-established on a non-provisional basis in February 1970, and continued until 30 April 1972 when it was re-designated US Army Engineer Group, Vietnam. This command handled the various non-divisional engineer troops, by 1968 totalling twenty-seven thousand plus, assigned to Vietnam. The two primary sub-commands were the 18th Engineer Brigade, which arrived in Vietnam 25 September 1965, and departed

20 September 1971, and the 20th Engineer Brigade, which arrived in Vietnam on 3 August 1967, and departed 20 September 1971. There were also various non-divisional engineer groups, battalions, and companies.

In simplest terms, Army engineers in Vietnam had two main missions. As Construction Engineers; they built ports, roads, bridges, airfields and base camps. They also worked on civic action projects building hospitals, schools or local government facilities. As Combat Engineers, they gave direct support to maneuver units by clearing LZs, clearing fire support base sites, clearing ahead of routes of advance, keeping logistical roads open, helping destroy enemy base camps or logistical sites and other such missions. Normally, the divisional engineer battalion carried out these direct support missions, but if additional engineers were needed, they would be pulled from US Army Engineer Command, Vietnam.

Army engineers frequently came under fire in Vietnam, especially when working on LZs of FSBs or when doing road clearing when they were prime targets for ambushes. During Tet, many engineer units were heavily engaged in combat, troops of the 69th Engineer Battalion even taking part in an air assault on Vinh Long airfield at Can Tho.

Divisional Engineer Battalions serving in Vietnam included:

1st Cavalry Division (Airmobile)
   8th Engineer Battalion
1st Infantry Division
   1st Engineer Battalion
4th Infantry Division
   4th Engineer Battalion
9th Infantry Division
   15th Engineer Battalion
23rd Infantry Division (Americal)
   26th Engineer Battalion
25th Infantry Division
   65th Engineer Battalion
101st Airborne Division (Airmobile)
   326th Engineer Battalion

Additionally, thirteen other Combat Engineer Battalions and fifteen other Construction Engineer Battalions served in Vietnam.

Signals

In Vietnam, the Signal Corps had responsibilities ranging from land telephone lines through satellite links, photography and meteorology to counter surveillance of the enemy. Eventually, to accomplish these tasks, the 1st Signal Brigade, which was the controlling

Radio equipment located at Special Forces Nha Trang Headquarter's MARS Station.

command for all non-divisional signals units in Vietnam would become the largest signals command ever formed in the US Army with a strength of twenty-three thousand troops by 1968. The 1st Signal Brigade, which arrived in Vietnam in April 1966, was broken into four main groups – 2nd Signal Group for III and IV Corps; 12th Signal Group for I Corps; 21st Signal Group for II Corps; and 160th Signal Group for the Saigon area. Serving under these four groups at various times would be varying numbers of signal battalions. Additionally, each division had its own signal battalion organised as follows: A divisional signals battalion would normally have twenty-five officers, four warrant officers and 612 enlisted personnel assigned. The battalion, according to TOE 11-35G, had the mission to:

Install, operate, maintain a division communications system for support of division-level functions including: a. Command control, intelligence, firepower and combat service support; b. To provide special staff and technical assistance for planning and control of all division communications by the division command and staff; c. To provide direct support cryptologistics for the division; d. To provide photographic service (excluding aerial photography and development of color film) for the division.

Members of the battalion were expected to be able to defend their installations if necessary.

To give some idea of the complexity of equipment assigned to the signals battalion, a partial list of communications, surveillance and detection equipment follows: eighty-one trailers of various sorts; 237 trucks of various sorts; two mine detecting sets; eighteen TSEC/KL-7 cipher machines; nine AN/GSA-7 Control Radio Sets; four AN/PDR-27 Radiac sets; thirty-four IM-93/UD Radiacmeters; seven IM-174/PD Radiacmeters; six AN/GRC-26 truck mounted radio sets; eleven AN/GRR-5 radio sets; two AN/GRR-5 truck mounted radio sets; four AN/GRC-106 truck mounted radio sets; thirteen AN/PRC-25 radio sets; two AN/VRC-24 truck mounted radio sets; two AN/VRC-46 radio sets; twenty-two AN/VRC-46 truck mounted radio sets; seven AN/VRC-47 truck mounted radio sets; six AN/VRC-49 truck mounted radio sets; nine AN/GRA-39 Radio set control groups; four AN/GRA-74 Radio set control groups; twelve OA-1754/GRC Radio set control groups; twelve AN/GRC-46 RATT sets; thirty-three AN/MRC-69 Radio terminal sets; six ASN/MRC-54V Radio repeater sets; eleven SB-22/PT Manual telephone switchboards; 274 TA-312/PT telephone sets; three AN/MSC-29 Terminals; and four AN/TCC-7 Telephone carrier systems.

The Signals battalion was broken into four companies, each with its own capabilities and missions. The HQ and HQ Detachment, handled administration and logistics for the battalion, intelligence, motor maintenance and command and control. The Command Operations Company was charged with providing internal communications facilities within the division including the divisional artillery and also for maintaining cryptographic equipment assigned to divisional command units. Additionally, the battalion air support signal section was within this company. The Forward Communications Company provided the division's communications facilities in forward areas. The Signal Support Operations company provided communications facilities for the division support command, provided photographic services, and provided the battalion's field cable installation teams among other duties.

Non-divisional signal battalions were organised basically the same as divisional ones. However, adjustments might be made in the TO&E to fit specialised missions.

US Army Signals Corps units had been in Vietnam since 1951 and by 1962 had built a sophisticated communications network throughout Vietnam. However, this network did not anticipate the massive buildup of troops which would begin in 1965 and the

A UH-1C helicopter flies in a resupply mission to a 125th Signal Company and 5th Special Forces Troops manning a mountain top at Nui Ba Den.

crowded airwaves and land lines which would result. One practice which proved different than anticipated was the use of far less wire than normally anticipated. Instead, the use of radios became almost universal among maneuver units, resulting in the need to install radio retransmission sites on various hilltops. Four around Saigon were particularly important, even though the VC often controlled the slopes, the signalmen were perched atop. As a result, resupply for many of these retransmission sites was possible only via helicopter.

Airmobility had also influenced signal practice, necessitating certain changes such as the field expedient removal of radio equipment from an MRC-69 VHF van and installing it in a jeep trailer or light truck by the 25th Infantry Division's 125th Signal Battalion, thus making the equipment air portable. This practice was soon adopted by other signal units. With the 1st Cavalry, particularly, the 13th Signal Batalion had to work at establishing airborne transmission nets.

Assigning radio frequencies to the multitude of US, Viet, and allied units soon proved extremely difficult as well, often necessitating delicate negotiations.

Signal Corps troops were frequently among the first to go into action on major operations as they established the basis for the communications net which would control diverse brigades and/or divisions over wide areas. Prior the launch of Operation JUNCTION CITY, for example, on 22 February 1967, members of the 53rd Signal Battalion began preparing on 17 February in great secrecy.

So critical did the NVA/VC view the US communications network that during the Tet Offensive signals installations were given top priority as targets in order to slow the US response. However, though communications were disrupted in a few cases, the signalmen managed to keep the net functioning – in some cases just barely – by staying on duty in many cases for forty-eight hours and by fighting as infantry to defend their installations. The 1st Signal Brigade suffered 183 casualties during the Tet Offensive, more than in the entire previous year, as a result.

The Signal Corps helped immensely with civic action projects and US morale as well, establishing village radio sets to help with the pacification program and using the MARS (Military Affiliate Radio System) so that soldiers could call home using ham radio systems. Across the populous portions of the country, troops of the 1st Signal Brigade laid telephone cable rapidly to modernise and expand the Vietnamese telephone system. Additionally, the Signal Corps ran the strategic Communications Command. Automatic telephone and teletype facilities as well as computers linked by data networks and satellite links and undersea cables allowed encrypted messages to be sent to CONUS or almost any other military command in the world. Various specialized radio functions were carried out by the ASA (Army Security Agency) operating under the codename of radio research units, but these operations are discussed in Chapter 10, Intelligence.

One of the greatest difficulties faced by the 1st Signal Brigade was keeping all of its slots filled with trained personnel as the one year tour hit the Signal Corps within Vietnam especially hard. Signalmen normally needed higher than average intelligence and aptitude scores thus creating a problem even finding qualified recruits to attend the schools. The schools themselves were complicated, too, the twenty-six-week Signals course at Fort Monmouth, for example, being extremely comprehensive. As a result, although non-tactical training continued at Fort Monmouth, a shorter eight-week course for tactical signalmen was given at Fort

Gordon. This course was so overcrowded, however, that the school was forced to operate around the clock on three training shifts. Exacerbating the problem was that trained signalmen, unless they were career officers or NCOs, rarely re-enlisted since their skills brought good pay in the civilian market. It soon proved necessary, in fact, to require those enlistees or draftees choosing to attend the Fort Monmouth course to enlist for a third year before being allowed to attend. A shortage of signals officers soon occurred as well, requiring Signals officer's OCS to be established at Fort Gordon along with the officers basic signals course for ROTC graduates. Some technical graduates with special skills received direct commissions into the signal corps as well. Advanced signal officer's training was carried out at Fort Monmouth. As the war progressed, there also arose a substantial shortage of majors and lieutenant colonels in signals since the number chosen for the Command and General Staff college had been somewhat disproportionate in favour of the combat arms during the late 1950s and early 1060s, thus limiting the number of qualified field grade officers in the Signal Branch. As the two signals schools in the USA labored to turn out qualified troops for Vietnam service, the 1st Signal Brigade established its own training facility in Vietnam to supplement the training at the Stateside schools and to train or retrain men in country.

By 1969, the 1st Signal Brigade and its training facility were becoming involved in the Vietnamization process as they attempted to train the Vietnamese to assume responsibility for their own communications. Although divisional signal battalions pulled out with their parent unit, the twenty-five non-divisional battalions normally remained in country until mid-1971 or later. The last of the four Signal Groups to leave was the 160th at Long Binh, which closed up shop in June 1972. The 1st Signal Brigade departed Vietnam on 7 November 1972, though other elements would remain until March 1973.

Military Police
Although the controlling unit for the Military Police in Vietnam was a brigade with subsidiary MP groups and battalions, probably the most important organisational MP unit in Vietnam was the company. A normal MP company consisted of nine officers, one warrant officer and 184 enlisted personnel. Such a company, whether independent or assigned to a division, would be capable of handling motor patrols, traffic control posts, securing divisional or other command posts, providing security at prisoner collection points, carrying out criminal investigations, carrying out escort

An XM706 Security Vehicle in use by the Military Police for convoy security duties.

assignments and road security details and other law enforcement or security missions. The divisional MP company was normally broken into a Divisional Provost Marshal Section, which included the division's provost marshal as well as the Criminal Investigation Division (CID) agents assigned; the company HQ, four MP platoons, each commanded by a lieutenant and with thirty enlisted men assigned; and a security platoon, commanded by a lieutenant and with thirty-eight enlisted men assigned.

The 560th Military Police Company was the first MP unit to arrive in Vietnam in September 1962, while the next major deployment did not occur until March 1965, when the 716th MP Battalion arrived in country. The next year, however, saw the arrival of many of the MP units which would serve throughout the war, including the 18th Military Police Brigade in September 1966. Based at Long Binh, the 18th MP Brigade would control the various MP formations within Vietnam. The stockade at Long Binh would become known as the Long Binh Jail and in GI slang as the 'LBJ Ranch,' playing on the initials of the President.

Operating directly under the brigade were three MP Groups – the 8th MP Group in charge of criminal investigation: the 16th MP Group in charge of MP operations in I and II Corps; and the 89th MP

Group in charge of MP Operations in III and IV Corps. CID agents of the 8th MP Group carried out investigations of various military crimes, but as the war progressed, black marketeering and drug offenses would occupy a substantial proportion of its efforts. CID agents generally operated in civilian clothes and in many cases carried out undercover operations.

The various MP formations had the responsibility for enforcing military laws and regulations, controlling traffic, protecting installations, handling POWs, manning checkpoints and providing route security. Due to the danger of ambush by VC or NVA, convoy protection duties using armored cars and armed jeeps became an especially important mission for the MPs. To help control the traffic on waterways in the Mekong Delta and around Saigon, the MPs even had their own 458th Transport Company (River Patrol Boat).

During the Tet Offensive, MPs saw heavy fighting, in many cases functioning as light infantry around the environs of Saigon and near other US compounds. The 716th MP Battalion was responsible for security of well over a hundred US buildings around Saigon, in many of which were Americans isolated by the fighting. To reinforce the 716th and aid in its evacuation missions, the 89th MP Group sent two V-100 Commando armored cars, which were normally the mainstay of MP convoy security teams.

During the latter years of the US Army involvement in Vietnam, as troop morale declined, the MPs found themselves being used more and more to enforce military discipline. In September and October 1971, for example, MP assault forces had to be used to quell disturbances by engineer and signal troops respectively. In the attempt to detoxify troops before they returned from Vietnam as well, the MPs became increasingly involved in providing heavy security at drug treatment centers during 1971 and 1972.

As a result of these commitments and the need to provide security for US installations after the departure of major combat units, Military Police formations were among the last to leave Vietnam. Responsibilities, too, often far exceeded the strength of the MP units remaining. Upon the departure of the 1st Infantry Division, for example, the 300th MP Company assumed responsibility for securing the division's base camp at Di An. The 720th MP Company had even broader responsibility as it covered the areas of Phu Loi and Xuan Loc formerly the responsibility of the 3rd Brigade, 82nd Airborne Division and 199th Infantry Brigade (Light). Other MP companies found themselves stretched equally thin. CID activities necessitated that the 8th MP Group remain until July 1972, when it was succeeded by the US Army Criminal Investigation Center,

While on a road security mission, a member of the 173rd Airborne Brigade fires his jeep-mounted M60 MG at suspected enemy positions.

Vietnam Field Office. The 16th MP Group had left Vietnam in December 1970, followed by the 89th MP Group in December 1971. Most MP battalions and independent companies had left Vietnam by fall of 1972, though the 716th Military Police Battalion and 18th Military Police Brigade remained until 29 March 1973, placing them among the very last US units to depart as they helped provide final security for US pullout.

Service Units

Medical
In Vietnam the Army Medical Corps performed the most effective job of saving lives in any US war. Of soldiers admitted to a hospital in Vietnam, only 2.6 per cent died as compared with a rate of 4.5 per cent in World War Two. More telling, and probably directly

attributable to the rapid medical evacuation capability of helicopters, was that only 19 per cent of hits resulted in deaths in Vietnam, while in World War Two this percentage ran to 29.3 per cent. Of those wounded, 40 per cent returned to active duty.

Medical battalions serving in Vietnam were either divisional or non-divisional. Both had similar organisation and responsibilities. Primarily, the battalions were charged with initial receiving and temporary medical or surgical care of the injured, then evacuation to other medical facilities when needed. Emergency dental care and some psychiatric care were also available within the medical battalion. The normal medical battalion in Vietnam would be divided into an HQ and Support Company, which would include the medical supply and administrative personnel as well as some ambulances and physicians, and three medical companies. Each of the medical companies had a strength of eight officers and eighty enlisted personnel, and were broken into a company HQ, an ambulance platoon and a clearing platoon. The clearing platoon handled most of the direct work with patients. In the 1st Cavalry division, twelve helicopter air ambulances were included within the 15th Medical Battalion serving that unit.

The 8th Field hospital arrived in Vietnam as early as April 1962, accompanied by the 57th Medical Detachment (Helicopter Ambulance) flying the first UH-1s in country. Much of the early 'Dust Off' (helicopter medical evacuation) technique was developed by this unit during these early stages. In April 1966, the 44th Medical Brigade arrived in Vietnam to control all of the non-divisional or non-independent brigade assets. By early 1967, the 44th was already commanding over seven thousand eight hundred personnel. Major subordinate commanders were the 67th Medical Group in I Corps, the 55th in Northern II Corps, the 43rd in Southern II Corps, and the 68th in III and IV Corps. By 1968, under these four groups were organised an assortment of other medical installations and units. These included four non-divisional Medical Clearing Battalions, the 58th, 61st, 70th and 74th; 2nd, 3rd, 7th, 18th and 27th Mobile Army Surgical hospitals (MASH); 3rd, 8th, 9th, 17th, 51st, 74th, 311th and 523rd Field Hospitals; the 12th, 24th, 29th, 36th, 67th, 71st, 85th, 91st, 93rd, 95th, 312th Evacuation Hospitals (Semi-Mobile); 22nd and 45th Surgical Hospital Medical Unit, Self-Contained, Transportable (MUST); the 6th Convalescent Centre at Cam Ranh Bay with 1,300 beds; and the US Army prisoner of War Hospital at Long Binh.

MASH units provided resuscitative surgery or other treatment necessary to prepare patients for evacuation. During the period

1967-68, various MASH were in the process of being converted to MUST. These offered more sophisticated mobile facilities than a MASH, including hospital facilities, accommodation for hospital personnel, helipads, etc, all of which could be moved by 2½-ton M35 6x6 truck. The Field Hospitals provided more permanent hospital facilities near large troop concentrations than either a MASH or a MUST. Evacuation Hospitals provided both out-patient care and hospitalisation, and prepared patients for evacuation to more specialised installations.

The air ambulance units flying medevac missions played a critical role in the operations of the 44th Medical Brigade, snatching wounded troops from combat and then being vectored via radio to the hospital nearest or best suited to dealing with the injuries aboard. Each of the four Medical Groups handled their medevac except for the 55th as the 43rd handled medevac for all of II Corps. Over eight hundred and fifty thousand casualties were moved by the Dust Off pilots during the war. Two of the pilots won the Medal of Honor for heroism under fire, while many others died attempting to save others. Although the Dust Off pilots and front line medics were the most likely medical personnel to see combat, the frontless nature of the war left virtually all medical installations open to attack. The 3rd Surgical Hospital at Dong Tam, for example, came under attack thirteen times during 1968.

As the US combat commitment wound down so did the need for US medical units, therefore many, including the 44th Medical Brigade left in 1970. US Army Medical Command, Vietnam, Provisional took over for the 44th Medical Brigade when it left and continued in operation until replaced in April 1972 by the US Army Health Services Group, Vietnam, which remained until the final pullout of US troops in March 1973.

Logistical Support
When the 173rd Airborne Brigade arrived in Vietnam as the first major US Army combat unit, logistical support was sorely stretched to keep the brigade supplied. Upon arrival, for example, only fifteen days of ammunition was available, and special flights had to be laid on from Okinawa just to enable the brigade to carry out operations. Later, as the new port facility at Cam Ranh Bay opened, supplies accumulated there through lack of transportation units to deliver the supplies to the units in the field. Ironically, considering the later preponderance of troops in support units, in the early days of the US Army Buildup, the per cent of troops assigned to logistics units was very low in comparison to those in maneuver units.

Initially, troops in Vietnam had been supported by the Pacific Command through the US Army Support Group, Vietnam, but on 30 March 1965 the 1st Logistical Command began operations, thus laying the groundwork for the massive logistical system which would eventually supply almost a million troops spread over 66,000 square miles. In fact, some experts feel that the 1st Logistical Command would eventually do its job too well, supplying troops not just with necessities but luxuries as well which helped erode their willingness to stay in the field.

One of the first steps in coping with the massive logistical needs was to expand the available port facilities within South Vietnam. The first to be built was the complex at Cam Ranh Bay, a project carried out rapidly by the Army Engineers. Other port facilities were then either built or expanded at Saigon and Qui Nhon. By late 1966, the 1st Logistical Command was supplying 700,000 tons of supplies per month through these facilities and others. Subsidiary to the 1st Logistical Command were four support commands at Da Nang, Cam Ranh, Qui Nhon and Saigon. Late in 1967, the 1st Logistical Command moved its operations to the massive Long Binh complex, where by 1968, with over fifty thousand troops assigned, it had become the largest US Army command in Vietnam. To help keep track of the thousands of tons of supplies flowing through the system every day, one of the world's most sophisticated computer systems was installed; however, the vast number of Vietnamese civilian employees still guaranteed that supplies and equipment ended up on the black market or in enemy hands.

In addition to bringing in supplies, the 1st Logistical Command was charged with returning bodies to the USA through its mortuaries at Da Nang and Saigon. Other units falling within its sphere included maintenance units, transportation units, ordnance units, quartermaster battalions specialising in supplying petroleum products, and various transportation commands. Within transportation units, especially, ambushes accounted for a substantial number of casualties as well as destroyed supplies or equipment. In some cases, transport trucks had to have armor plating added and convoy escort absorbed resources of the Military Police, helicopters and armored units. The arrangement of convoys was designed to minimize losses, too. As a result, trucks carrying subsistence (food, etc) items were placed in the front of the convoy, partially, too, so they did not have to drive through the dust created by other trucks. Then, came trucks carrying clothing, construction materials, etc, followed by the trucks carrying explosive items such as fuel or ammunition. By placing this latter group at the rear of a convoy, should one be hit it would not block the road and prevent the remainder of the convoy from moving forward. One driver assigned to the 7th Transportation Battalion – Sgt William W. Seay – won a Medal of Honor fighting off members of an NVA ambush, killing at least ten, before being killed himself by a sniper. With the enemy likely to turn up anywhere in Vietnam, truck drivers and other logistical personnel frequently became front line troops, if only for a few hours.

Within the divisions, the Support Command, within an infantry division comprising 149 officers, twenty-eight warrant officers and 2,203 enlisted personnel, handled supply, maintenance, transport and medical services. The Administration Company of the Support Command, particularly, handled many diverse tasks for the division including: Inspector General, Judge Advocate, Finance, Disbursements, Examination (accounting), Chaplain, Information, Adjutant General, Administrative Services, Postal, Special Services (entertainment and recreation), Personnel Services, Payroll, Personnel Records, Personnel Management, Personnel Actions, Administrative Machines Branch, and Replacements. Also illustrative of the diversity of operations carried out by divisional support and logistical personnel is the organisation of the Infantry Division Supply and Transport Battalion. Within the HQ and HQ Company, for example, the Division Supply Office was broken into an Engineer Section, an Ordnance Section, a Quartermaster Section, a Signal Section, and a Transportation Section; each charged with keeping supplies flowing to the troops within their venue. Within the same battalion, the Supply and Service Company handled forward supply; baths for the troops (one sergeant and eighteen PFCs assigned); graves registration, collection, and evacuation; and other such tasks.

Support Command

Mission

To provide division level supply, field maintenance, medical service and miscellaneous services for all elements of the division assigned or attached.

Assignment

To Armored, Infantry and Infantry (Mechanized) Division.

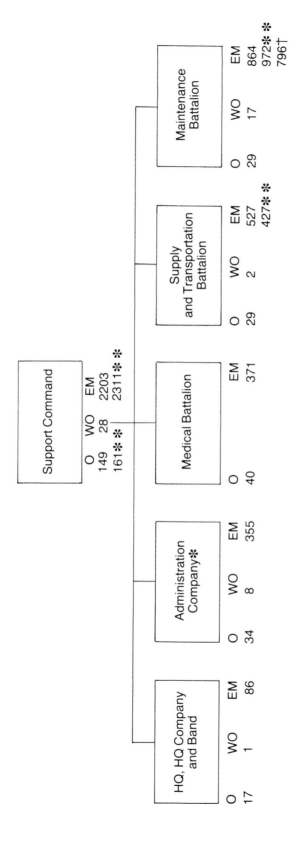

Support Command

O	WO	EM
149	28	2203
161**		2311**

HQ, HQ Company and Band

O	WO	EM
17	1	86

Administration Company*

O	WO	EM
34	8	355

Medical Battalion

O	EM
40	371

Supply and Transportation Battalion

O	WO	EM
29	2	527
		427**

Maintenance Battalion

O	WO	EM
29	17	864
		972**
		796†

* Support Command Commander's responsibilities for the Administration Company are limited to tactical, security and movement aspects. Figures relate to an Infantry Division, except:
** Armored Division
** Infantry Division (Mechanized)
† Infantry Division (Mechanized)

Capabilities

a. Provides division level logistical support to include mobile intransit storage and distribution of Class I, III, and II and VI supplies and control of Class V supplies, limited bath service and graves registration;

b. Provides direct support maintenance except for cryptographic and medical items;

c. Provides divisional level medical service including evacuation, clearing stations, emergency dental treatment and medical supply;

d. Has a limited capability to carry division reserve supplies or independent or semi-independent division mission;

e. Provides staff advice to division commander on quartermaster and ordnance operations, on all supply and maintenance matters except water supply and maintenance of medical and cryptographic material, and on transportation matters pertaining to the operations of the support command;

f. Furnishes music for division functions and performs such combat duties as the exigencies of the service might demand;

g. Provides maintenance and salvage collection points;

h. Individuals of this organization, except Chaplain and medical personnel, can engage in effective, coordinated defense of the unit's area of installation;

i. For mobility of the organizational components, see Section I of the respective TOE.

EPILOGUE – THE AFTERMATH

Although by the end of March 1973, virtually all US troops had been pulled out of Vietnam and on 30 April 1975 the Republic of Vietnam fell to the invaders from the North, the effects of the war are still being felt in the United States both militarily and politically. The United States, which had maintained conscription throughout the 1950s and 1960s, was forced by the unpopularity of the war to first adopt a lottery system for the draft and then, finally, to eliminate conscription completely and go to an all volunteer armed forces. Only during the Reagan Administration and the ensuing resurgence in popularity of the military has the profession of arms re-assumed the luster it lost in the red clay of Vietnam. Once again eighteen-year-old males have to register for the draft, though the likelihood of a callup is considered remote. Even so, this token return of Selective Service still draws protests from some.

That the memories of Vietnam are still fresh in the American psyche can best be illustrated by two political expressions; Jane Fonda, the symbol of Vietnam War protest, now finds herself the target of protest by veterans almost anywhere she appears and just having one of her exercise tapes in a military post exchange can create controversy. The 1988 Presidential Election saw the Vietnam issue arise as well when Republican Vice-Presidential candidate Dan Quayle's service in the National Guard during the conflict became front page news.

At least a goodly portion of the political controversy surrounding US involvement with the Nicaraguan Contras stems from the deep-seated reluctance most Americans feel to get involved in another guerrilla war, especially one the US is not willing to fight to win.

A television documentary purporting to show that Gen William Westmoreland knowingly conspired to underestimate VC/NVA troop strength, thus contributing to the Tet Offensive in its effect, was another example of the lasting polarization among certain segments of American society. Veterans' groups, always suspicious of the coverage given to the War by the media, rallied to contribute to a legal fund so that Gen Westmoreland could sue the television network which had aired the series, while liberal members of the media claimed that supporters of the general were attempting to inhibit the freedom of the Press. To this day, many veterans, with much justification, believe the Vietnam War was not lost on the battlefield, but on the front pages of American newspapers and on the flickering screens of American televisions.

Even the Vietnam Veterans Memorial has been a controversial subject since it was designed by a non-veteran and initially was criticised for being an 'ugly gash in the ground.' It has now gained acceptance and is considered a moving tribute by its very simplicity. However, those who died in the war are often a reminder of the inequality in those who served in combat and those who did not. It has been astutely pointed out that one division which will remain in American society for many years is between the segments of society – Black, Hispanic, lower or lower middle class whites – whose sons died in Vietnam and those segments – upper middle class and upper class – whose sons did not die in Vietnam.

The fate of American MIAs unaccounted for after the war has also created accusations of a coverup by the Defense Department which, according to critics, is aware of Americans still being held in Vietnam, Laos or Cambodia. Among the results of this belief have been private rescue operations launched by veterans of the Special Forces, reportedly with government assistance in at least one case.

The 'respectability' the war has now achieved is nowhere more apparent than in the media. The number of books, both fiction and non-fiction, written about Vietnam continues to burgeon yearly, while films and television series have made the war a subject of pop culture. Some films such as *Platoon, Full Metal Jacket* or *Hamburger Hill* attempt to portray the war with some reality, while others such as *Rambo* or *Missing In Action* seem to be comic book attempts to 'go back and win this time'.

The Post-Vietnam US Army

The US Army of the late 1970s and the 1980s at times has had to work at filling all of its manpower requirements. However, the professionalism of longer-serving volunteers has enabled the Army to modernise and prepare for possible missions in Europe, Korea, the Middle East or elsewhere.

Some of the most famous Vietnam era units are no longer in existence, while others have evolved to carry out different missions. The 173rd Airborne Brigade, the airborne workhorse of the war, has had its colors honorably retired, while the famous 1st Cavalry Division is no longer an airmobile division, but with its four armored and four mechanised battalions (plus two armored and one mechanised 'roundout' battalions which would join from the reserves in time of war) maneuvers through the dust of Fort Hood, Texas. The 1st Cav, which had lost its colours in Korea, certainly restored its reputation in Vietnam as America's 1st Airmobile Division, but now the 1st Cav is grounded once again, though its current air cavalry elements can certainly claim a sterling combat heritage. Airmobility is now the specialty of the 101st Airborne Division (Air Assault), which from Fort Campbell, Kentucky, carries on the traditions of the 'Screaming Eagles.'

Among the infantry divisions which served in Vietnam, the ill-starred 23rd (Americal) Division has gone out of existence with little mourning. The others have returned to their traditional posts and new missions or, in the case of the 9th Infantry Division, a new post and a new mission. The 1st Infantry Division, now a mechanized division at Fort Riley, has had a brigade deployed to Europe for much of the 1980s. The 4th Infantry Division, also now mechanized, is at Fort Carson, with a brigade in Europe. The 25th Infantry Division has remained a standard infantry division at its traditional home in Hawaii. Now at Fort Lewis, Washington, the 9th Infantry division has become a test bed for new high technology concepts in light infantry equipment tactics, just as it tested and proved the value of riverine infantry in the Mekong Delta. The famous 'Black Horses' of the 11th Armored Cavalry Regiment who proved the value of armor in Vietnam have been assigned to Fulda, Germany, where it is not too uncommon to see soldiers wearing the distinctive black horse patch on both shoulders indicating service with the regiment in Vietnam as well as currently. One regiment particularly has thrived since Vietnam as the 75th Infantry (Ranger) has been expanded with the addition of a third battalion and now holds a key place among US special operations forces.

The lessons of Vietnam have resulted in a emphasis on airmobility as well as a resurgence of the belief in the value of light infantry, particularly for possible use in the Middle East. The early logistical problems encountered in Vietnam have also been analyzed and have resulted in substantial logistical planning for use of rapid deployment forces around the world, among other steps resulting in the pre-positioning of critical supplies near likely trouble spots.

One of the hardest lessons to learn from any conflict is that an Army must prepare for the next war, not the last one; many indications point towards the US Army being more than willing to put Vietnam behind it and to get on with preparing for future conflicts. Whether self-serving members of the Congress and the 'Military Industrial Complex' will allow them to do so is another question.

APPENDIX – UNIFORMS
AND INSIGNIA

In terms of general issue uniforms and insignia the Vietnam War was very mundane, with black 'subdued' insignia on jungle green uniforms being the norm. Only the flamboyant, often vulgar, unauthorised insignia produced in the local tailor shops, gave the GI the chance to express individuality.

The standard field headgear for line infantry, artillery or combat support units was normally the M1 steel helmet. In most cases it was covered with a camouflage cover with slits for inserting branches or twigs for additional camouflage. Around the base of the helmet a wide, sturdy rubber band was frequently affixed and used to carry insect repellent ('bug juice'), cigarettes, matches, and so on. Especially among LRRPs but also among many grunts, the olive drab or camouflage 'boonie hat' or bush hat was preferred since it was less noisy and less hot. OD bandannas or headbands made from OD bandages or towels also saw at least some use.

Various types of berets were worn by special mission or advisory units. Most famous was the green beret of the Special Forces. Other berets saw limited wear, however, as the LRRPs and Rangers sometimes wore black berets, though rarely on operations, and the US advisors to the ARVN Rangers wore their maroon beret.

In rear areas, the olive green garrison or side cap might occasionally be seen in wear with the tan 'Class A' uniform but far more common was the baseball-style fatigue cap often associated with Gen Westmoreland, who wore his with his 'Master Blaster' parachute wings affixed along with his general's stars. Armor crewmen wore the CVC (Combat Vehicle Crewman) fibreglass helmet, while helicopter crewmen normally wore the light aviation helmet, also of fibreglass. Helicopter pilots often showed a certain independence in headgear, however, wearing old-style cavalry Stetsons, though rarely in action.

The green utility uniform with four pocket jacket and trousers was standard throughout the US Army, with the jungle utilities with their bellows-pocketed jackets being in general use by 1966. The earliest versions had exposed buttons at the pockets and epaulets, while later versions had the buttons covered by flaps and were constructed of the more durable fabric. Initially, camouflage utilities were available only to the Special Forces and advisors to Vietnamese units. The most popular camouflage pattern was the Tiger Stripes pattern worn by the Vietnamese, but except for some utilities made up in this pattern for Special Forces, it was not readily available in sizes which would fit Americans. Some LRRPs who liked this pattern made up their own field expedient versions using black paint and green jungle fatigues. Also available primarily to Special Forces was the spotted 'duck hunter' camouflage of the type sold to hunters in the USA. Most troops did not like this pattern as it did not blend in well in Vietnam. In 1967, Leaf pattern camouflage was introduced, though it, too, was rarely issued to the average grunt. LRRPs, however, did receive Leaf pattern utilities.

The heat and humidity in Vietnam often dictated that in rear areas support troops often wore olive drab T-shirts rather than utility jackets; however, in the bush, grunts were usually willing to tolerate the heavier utilities for the greater protection they offered against thorns, bamboo, leeches and other flora or fauna.

Armored crewmen normally wore the same basic utilities as other troops, as did helicopter crewmen during the earlier stages of the war. However, after 1969, most helicopter crewmen were issued the nomex fire resistant two-piece flight suit. The Class A tan summer uniform was not widely worn in Vietnam since even those not likely to be engaged in combat affected utilities since they were in a 'combat zone.' Since the front lines were so nebulous in Vietnam, perhaps this was not really that much of an affectation.

Initially, full color insignia was worn in Vietnam, though during the period 1966–67 these were switched to black 'subdued' insignia. Normally worn on the right breast was the name tape and on the left breast the US ARMY tape. Also on the right breast would be worn parachutist's wings and/or helicopter pilot's wings and the Combat Infantryman's Badge. Enlisted rank insignia was worn on the shirt sleeves, though by 1969, the practice of wearing small metal pin-on insignia on the collars had become common. Officer's rank was worn on the collar. Unit shoulder sleeve insignia was worn on the left sleeve, while on the right sleeve might be worn the insignia of a unit with which the soldier had previously seen combat service. Particularly on officer's utilities, branch insignia was also worn on the collar. Pocket patches – for the most part unauthorized – were worn for battalions, companies, recon teams, snipers or other special groups. 'Ranger' or 'Airborne' tabs were authorized for wear over the shoulder sleeve insignia, but other unauthorized tabs might also be worn such as for 'LRRP' or 'Dog Handler.'

Initially troops deployed to Vietnam wore the standard black combat boot, but by 1966, the fabric, leather and rubber jungle – or tropical – boot was gaining wider distribution. Initially, these boots had buckles at the ankle, but these were replaced by the more comfortable and more durable boot with nylon reinforcement at the ankle, an aluminium insole to offer protection against punji spikes, and grommets to allow water to drain out. Although LRRPs and Special Forces personnel normally wore the standard jungle boots, there were some who preferred the tennis-shoe style 'bata boots.' Special Forces recon teams also tested a strange version of the jungle boot with rubber bare feet of Vietnamese size on the soles, theoretically to leave footprints which would appear to be those of local peasants. In addition to leaving footprints far deeper than normal for the small Vietnamese, these boots proved uncomfortable to walk in and did not get past the test stages.

Vietnam was the first US war where individual body armor saw such wide usage. The earliest type of flak jacket was collarless, while the latter version had a three-quarter collar. Both of these were fabricated of ballistic nylon and included pockets and grenade loops. Primarily, these jackets were intended to stop stray grenade fragments or richochets rather than direct hits from a 7.62 x 39mm round. Able to stop a direct hit from a rifle round was the heavy 25lb 'chicken plate' armor used by helicopter door gunners or others particularly exposed to enemy fire.

For load bearing, an infantryman used the M56 harness, pistol belt, universal pouches each holding four M16 magazines, canteen and canteen cover, field dressing pouch at the shoulder, and buttpack and/or rucksack, the latter usually deleted in fighting order. In addition, the M7 knife bayonet would be usually worn on the belt and the OO angle-headed flashlight on the same harness. Grenades might be carried affixed to the universal pouches, the harness or in special pouches. Helicopter pilots had a mesh survival vest, which carried various items useful if shot down in pockets and also had a built-in holster for their pistol. Some Special Forces troops acquired these and used them to carry escape and evasion items. Special Forces troops used an indigenous rucksack which resembled that used by the NVA/VA. LRRPs and members of Special Forces Recon Teams often wore or used certain items of captured gear to break up the distinctive US infantryman's profile should they be glimpsed passing through the bush. Special Forces troops almost invariably carried extra canteens either for the special LRRP rations which had to be rehydrated or because the enemy was in control of local water sources in areas of operations.

BIBLIOGRAPHY

Bergen, John D. *Military Communications: A Test for Technology,* 'The US Army in Vietnam' (Washington, DC, Center of Military History, US Army, 1986)

Berry, E. Clifton, Jr. *Sky Soldiers* (Toronto, Bantam Books, 1987)

Casey, Michael, et al. *The Army at War,* 'The Vietnam Experience' (Boston, Mass., Boston Publishing Company, 1987)

Collins, Brig Gen James Lawton, Jr. *The Development and Training of the South Vietnamese Army, 1950-72,* 'Vietnam Studies' (Washington, DC, Department of the Army, 1975)

Dorland, Peter, & Nanney, James. *Dust Off: Army Aeromedical Evacuation in Vietnam* (Washington, DC: US Army, 1982)

Drendel, Lou. *Gunslingers in Action* (Carrollton, Tex, Squadron/ Signal, 1974)

Dunston, Simon, *Vietnam Tracks: Armor in Battle, 1945–75* (Novato, Calif., Presidio, 1982)

Esper, George. *The Eyewitness History of the Vietnam War* (New York, NY, Ballantine Books, 1983)

Forbes, John, & Williams, Robert. *Riverine Force* (Toronto, Bantam Books, 1987)

Fulton, Maj Gen William B. *Riverine Operations, 1966–1969,* 'Vietnam Studies' (Washington, DC, Department of the Army, 1973)

Gadd, Charles. *Line Doggie: Foot Soldiers in Vietnam* (Novato, Calif., Presidio, 1987)

Hay, Lt Gen John J., Jr. *Tactical and Material Innovations* (Washington, DC, Department of the Army, 1974)

Katcher, Philip. *Armies of the Vietnam War, 1962–75* (London, Osprey, 1980)

McChristian, Maj Gen Joseph A. *The Role of Military Intelligence, 1965–1967* (Washington, DC, Department of the Army, 1974)

Mangold, Tom, & Penycate, John. *Tunnel Warfare* (Toronto, Bantam Books, 1987)

Mesko, Jim, *US Infantry – Vietnam* (Carrollton, Tex, Squadron/ Signal, 1983)

Mutza, Wayna *UH-1 Huey In Action* (Carrollton, Tex, Squadron/ Signal, 1986)

Nalty, Bernard C., et al. *An Illustrated Guide to the Air War Over Vietnam* (New York, NY, Arco, 1981)

Oberdorfer, Dan. *Tet* (New York, NY, DeCapo, 1971)

Ott, Maj Gen David Ewing. *Field Artillery, 1954–1973,* 'Vietnam Studies' (Washington, DC, Department of the Army, 1975)

Pearson, Lt Gen Willard. *The War in the Northern Provinces, 1966– 1968,* 'Vietnam Studies' (Washington, DC, Dept. of the Army, 1975)

Prugh, Maj Gen George S. *Law At War: Vietnam, 1964–1973,* 'Vietnam Studies' (Washington, DC, Department of the Army, 1975)

Rogers, Lt Gen Bernard. *CEDAR FALLS – JUNCTION CITY: A Turning Point* (Washington, DC, Department of the Army, 1974)

Russell, Lee. *Armies of the Vietnam War (2)* (London, Osprey, 1983)

Spector, Ronald H. *Advise and Support: the Early Years,* 'The US Army in Vietnam' (Washington, DC, Center of Military History, US Army, 1985)

Stanton, Shelby, L. *Anatomy of a Division: The 1st Cav in Vietnam* (Novato, Calif., Presidio, 1987)

— *The Rise and Fall of An American Army: US Ground Forces in Vietnam, 1965–1973* (Novato, Calif., Presidio, 1985)

— *Vietnam Order of Battle* (Washington, DC, US News Books, 1981)

Starry, Gen Donn A. *Mounted Combat in Vietnam,* 'Vietnam Studies' (Washington, DC, Department of the Army, 1978)

Terry, Wallace. *Bloods: An Oral History of the Vietnam War by Black Veterans* (New York, NY, Ballantine, 1984)

Thompson, Leroy. *DE OPPRESSO LIBER: The Illustrated history of the US Army Special Forces* (Boulder, Colo., Paladin Press, 1987)

— *Uniforms of the Indo-China and Vietnam Wars* (Poole, UK, Blandford Press, 1984)

— *US Elite Forces – Vietnam* (Carrollton, Squadron/Signal, 1985)

— *US Airborne Forces, 1941–1986,* 'Blandford War Photo-Files' (Poole, UK, Blandford Press, 1986)

— *US Special Forces, 1941–1987,* 'Blandford War Photo-Files' (Poole, UK, Blandford Press, 1987)

Tolson, Lt Gen J. *Airmobility, 1961–1971,* 'Vietnam Studies' (Washington, DC, Department of the Army, 1973)

Official

HANDBOOK FOR US FORCES IN VIETNAM (Washington, DC, Department of Defense, 1966)

INFANTRY REFERENCE DATA (Fort Benning, Ga; US Army Infantry School, June 1967)

A POCKET GUIDE TO VIETNAM (Washington, DC, Department of Defense 1962)

VIETNAM ERA MEDAL OF HONOR RECIPIENTS, 1964–1972 (Washington, DC, US Government Printing Office, 1973)

INDEX

Page references in italics indicate illustrations